Where Are

YOU|SPIRITS

Style and Theme in Berawan Prayer

Where Are
YOU|SPIRITS

Peter Metcalf

Smithsonian Institution Press   Washington and London

This book was edited by Leigh Alvarado Benson and designed by Janice Wheeler.

Library of Congress Cataloging-in-Publication Data
Metcalf, Peter.
    Where are you, spirits.
    Bibliography: p.
    1. Berawan (Malaysian people)—Religion. 2. Prayer.
I. Title.
BL2083.B45M48   1989   299'.92   88-31119
ISBN 0-87474-620-5
British Library Cataloging-in-Publication Data is available.

∞ The paper used in this publication meets the minimum requirements of the American National Standard for Performance of Paper for Printed Library Materials Z39.48-1984.

This book was manufactured in the United States of America.
10 9 8 7 6 5 4 3 2 1
98 97 96 95 94 93 92 91 90 89

For Pam Brady

Smithsonian Series in Ethnographic Inquiry
Ivan Karp and William L. Merrill, Series Editors

Ethnography as fieldwork, analysis, and literary form is the distinguishing feature of modern anthropology. Guided by the assumption that anthropological theory and ethnography are inextricably linked, this series is devoted to exploring the ethnographic enterprise.

ADVISORY BOARD

Table of Contents

Preface

This book is a description of Berawan prayer, considered from several perspectives. It is designed to be used in different ways, according to the tastes of the reader. Someone simply curious to see what people in Borneo pray about can go directly to the translations that appear in each chapter after the first two. This reader will soon discover that there are things in the prayers that are not transparent, and so be led to consult the endnotes, and the summary, and then perhaps the account of the rite at which the prayer was spoken. A reader with technical or linguistic interests might begin with the Berawan texts. With interest whetted in these ways, one might then wish to explore the analyses offered in chapters one and two. Alternatively, the reader who sees the theoretical challenges that the phenomenon of prayer presents to the comparative study of religion may prefer to follow my unfolding of them, beginning with the statement in the introduction.

The book has taken several years to arrive at its present form. It would not have completed its evolution without the help and encouragement of four valued colleagues. David Sapir first made me aware of the inherent interest of a neglected corner of my field data. Rodney Needham worked through the transcriptions of the prayers as they were completed, and pointed out, among other things, dozens of etymological connections. Ellen Contini-Morava helped me revise my orthography, and offered advice on other linguistic matters. Finally, Dell Hymes read an early draft, and his extensive comments prompted me to recast the presentation of the texts, and attempt a new level of segmental analysis. To all four, I am grateful for their help in developing a different facet of the project. The flaws that remain in it must, of course, be attributed to me.

Initially, my objective was simply to transcribe and translate some recordings made during fieldwork in Borneo in the early 1970s. I began with notes made at the time, and they reminded me, as always, of the debt that I owe to the Berawan people, who responded goodhumoredly to my fumbling attempts to comprehend their ways. I am particularly indebted to the men who spoke the prayers set out in these chapters, preserved as none ever were before, and to those who helped me write them down. The man who did most of this tedious work was Michael Melai Usang. Without his help then, there would be no book now.

When I came to look again at those transcriptions, however, I soon discovered that they were full of errors. They had sufficed for my purposes during fieldwork, when all I needed was the gist of what was said, but a proper treatment of prayer as a genre required precision. Consequently, I have been obliged laboriously to rework my tapes, this time without the help of a native speaker of Berawan. I would not do it that way again, and it was only possible because of the repetitiveness—that is, structure—of the prayers. As I played the tapes over and over, I learned to recognize phrases and passages. Once identified in one context, they could be made out in others that I had not previously been able to decipher. The same painstaking process of cross comparison enabled me to track down glosses for unfamiliar words used in the prayers. No doubt, errors remain. But I am confident that the texts set out below have a high degree of accuracy.

From my corpus of prayers, I prepared seven for publication. They were chosen to represent different occasions illustrative of the life of the community, and different levels of skill in performance. As I polished them, each prayer developed a whole academic apparatus: endnotes, summaries, outlines of ritual circumstances, and biographies of the speakers. To my surprise, the volume of this supporting material rapidly outgrew the texts themselves. At first I found this embarrassing because it seemed to accuse me of verbosity, the vice of academics. Why couldn't I let the prayers speak for themselves? I hope it is more than self justification to argue that that is not possible. After all, these prayers were in themselves the most ephemeral of things, mere splashes in a torrent of discourse. Why should they be preserved? The best analogy is an archaeological one: The prayers are like potsherds taken from a dig. They may be attractive in themselves, and they may suggest the shape of the whole vessel, but much of what the specialist can learn from them is in their context, meticulously recorded with theodolite and tape measure. Not to preserve this data is to be a mere seeker of curiosities, a despoiler of sites. The notes that accompany the prayers are designed to record their locations in the stratigraphy of Berawan life. Like a shard, each prayer may be examined repeatedly, first observing one feature, then another. In this way they teach us about the totality of Berawan culture.

The production of the book was made enjoyable by the people at the Smithsonian Institution. I thank Ivan Karp and William Merrill for their many helpful suggestions, and Daniel Goodwin and Leigh Alvarado Benson for being the most amiable and supportive editors. For support during part of the time when I was working on the book, I thank the National Endowment for the Humanities and the Wilson Gee Fellowship Program at the University of Virginia.

Orthography

Most features of the orthography of Berawan utilized in these analyses will be readily accessible to those familiar with Austronesian languages. In particular, I have conformed where possible to the spelling conventions of the national languages of Malaysia and Indonesia. Nevertheless, there are features that are peculiar to Berawan and call for comment.

Vowels: In contrast to Malay, Berawan has two pairs of front vowels. The mid front vowels /é/ and /è/ are similar to those found in Malay, but the distinction between /í/ and /ì/ has no counterpart. As the diacritics indicate, the contrast is similarly one of relative height. Note that both of the mid front vowels require diacritics in order to distinguish them from /ə /, which in current usage is written "e." The same restraint does not apply to the high front vowels, but it was judged desirable to retain both diacritics in order to mark the contrast. Consequently, there is no "i" in Berawan as there is in Malay. The remaining vowels present no unusual features.

	front	*mid*	*back*
high	í ì		u
mid	é è	e	o
low		a	

Syllables: Most Berawan words have two syllables, but one and three syllable words are also common. No Berawan words are longer than three syllables. The canonical forms of the syllables are: V, VC, CV, CVC, CVV, and CVVC.

Stress: Stress is invariably on the final syllable of a word, with one exception. If the final syllable has the V form, then the stress is on the penult. For example, in the word **píléo** the stress lies on the syllable /lé/. (Note that the juxtaposed vowels do not comprise a diphthong.) Since the occurrence of stress is regular, it is not marked in the orthography.

Vowel length: In final syllables, some vowels (í, a, u, o) occur with greater length. Indeed, there are at least two words that differ only in this feature, the particles **ka** and **kaa**, indicating futurity and prohibition respectively. Not all vowels show this contrast, and it is found only in final syllables. Lengthened vowels are symbolized by a double letter.

Consonants: Although Berawan lacks some consonants found in Malay or Indonesian, it does include one not found, namely /v/. In accordance with modern convention in those languages, "c" is used to represent /č/, as in English /ch/. The sounds /ng/ and /ny/ are written with two letters, in conformity with practice in Malay orthography, but they are singular nasal consonants. Their production is like that of single consonants, and they are distributed in words like single consonants.

Several consonants occur in geminate form, and this is indicated by doubling the letter. These are: **pp, tt, cc, dd, jj, ll,** and **yy.**

	labials	*dentals*	*palatals*	*velars*	*glottals*
voiceless stops	p	t	c	k	'
voiced stops	b	d		g	
affricatives			j		
nasals	m	n	ny	ng	
liquids		r			
spirants:					
voiceless		s			
voiced		v			
semivowel	w		y		

The Long Jegan isolect: Central northern Borneo is a region of considerable ethnic and linguistic complexity, and our knowledge of the variation and relationships of dialects is incomplete. Ambiguity is avoided by dealing with the languages of particular speech communities, that is, isolects. This orthography was devised for the isolect of the village of Long Teru, where all but one of the prayers set out was recorded. The final prayer, however, was collected at Long Jegan. (For the locations of Berawan communities, see the introduction.) Even without a comprehensive study of the two isolects, there are differences that are noticeable in the texts. Phonologically, the most obvious and systematic difference is that the Long Teru isolect often has V' at the end of a word, where the Long Jegan isolect has VV:

Example 1: **líko'** (river) becomes **líkau**
Example 2: **bílì'** (spirit) becomes **bílíe.**

The same applies to final /é/:

Example: **kamé** (we, exclusive) becomes **kaméí.**

Other differences also occur. For instance, note the name of the deity called at Long Teru **bílì' puwong bílì' ngaputong** (**puwong** means "hold," **ngaputong** means "create"). In prayer seven, the speaker refers repeatedly to **bílíe ngaputíeng**, demonstrating a modification of the vowel in the final syllable. In one or two of the other prayers, the Long Jegan pronunciation is borrowed in this one phrase only, so that **bílì' puwíeng bílì' ngaputíeng** appears alongside the proper Long Teru form. Occurrences of this are noted in the prayer summaries, and their significance explained. Nonfinal /o/ can be modified in other ways, for example Long Teru **wong** (to be) is pronounced **wíong** at Long Jegan. In the glossary, the Long Jegan variants of words that occur in the texts are given in parentheses after the Long Teru form.

Syntax: In most respects, Berawan is a typical Austronesian language. For a general discussion of the family, including its history and distribution, the reader is referred to the article in the *Encyclopaedia Britannica* (Pawley, 1974). Pawley characterizes Austronesian languages in this way:

> Structural features retained by a majority of languages . . . include a fairly constant form for each grammatical and vocabulary element, with boundaries between elements in words being clearly definable, and a relatively simple morphology of verbs and nouns. In addition, in the verb phrase, a number of elements indicating tense, aspect, and voice, are present . . . Most roots are capable of being used as nouns or verbs.

It might also be worthwhile to point out that Berawan is a SVO language, that Berawan verbs do not inflect for tense or person, that nouns do not inflect for number, and that there is no inflection for agreement.

Typeface: Words in Berawan or other languages of Borneo appear in boldface type in the chapters. This typeface, however, is suppressed in the prayers themselves. Italics are not used for Berawan.

Proper names: When Berawan proper names appear in the translations of prayers or in the discussion, diacritics are omitted. For example, **Sadí Pejong** is written Sadi Pejong.

Introduction

Of all religious phenomena, there are few that, even if considered only from a distance, give so immediately as prayer the impression of life, of richness and complexity. It has a marvelous history: from the outset, it has elevated itself little by little to the summits of religious life. Infinitely supple, it has taken on the most various forms, in turn adoring and coercive, humble and menacing, dry and profuse in imagery, immutable and variable, mechanical and mental. It has fulfilled the most diverse roles: here it is a brutal demand, there an order, elsewhere a contract, an act of faith, a confession, a supplication, a commendation, an hosanna. Sometimes the same type of prayer has passed through all these vicissitudes; almost empty at the beginning, the one has in the end become filled with meaning, the other, almost sublime at the outset, reduces itself bit by bit to a mechanical psalmody (Mauss [1909] 1968:357, my translation).

Prayer is talking to God. (Phillips 1966:43)

Cutting through the sociable din of a Berawan ritual, the voice raised in prayer is unmistakable. First, a sort of prolonged moan like someone practicing French rounded vowels in a bass voice, a noise designed to attract the attention of audiences both seen and unseen. Then an intake of breath, and a direct appeal, "where are you," its flat intonation making it plain that this is a summons, not a rhetorical question. Another breath, and a list of supernatural agencies spills out, "spirits of" this, "spirits of" that. By the second line, the phonetic pattern of prayer is established. Lines are crisply delivered, uniformly voiced. Sometimes they follow one another in stately fashion, each a clear declaration. Sometimes they tumble out in balanced phrases so fast that only the quickest ear can sort them out, or else they decline into a breathless mutter, only to be followed an instant later by a reasserted stridency.

That a people of interior Borneo should be making prayers in this way, or making prayers at all, is not something to be taken for granted. To what end is this theatrical style employed, and by whom? What are its devices and conventions? Who or what are these spirits that are invoked? These are the questions that this study answers. Its focus is a corpus of seven prayers recorded between 1972 and 1973 at gatherings large and small, from quiet family affairs to great community gatherings. Set out in the Berawan, with English translation on the facing pages, they constitute about a quarter of the book. The rest of the book is commentary and analysis, and fully necessary if we are to appreciate the prayers and what they can tell us about a host of things that are interesting both ethnographically and comparatively.

Prayer, Ritual, and Exegesis

It is twenty years since S. J. Tambiah pointed out forcefully that anthropologists constantly underrate the importance of the spoken parts of rituals, or even ignore them altogether. His essay *The Magical Power of Words* has been cited earnestly many times. Moreover, the appearance of the essay in 1968 was timely. A major revival of interest in comparative religion was just getting under way within anthropology—Victor Turner's *Forest of Symbols*, published the previous year, provides as good a benchmark as any—and the subsequent decades saw the production of many excellent studies in ritual and symbolic analysis. Yet it is difficult to think of one that makes sustained use of the words employed in ritual, though speech is often a routine and essential element in it, as Tambiah insisted.

A couple of explanations for this state of affairs suggest themselves. The first is a simple, practical point. Rituals have their own rhythms; the normal procedure among the Berawan—and I suspect that they are not unique in this—is for a crowd languidly to assemble. No one quite knows when things will start. Always there are delays and excuses, providing an opportunity to socialize perhaps over a glass of rice wine. Then suddenly the rite begins, and such is the manic intensity of the participants that you might imagine that its success depended upon the speed with which it is concluded. It finishes as suddenly as it began, and everyone is relaxed again—a striking experience of the social construction of time. During the artificially hectic moments of the rite-in-execution, the poor anthropologist is hard pressed to keep track of all that is going on. It takes some nicety of judgement to be in the right place at the right time, with a functioning tape recorder to catch the words of the relevant elder, or ritual specialist, or whomever. Surely it is sufficient to listen in for a moment to what is being declaimed or muttered, just to get the drift. Alternatively, some bystander can be quizzed later about what was said. The temptation is to reserve the tape recorder for occasions that lend themselves more easily to its use, a quiet evening perhaps when some old man or old woman, tongue loosened by a drink or two, can be cued to recite a narrative of some kind. Surely this is one reason why we have so many myths on record, and so few prayers.

The second reason is more abstract, and has to do with a category problem that we have generated for ourselves. In the last century, W. Robertson Smith founded a novel theory of religion on the radical distinction of ritual on the one hand, and dogma on the other. Smith's purpose was to move the discussion of comparative religion, and especially of folk religions, away from theology. In Smith's view, what came first was not dry doctrine but social activity: "What conceptions men did at first hold received their clearest expression, not in words, but in ritual acts. In part Smith was attacking those who sought to analyze and explain ritual through recourse to myths and legends alone, thus making ritual merely magical, mimetic replication of myth" (Beidelman 1974:64). Smith's views were largely adopted by Emil Durkheim, and so became central to the anthropological tradition, the same tradition that is revived in the work of Turner and others. The consequent emphasis on ritual analysis is the distinctive contribution of anthropology to the comparative study of religion, and has been enormously productive. But Smith's initial distinction had the strange consequence of making ritual language in general, and prayer in particular, appear anomalous. This cleavage between myth and ritual is made by the separation of words and actions. What then are we to make of ritual words? Myth and ritual need to be kept separate, because the former is, in Smith's view, a post-facto rationalization of the latter. How can the same words be the action and the explanation for the action? It is a commonplace of anthropology that a usual reaction to anomalous things is avoidance.

It might well be urged that this difficulty is artificial. Speaking is, after all, a type of behavior. Tambiah quotes with approval remarks made by Edmund Leach to that effect: "Ritual as one observes it in primitive communities is a complex of words and actions . . . it is not the case that words are one thing and the rite another. The uttering of the words itself is a ritual" (Leach 1966:407, quoted in Tambiah 1968:175). But this common-sense position is not so easily maintained. How are we to know when an utterance is *not* a ritual? Taking the bull by the horns, Leach in a subsequent article argues that ritual is simply the communicative aspect of human actions (1968:524). He concedes, however, that not all anthropologists will be willing to follow him this far. The reason that they will not is presumably that the definition is so imperialistic, incorporating without distinction virtually every context in which speech occurs. Smith's original distinction is confounded, if not inverted, and the anthropological tradition of ritual analysis is set at naught. Moreover, this new study of ritual is open to Ernest Gellner's objection, cited by Tambiah a few lines below his quotation from Leach, that linguistic philosophy has failed in its attempt to see the word as deed.

My concerns are not philosophical, and I need not attempt to rectify this situation. My purpose is to sharpen our perception of the Janus-like quality of Berawan prayer. At one moment it seems formulaic, part of the prescribed forms of the rite. At the next, it becomes reflective, summarizing and justifying the rest of the rite. Sometimes it takes on the tone of a briefing for inattentive deities. It is in this latter mode that the prayers initially attract attention. Prayers may last from two to ten minutes, seldom longer. They are only tiny fragments of the rites that house them—rites that may last hours or days—but they frequently contain an invaluable key to the entire event. An example of this characteristic is provided by the opening sections of prayer three (see chapter four). The speaker is instructing the sacrificial animal:

> Go and meet grandfather Tenangan,
>> grandfather Tenangan,

who gives life, gives life.

Tell him:

> I am coming,
> because asked by Tama Itang Gumbang,
>   asked by Tina Itang Keleing,
> to request a good life for little Ukat.

> That's the reason I come,
> to meet you grandfather Tenangan,
>   to ask for a good life, a cool life,
>   for the child of those two,
>   about whom they worried,
>   anxious all night long.

Tell this, spirit of the chicken:

> Today they celebrate,
> his recovery,
> because he is alright now.

Tama Itang Gumbang and Tina Itang Keleing are the father and the mother of Ukat, who had been seriously ill in infancy, so that the tired parents sat up "worried, anxious all night." At that time they made a prayer, promising that if their son recovered they would make appropriate offerings, and the purpose of the rite then in progress is to redeem that pledge. "Grandfather Tenangan" is the speaker's title for the spirit agency that "gives life."

This section of prayer is expository in nature. Had any participant—not to mention the anthropologist—misunderstood the purpose of the gathering, it is stated here by the senior member of the family. It is true that the statement is couched in indirect language. Using a device that has its own charm, the words are provided as a speech to be made to grandfather Tenangan by the spirit of the chicken, which is all the while being waved around by its legs. Also, the chattiness of the narrative is constrained by the conventions of prayer. There is some use of stylistic repetition and redundancy. Nevertheless, the prayer appears basically as a commentary on the rite rather than a part of the rite. However, just a few lines later this tone changes. When speaking of the sacrifice that will terminate and somehow seal the prayer as rite, the phraseology becomes formulaic and mystical. Lines very much like them occur in almost all prayers, and they are difficult to gloss. As literally as possible they say:

> Transform potency to grow, potency to grow,
> > potency stomach, potency life elixir,
> > potency to carry on the shoulder, potency to feed,
> blood of the chicken,
> > enter into the body, into the body,
> > of grandchild Ukat afterwards.

Since the nature of sacrifice is a classic and thorny issue in the anthropology of religion, it would be interesting to get to the bottom of what these lines imply. Instead of supplying an exegesis, they themselves require exegesis, which is not easy to obtain. Old men say only that they learned these phrases from their fathers; that they have always been used. They have almost the quality of spell.

An Integrated Approach to Prayer

It would be misleading to imply that the two faces of prayer, both of and about ritual, can be distinguished by sorting out passages that are of one type or the other. On the contrary, the two aspects coexist everywhere in the texts, and it is that realization that prompts a new, integrated approach to their analysis.

My first interest in the prayers was as supporting evidence for my interpretations of rituals, in the course of which, like others before me, I erected whole systems of symbolism. Such procedures have been met with skepticism in some quarters from the outset. In one of his early papers, republished in *The Forest of Symbols*, Turner felt obliged to justify that the polysemy of the **mudyi** or "milk tree" included meanings that the Ndembu people would not or could not state directly. Turner argues that these unstated meanings, having to do with potentially disruptive oppositions, are clearly expressed in ritual. This argument would seem modest enough, but Turner was well aware that it went counter to the opinions of established figures in the field. He quoted S. F. Nadel's reprimand that "uncomprehended symbols" can have no part in any social inquiry because the participants in a rite cannot act out meanings of which they are not aware. Monica Wilson had taken a similar position in her account of another African culture, preferring "Nyakyusa interpretations of their own rituals, for anthropological literature is bespattered with symbolic guessing, the ethnographer's interpretations of the rituals of other people" (Turner 1967:20–26, quoting from Wilson 1957:6). Wilson's "symbolic guessers" were in the main those who imposed models upon the primitives lifted from psychoanalysis, rather than those practicing the kind of analysis that Turner advocated. Nevertheless, two decades later the skepticism persists, now fed by a reaction to the perceived excesses of structuralism. Once again it is urged that no meaning has validity unless stated by an indigene (Lewis 1980). The radical relativism, bordering upon flippancy, with which some symbolists have met this challenge has served only to provoke further odium. For my part, I remain interested in substantiating my interpretations, in building my case that the systems of meaning that I hit upon are more than imposed "symbolic guesses." Conviction grows when a meaning that is deduced or hypothesized on the basis of one element of ritual or mythology can also be made out in another. In this way, apparently unrelated elements can be seen as parts of an intelligible whole. Here is the great virtue of the prayers; they provide in a compact way direct expression of ideas about ontology and cosmology, about the speaker's sense of place and of communal identity, about augury, sacrifice, the living and the dead, and much else besides. Moreover, as an added bonus, they are immune to charges of manipulation by the observer. Without provocation, senior men of the community leap to their feet and deliver their deepest religious thought.

What matters about the prayers transcribed in this book is that they are Berawan words from Berawan mouths. They constitute a storehouse of useful data. But, and here we must drop the other shoe, the words were not spoken in order to provide that data. Instead each is the creation of some specific social context that at every moment impinges on the prayer. This context goes beyond the immediate circumstances calling forth the rite. There is no Berawan *Book of Common Prayer*, with set wordings for each occasion. Every prayer is unique, and liable to refer to any detail that the speaker finds relevant: the personal histories of those involved, their family quarrels, their previous ritual participation, and so on. The speaker may angle his delivery to reflect his own religious preferences, or sneak in a lecture directed to some part of his audience, and he can do this because of his own status, for prayers are not made by just anybody. Those who do make them are always playing to an audience, a living human audience, in addition to whatever spirit agencies are invoked. All these subtle factors must be grasped in order to obtain a proper reading. It follows that prayer must also be considered in its guise as performance. Each prayer is unique but each contains formulae and figures that are utterly familiar to its hearers. Each is structured, constrained, and given force by conventions inculcated in each adept; in short, prayer is a genre.

The approach of this study is integrated in the sense that it attempts to keep both aspects of prayer that were outlined in the preceding paragraphs in view throughout. It is integrated in a simpler sense because it desegregates the subdisciplines of social and linguistic anthropology. So far, I have dealt with prayer as an adjunct to ritual analysis, but the use of the term genre in the previous paragraph serves to remind us that there is an alternative way of dealing with it, one that would come more easily to many of my colleagues. The study of oral literature for its own sake has always been prominent in American anthropology. From its inception, the Bureau of American Ethnology (BAE) encouraged its fieldworkers to collect and record texts of all kinds. This painstaking labor produced a vast corpus of material published in the bulletins of the BAE, which in latter years was the inspiration of much of Claude Levi-Strauss's work on myth. Franz Boas and his students maintained and even intensified the interest of the BAE. In 1905, Boas wrote to the then editor of the BAE bulletins, William Holmes, to urge him to publish in full some texts collected by John Swanton. He argues the lasting importance of these texts: "My own published work shows, that I let this kind of work take precedence over practically everything else, knowing it is the foundation of all future research" (Boas and Stocking 1974:123). Finally, it is in the writings of Edward Sapir that the texts are put in their full linguistic context. The concluding chapter of his book *Language*, which is comprehensive in its treatment and has been widely influential, is called "Language and Literature." Early in his discussion, he emphasizes the material of verbal art:

> Language is the medium of literature as marble or bronze or clay are the
> materials of the sculptor. Since every language has its distinctive
> peculiarities, the innate formal limitations—and possibilities—of one
> literature are never quite the same as those of another. The literature
> fashioned out of the form and substance of a language has the color and
> texture of its matrix. The literary artist may never be conscious of just
> how he is hindered or helped or otherwise guided by the matrix, but

when it is a question of translating his work into another language, the nature of the original matrix manifests itself at once. All his effects have been calculated, or intuitively felt, with reference to the formal "genius" of his own language; they cannot be carried over without loss or modification. (E. Sapir 1921:222)

Sapir's remarks about the difficulties of translation are obviously relevant to the enterprise outline above, employing prayer as data on ideology. Even the English tradition has been self-conscious about the business of translating key concepts (Beidelman 1974). What is different about Sapir's approach is that he directs attention to the "color and texture" of the medium, to the "distinctive peculiarities" of the language in which the concepts are cast. He illustrates it by comparing several classic forms of prosody, and summarizes his findings with elegant conciseness:

Latin and Greek verse depends on the principle of contrasting weights; English verse, on the principle of contrasting stresses; French verse, on the principles of number and echo; Chinese verse, on the principles of number, echo, and contrasting pitches. Each of these rhythmic systems proceeds from the unconscious dynamic of habit of the language. (E. Sapir 1921:230)

Weight, stress, number, echo, and pitch: these are the qualities that he discovers and uses to characterize the different genres. They bring us a long way from cosmology and sacrifice, but they, or others like them, are every bit as much inherent in the prayers, as Sapir's demonstration establishes. It is not only that we will need to grasp the metrical structure of prayer in order to utilize it to learn about ideology—although that is true—but also that a full "translation" of the prayers goes beyond such a limited utilization. The prayers are a special creation of Berawan culture, a rare embodiment of its "genius."

The Distinctive Character of Berawan Prayer

Robertson Smith might have applauded the conclusion that Berawan cosmology as much exists because of the institution of prayer as the reverse. However, it would be a mistake to generalize this proposition. Presumably, all religions have a cosmology, whether simple or elaborate. But, contrary to received opinion, not all religions have prayer.

In a standard work on the terminology of religion, slanted—as they all are—toward the world religions, prayer is asserted to be a "central element in most forms of religion" (Kauffman 1957:351). No evidence is brought forth to support this assertion, and it would require some nice distinctions about what is "central" and what is not, let alone what it is that constitutes prayer. There may be relatively few religious systems that totally lack anything that might be called prayer—though there are certainly some—but I suspect that there are many where it is a marginal activity. Even where it exists and is not marginal, it may take innumerable forms, as Marcel Mauss points out in the quotation with which we began.

What is needed at this point is a working definition of prayer. My formulation is simple: invocation and supplication. To qualify as prayer, an utterance needs to be directly and unambiguously addressed to some supernatural agency, requesting some kind of boon. As D. Z. Phillips urges, prayer is predominantly spoken in the second person. The volitional nature of the agency is clearly acknowledged.

The usual fate of definitions in anthropology is to be outflanked by ethnographic realities, and that may well be the case here, since the comparative study of prayer is at such a rudimentary stage. Nevertheless, it is necessary to make a beginning. The definition has some utility in Borneo; a few examples from other corners of the Malayo-Polynesian world will serve to show its ability to discriminate, while encompassing a great diversity of speech forms.

An obvious source on supernaturally charged language is Bronislaw Malinowski's *Coral Gardens and their Magic* (1935). It contains barely a mention of prayer, and the category does not appear in the indexes of his major works on the Trobriands. There is a body of re-analysis building upon Malinowski's work, and showing how the spells gain their force from the use of tropes (Nadel 1957; Tambiah 1968; Weiner 1983). The impression remains, however, that Trobriand religion is all but devoid of prayer in the sense outlined above.

Among the Maori of New Zealand, there are sacred incantations called **karakia.** But, Elsdon Best tells us:

> Perhaps the most remarkable feature of Maori **karakia** is the fact in but a few cases do we find a true invocation, anything that can be called an appeal to higher powers . . . Many of the better type of **karakia** consist of a repetition of matter seemingly quite foreign to the subject under treatment. (Best [1924] 1976:308)

Apparently, this foreign matter is largely lists of names of chiefs and priests. There is no form of Maori prayer distinct from **karakia.** By contrast, prayer is a significant part of the religious observance of the Manus of the Admiralty Islands, as described in Reo Fortune's classic account. It takes a strange form, however, which parallels Manus cosmology:

> Each Manus man worships his father, not in Heaven, but in his house front rafters, not one Father for all, but each man his own. The skull of the father of the house owner has an honored place in a finely carved wooden bowl hung high above, and just inside, the entry at the front of the house. The spiritual presence, of which the skull is the material relic, guards the house and supervises the morals of its people. (Fortune 1935:1)

Fortune refers to the protective spirit of the skull as Sir Ghost, and describes the close interaction between it and the members of the household:

> On public occasions when a feast is brought to the verandah of his house, the ward addresses Sir Ghost in front of the assembly. He tells Sir Ghost that the feast is given in Sir Ghost's honour . . . Finally the ward takes up a rolled handful of food and robustly concluding his speech with, "Food offering to you, this," hurls the food at the outer thatch, inside of which the skull bowl hangs. (Fortune 1935:14)

In return for protection from the weather, for food offerings, and for the respect of his ward, Sir Ghost is expected to provide health and good luck. A series of reverses will bring forth prayers of a different kind:

> If at any time Sir Ghost appears not be giving what had been asked of him, his ward will easily be fired to anger. He will then threaten Sir Ghost with a final breaking of their compact. Does Sir Ghost wish to be thrown out of the house into the open, "to be washed by all rains, scorched by all suns," to have his name called upon by no one, to be homeless and forgotten? If Sir Ghost continues to withhold good fortune from him, then out Sir Ghost must go. (Fortune 1935:14–15)

This is a form of invocation that—to say the least—does not readily fall within our standard dictionary characterization of prayer as "adoration, praise, thanksgiving, petition, confession, repentance, meditation and dedication" (Kauffman 1957:357). There is nothing in that list that includes "threaten."

At the other end of the spectrum, some accounts of the traditional religions of central Polynesia emphasize the place of regular, individual prayer. Robert Williamson (citing Moerenhout 1837 and Ellis 1839) says that:

> The Society islanders repeated their prayers on getting up in the morning, before meals, before going to sleep, and, indeed, before every act of their

lives . . . prayer was offered by these people before eating, tilling the ground, planting gardens, building houses, launching canoes, casting nets, and at the beginnings and ends of journeys. In addition to the family payers offered up at the domestic **marae** by the head of household, any member of the family might go there to present petitions to the gods. (Williamson 1937:102)

The Society Islanders were evidently well situated to adopt the Christian practices that would rapidly sweep away their old order. Williamson provides us with a specimen of an evening prayer which is a reasonable approximation of the Lord's Prayer:

> Save me! Save me!
> It is evening;
> It is evening of the gods.
> Watch near me, O my God!
> Near me, O my Lord!
> Keep me from enchantment;
> Keep me from sudden death;
> From evil conduct;
> From wishing evil (cursing) or from being cursed;
> From secret practices (plots)
> And from quarrels over boundary marks.
> Let peace reign far and wide around us, O my God!
> Preserve me from the furious warrior,
> From him who roams about furious (delights to terrify)
> Whose hair is always standing on end.
> Let me and my spirit live
> And rest in peace this night, O my God! (Williamson 1937:102–103)

This is not the place to attempt a survey of prayer in the religions of Oceania, though such a study would be interesting and useful. The point is that there is little that can be taken for granted about the place of prayer in any one of them; each case is remarkable when compared to others. As it happens, prayer is important in Berawan religion. In fact, I would be inclined to call it a "core ritual" in the sense that Clifford Geertz calls the **slamatan**, a simple sharing of food with neighbors, a core ritual of Javanese society (Geertz 1960:11). That does not mean, however, that Berawan pray in the same manner as the Society Islanders. As we shall see in chapter one, Berawan do not pray individually, and they do not pray regularly. None of their prayers much resembles the Lord's Prayer.

Prayer is central to Berawan religion because it is a concomitant of ritual. Ritual in turn is a part of **adèd** "the way things are done" (Metcalf 1982a:4–6). To be wise in the traditional religion is to know how things should be done, and that knowledge reposes in elders and experts within the community. Each community is slightly different from its neighbor, an autonomous congregation. It follows that the form of Berawan prayer is a product of those communities.

Prayer in the Community Context

Across central northern Borneo there are peoples that share a similar way of life. It is a land of dense rainforest, covering hills that rise toward the mountainous spine of the great island. Out of the central massif, rivers flow west into the South China Sea, and east into the Celebes Sea. It is along the banks of these rivers that the majority of the interior folk live, scattered in isolated communities. Over an area as large as New England there is a population of only a few tens of thousands (see figure 1).

Typically, whole communities are housed in a single, massive wooden structure, a longhouse. A longhouse may accommodate up to a five hundred people, and it is a rare village that requires more than one. Usually these structures are set beside the major waterways that are the arteries of the interior, a little back from the bank behind a grove of palms. The house is raised ten or more feet above the ground on solid piles. On the side facing the river, there is a wide veranda, which runs the length of the building. This is public space, the main street of the village. During the day men and women work here, mending fishing nets or pounding rice, or they sit and gossip, looking out over the river. Everywhere there are knots of children, peers of about the same age, scampering up and down the veranda, or playing in the open space directly in front of the house. The veranda is also the scene of most social gatherings, parties, and rituals. On festive evenings, wick lanterns twinkle along its length, mats are spread in a suitable spot, and people crowd in, sitting knee-to-knee. Various games are popular, and there may be singing and dancing. Rituals, however solemn their purpose, hardly seem much different from these parties. There are phases of the rites that occur during the day, or that require senior men and women of the community to huddle together earnestly, but almost every major rite will sooner or later call forth communal participation and so-ciability.

On the side of the veranda away from the river, a partition runs the length of the house, under the ridge of the high, wood-shingled roof. Behind the partition are the separate rooms for the families who share one

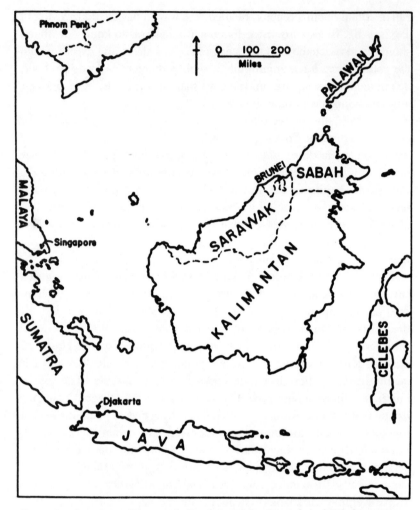

Figure 1. Location of Borneo in Southeast Asia. Sarawak and Sabah are states of the nation of Malaysia, Kalimantan is a part of Indonesia, and Brunei is independent.

hearth and the produce of a family farm. Each family apartment has a door opening onto the veranda, and the usual way of specifying the size of a longhouse is to say how many doors it has. Thirty-, forty-, and fifty-door longhouses are not unusual. Each apartment contains sleeping spaces (some closed off to give a minimum of privacy to married couples), mats to sit on, some simple imported furniture or a sewing machine perhaps, and whatever heirloom property the family owns, most conspicuously brass gongs and Chinese jars. Sometimes the kitchen is housed in a separate structure connected by a walkway at the back of the room, so as to reduce the risk of fire in the main building. Generally, family apartments are about the same size, but sometimes the apartments in the middle of the house are larger and belong to the noble families of the community. In former times, the households of aristocrats included clients and slaves.

At some distance from the longhouse, upriver and down, are the farms on which the economy of the community principally depends. The mode of agriculture is extensive, using the technique usually referred to as slash-and-burn. Despite a common prejudice against this technique, especially among government officials who do not approve of upriver ways, there is no evidence that the farmers are causing ecological degradation. There are large reserves of land so that the fallow period is long. Moreover, farmers practice methods of conservation, such as preserving the largest trees in their clearings. These techniques require that, to avoid exhausting the soil, new farms must be cut out of the jungle each year, and families must go far afield to look for suitable elevation to avoid flooding or erosion, to seek out promising-looking soils, and so on. The crop is hill rice, and there is almost no use of irrigation. The work is hard. During busy periods of the agricultural cycle, family groups can be seen in the misty dawn paddling away from the front of the longhouse toward the side stream that leads to their farm, and perhaps those of one or two neighbors. There is some cooperative labor, especially during planting and harvesting, and those receiving help must feed the helpers. But the crops belong exclusively to the coresidents of the apartment to which the farm belongs. Each has its own rice barn, and for the most part families do not come to each other's aid when stocks run low. At such times, people fall back on the produce of the jungle, particularly sago. Sago palms grow wild, but groves are often maintained by replanting whenever a palm is cut down. Fishing and hunting are important sources of protein year-round.

This generally is the lifestyle that is shared by the people that call themselves **orang ulu** (**orang** means "person, people;" **ulu** means "upriver"). Beyond this, there are innumerable differences in the details of culture and society. It is an area of ethnic fragmentation, reflecting migrations and countermigrations, wars and alliances, over many generations. Each community has its own story to tell, each has borrowed from here and there to produce its own combination of traits. If sufficient attention is paid to the minutiae of ritual, each is unique. Nevertheless, there are two major ethnic cohesions. The more homogeneous group is comprised of the Kayan people, who are found in every major watershed in central northern Borneo, both on what is now the Indonesian side of the central mountain chain, in Kalimantan to the east, and on the Malaysian side in Sarawak. The Kayan number about 14,000, and display only minor dialect variation (Rousseau 1978:78). Their cultural uniformity may be the result of rapid expansion in the nineteenth century, and in some river systems they are still considered newcomers. The reverse is the case with the Kenyah people, who are also found throughout the same region with areas of Kenyah predominance interspersed between those of the Kayan. The Kenyah are more numerous, about 40,000 strong, but far more diverse, comprising at least forty named subgroups (Whittier 1978:92). Not all Kenyah dialects are mutually intelligible, and there are a number of marginal groups whose ethnic status is unclear. Finally, there is a residual category of peoples that belong in neither of these major cohesions. This category is comprised of many small groups with complex ethnological linkages. The Berawan are one of these groups (Metcalf 1976a).

The Berawan number about 1,600 people and live beside two main tributaries of the Baram river, the Tinjar and the Tutoh (see figure 2). In each watershed, there are two major longhouse communities, Long Teru and Long Jegan in the Tinjar, and Long Terawan and Batu Belah in the Tutoh. All but one of the prayers included here were recorded at Long Teru, where the traditional religion has been maintained. That does not mean, of course, that belief and practice at Long Teru have gone unchanged. That could hardly be the case when so much has changed around them. In the late 1940s, after the disruption caused by the Second World War, a wave of mass conversion occurred among the Kayan and some other peoples near the headwaters of the Baram river. From there Christianity trickled downriver in a steady but less spectacular movement of conversion of individuals and of families. In the 1950s an indigenous revivalist movement sprang up, seeking to compete with the alien faith by copying some of its organizational features, such as missionaries, and by radically simplifying the observances of the old religions. This movement, called Bungan after its principal deity, met with considerable initial success, and for many years the Baram was the scene of intense religious struggle. By the early 1970s, Christianity had clearly gained the upper hand, and there were only a handful of communities that held out. At Long Jegan a Berawan variant of the Bungan persisted, under the leadership of its prophet Sadi Pejong. One of his prayers is set out in chapter

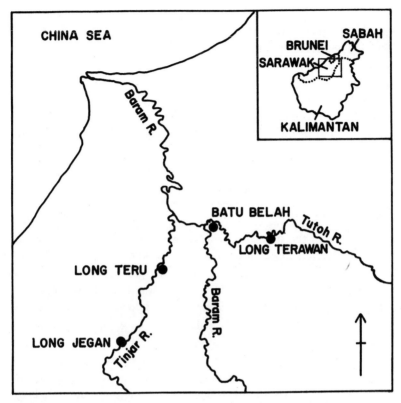

Figure 2. Locations of Berawan communities in the lower Baram area.

eight, together with more details of his version of Bungan. Of all the upriver communities, only Long Teru has maintained the traditional religion throughout this entire period.

At Long Teru there is still a vital religious tradition that is apparent in all aspects of the life of the community, giving coherence to the daily and the annual round, and to the trajectories of individual lives. It is expressed in innumerable observances, most of them casual enough, little more than gestures, but some that involve conscious effort and organization. Some festivals galvanize the entire longhouse. It is not possible to describe briefly the full range of this activity, but it is worthwhile to point out a few general features as background for chapters three to seven—in each of which prayers are presented in their various ritual contexts.

Of life crisis rituals, by far the most important are those having to do with death, and I have made them the focus of a separate study (Metcalf 1982a). The rites for an important person may take years to conclude. The immediate funeral (**pataí**) lasts up to ten days, and every family must participate. Every night there are boisterous gatherings, and no one is supposed to sleep. After the conclusion of **pataí**, the close family of the deceased must perform additional rites, but the community as a whole is not involved at this stage. However, if the family of the deceased decides on secondary rites, there is another longhouse festival, this one even more exuberant than the first. These rites, called **nulang**, must occur no sooner than one year after the death, and they involve recovering the remains of the corpse and bringing them back in triumph to the longhouse. This is the most important festival of the Berawan religion, drawing its awesome sacredness from the immediate contact with the ancestors, who are believed to arrive en masse to receive this new addition to their company. Prayer four was recorded during a funeral, and prayer five was recorded at the beginning of a **nulang** when the party that was to recover the remains of a dead man arrived at his temporary tomb. Chapters five and six give accounts of the associated rites of **pataí** and **nulang** respectively.

By comparison, weddings are simple affairs. For the most part, they involve summoning all the neighbors to have a drink and to witness that the union is now socially accepted. The rites themselves are brief. Even grand weddings between families with social pretensions are only bigger parties. Unlike some of the Kenyah who have elaborate ceremonies for giving names to whole generations of children, during which aristocratic or commoner status is emphasized, the Berawan name children at birth without ceremony. The only Berawan festivals to rival **nulang** in scale and solemnity of purpose were those concerned with headhunting. They too involved gathering large crowds of guests from other villages, and feasting with them for a week or more. Traditionally, massive posts, decorated with sacred leaves, were erected to mark these festivals and to symbolically renew the vigor of the community. These festivals ceased with the suppression of headhunting—the last occurring in 1946–1947 with heads taken from the retreating Japanese—and now they only exist as pale shadows of their former glories, appended to the mortuary rituals (Metcalf 1982a:112–35).

Currently the only occasion other than death that involves the participation of the entire longhouse population is the annual celebration of **papì' lamèng** "prayers for the house." It is described in chapter three, and two prayers that were said during the festival are recorded. I begin with them because they provide nice examples of prayer in its most general form, focused on the welfare of the entire community for the coming year. Apart from this, there are no other calendrical festivals. Ritual related to the agricultural cycle is not elaborate. This is surprising in view of the complex rice cults found in other parts of Borneo, for instance among the Iban (Jensen 1974:151–94), and suggests that rice cultivation may have been less important in the Berawan economy in former times.

Other rituals are smaller in scale, family based, but they are nonetheless significant for that. Some occur within the family apartment, and are as private as anything can be in the longhouse. Others, while still the prerogative and responsibility of the coresidential group, require that neighbors and kin be summoned. The usual locus is the veranda in front of the family apartment, and the hosts will serve at least rice wine. The beneficiaries of such rites are individuals or small groups with some particular problem or need. Many rituals of this kind concern healing, and a nice example is provided in chapter four, together with a prayer spoken at the time. Sometimes augury is involved in diagnosing the cause of the affliction. The most serious form of augury involves calling the major omen bird, the hawk **plaké**. It occurs after the completion of a funeral, to test whether there will be more deaths. Traditionally it was employed in assessing the fortunes of war and headhunting, but it is also used in cases of life-threatening illness. Chapter seven describes such an occasion, and records a prayer used at that time.

These smaller, more intimate rites bring together only a fraction of the population of the longhouse. But since they occur over and over again during the year, they exert a more profound influence on the social fabric than the occasional grand festival. They constitute to a large extent what the Berawan themselves see as their way of life. Moreover, they take on a shape that is characteristic of a particular community, regardless of which family is sponsoring the event. That finally is the most salient feature of the traditional religions, and the feature that is lost with them: the longhouse as a ritual community, its own religion, an autonomous congregation.

Prayer in the Regional Context
Because of the pace of religious change in central northern Borneo, the opportunity to study indigenous ritual language is rapidly slipping away. Unfortunately, the existing sources available for study are extremely thin. It seems likely that the prayers set out in this text will provide the principal

record of a genre that formerly must have been found over a wide area, with dozens of different variants. We shall now never know about most of these, but that makes it all the more important to assess, as far as possible, how representative these examples are of a more widespread phenomenon. This is especially true since the Berawan live on the western edge of the culture area that Edmund Leach labeled alliteratively the Kayan-Kenyah-Kajang complex (1950:46). "Kajang" is the term that Leach coined to cover the many small groups that are not part of the Kayan or Kenyah cohesions, yet are found within the same geographical area. My general conclusions are that the ethnographic evidence is sufficient to indicate, first, that prayer was an important feature of the religions of the region, and second, that the Berawan form of it displays features typical of prayer throughout the region.

The poverty of sources on prayer in central northern Borneo is only one result of a regrettably poor ethnographic record. For the most part, we are obliged to rely on accounts written early in the twentieth century by travelers and colonial administrators. Sometimes they are insightful, sometimes not. They suffer, however, from two pervasive faults: their coverage is frustratingly patchy, and they often fail to attribute particular traits to particular communities. The tendency to impose a false homogeneity on interior folk makes it difficult now to sort out how uniform particular beliefs and practices in fact were. This situation is exacerbated by the evident readiness of Bornean peoples, especially among the more marginal groups, to borrow the language of their more powerful neighbors when discussing abstract matters. A nice example is provided in the Berawan prayers, where terms from several different Kenyah isolects are freely adopted as synonyms for the indigenous Creator Spirit (see chapter one). What was needed, of course, was systematic fieldwork in several communities across the region, chosen strategically to provide the necessary coverage. Lacking this, we must draw what inferences we can.

Charles Hose, as one of the first district officers, traveled widely in the Baram river watershed. He tells us "all Kayans, men and women alike, invoke in their prayers the aid of Oding Lahang and Laki Tenangan." The latter is the supreme deity of the Kayan pantheon, so we have here a clear case of invocation and supplication, that is, of prayer. The reference to women praying is somewhat puzzling, since among the Berawan prayer is usually restricted to men, but Hose makes no further reference to it. Elsewhere he describes how a sick Kayan might address prayers to Laki Tenangan, asking the spirit of the augural hawk, Laki Neho, to act as intermediary. He has the invalid hold up an egg and say: "This is for you to eat, carry my message direct to Laki Tenangan that I may get well and live and bring up my children, who shall be taught my occupations and the true customs." It is not clear how much Kayan Hose spoke, and the prayer is suspiciously brief. Most likely it is a synopsis of what he took to be the general sentiments, and sufficient to indicate supplication with offerings, a typical feature of a Berawan prayer. Several times, Hose mentions the importance of sacrifice in Kayan ritual, so that a picture emerges of prayer as an element in Kayan religion (Hose and McDougall 1912, 2:5, 10, 25, 75).

Hose provides more convincing details about Kenyah prayer. Whenever any important matter was undertaken, he tells us, a pig would certainly be sacrificed as part of the ceremony:

> An attendant hands a burning brand to the chief, and he, stooping over the pig, singes a few of its hairs, and then, addressing the pig as "Bali Bouin," and gently punching it behind the shoulder . . . pours out a rapid flood of words. The substance of his address is a prayer to Bali Penyalong . . . and an injunction to the soul of the pig to carry the prayer to Bali Penyalong. (Hose and McDougall 1912, 2:61)

All this is highly reminiscent of Berawan ritual, and in both the prayers in chapter three, recorded during a longhouse festival, we find the speakers pouring out just such a "rapid flood of words" over a pig, charging it with a similar mission. They did not require a burning brand, but produced instead an old brass cigarette lighter. They addressed the pig as **bíli' bíkuí** (**bíli'** means "spirit," **bíkuí** means "pig") and prefer other names for the supreme deity. Aside from these differences, the process is identical. Hose recounts a particular incident when an important Kenyah chief of the epoch, Tama Bulan, was preparing to join Hose on a warlike expedition against rebels. Tama Bulan's people then lived far upstream in the watershed of the Pata, a tributary near the head of the Baram. Moreover, they were an influential group so that we may take their practices as representative of at least a segment of the Kenyah. Tama Bulan's preparations consisted of securing omens from the eagle **flaki,** and of making prayers before an "altar" to Bali Penyalong. As we shall see, Berawan also construct "altars" before which prayers are offered, but the striking thing here is the way that Hose describes the "prayer or incantation which he kept pouring forth in the same rapid mechanical fashion in which many a curate at home reads the Church service" (Hose and McDougall 1912, 2:52–53).

Hose's phrases in the two quotations convey what one would expect of an uncomprehending bystander listening to the style of speech described in chapter one.

This impression is consistent with the considerable evidence in the Berawan texts of borrowing from the Kenyah, suggesting a well-established genre widely distributed among the Kenyah and their close neighbors. Words loaned from the Kayan are much less frequent, reflecting the relative recentness of interaction. This is confirmed in the work of J. M. Elshout, who describes the Kenyah on the other side of the mountain chain in the eastern half of the culture area. Elshout worked as a medical officer in the Dutch administrative post at Long Nawang, an important center of the numerous and prestigious Lepo Tau Kenyah. Unlike Hose, Elshout includes segments of actual utterances rather than mere summaries. Most of them are, unfortunately, very brief, and not all of them could be safely classified as prayer. But he gives one, made at a name-giving ceremony, that is thirty-two lines long that clearly demonstrates some of the stylistic features described in chapter one, notably a use of rhyming parallel language (Elshout 1923:182).

More recent sources have the advantage of providing us with full length texts, but they also have the disadvantage of not being recorded in association with rites of the traditional religion. Most pertain to one or another variant of the Bungan cult, but some originated in communities now nominally Christian. Consequently, they are suspect as expressions of indigenous religious concepts. They are most convincing as evidence of continuity in linguistic style.

In the Berawan texts, the single Bungan specimen from Long Jegan is metrically less complex than the others, even dull, but it shows the same sort of structures that are found in the prayers of the old religion from Long Teru. It seems reasonable to assume that, if these same metrical structures are found in Bungan prayers from various Kayan and Kenyah communities, then they were also characteristic of prayer in the traditional religions of those communities. Or, to put it the other way around, it hardly seems likely that this style of speech originated with the Bungan cult. On the contrary, the effect of the Bungan was everywhere toward simplification. Moreover, the style certainly could not have in that manner found its way into prayer at conservative Long Teru.

All of the recent sources have appeared in the pages of the invaluable *Sarawak Museum Journal*. There are two sources by Bishop A. D. Galvin (1968, 1974), and several prayers are included in the collection put together by Carol Rubenstein (1973). Rubenstein is not an ethnographer or a linguist. She came to Sarawak interested in recording the poetry of Bornean peoples in general, and succeeded in obtaining funding and enlisting the aid of the staff of the Sarawak Museum. With her guides, she made trips to different areas, collecting whatever oral productions were offered in the short time available, without any attempt at coverage. Since dozens of different languages were involved, she was obliged to work through chains of interpreters. The project was from the point of view of an ethnographer a hopelessly ambitious one, and published results show the consequent technical faults. There is no attempt to sort out the different genres and traditions characteristic of one area or the whole region; instead everything from lullabies to liturgies is mixed in together and described as "song." There are no criteria for the segmentation of lines, the first step in metrical analysis. Transcriptions and translations are inconsistent and not articulated so it is impossible to recover the word-for-word glosses that she obtained from her informants. Yet these faults are offset by the sheer volume of the results. In two volumes there are over a thousand pages of text, over two hundred items of oral literature from the length and breadth of Sarawak. With all its faults, it is the most important source in existence on the oral literatures of the northern half of the island. To leaf through the pages of Rubenstein's collection is to become aware of the research efforts that would be needed to fully document the riches that are now being lost.

There are forty-seven items of Kayan or Kenyah origin in her collection. If we apply my definition of prayer, twenty items seem to qualify: ten of thirty-one Kenyah items, and no less than ten out of sixteen Kayan ones. This is already significant; granted, these are not random samples, and informants in different areas may have had their own motivations to emphasize or to repress one genre or another. Yet the fact remains that prayers are much less conspicuous in the collections from other ethnic groups to the north and the south, if not entirely absent. Of the Kenyah prayers, six come from the village of Long Moh. Long Moh was settled by Lepo Tau Kenyah who immigrated to the upper Baram from across the mountains a couple of generations ago. The community is predominantly Bungan, with some Catholics, and the most active center of non-Christian ritual activity in the area. Bishop Galvin's two prayers were also recorded from this village. The remaining four Kenyah prayers are from villages in the same area where Bungan influence is fading. The ten Kayan prayers come from another river system—from the Belaga to the south—thus widening the geographical representativeness of our sample. All of them display, in various degrees, the stylistic and metrical elements characteristic of Berawan prayer, as described in chapter one. Surprisingly, it is the Kayan ones that display the most parallelism, and consequently they resemble the Berawan examples most closely. This similarity may indicate a relatively greater conservatism in Kayan prayer.

In conjunction with the earlier ethnographic descriptions, these texts make it reasonably certain that prayer functioning in a manner similar to Berawan prayer was once to be found throughout central northern Borneo. One would like to know about other smaller ethnic groups in the complex. On its northern edge, the Kelabit in the central highlands and their cousins the Lung Bawang in the Trusan watershed should probably be included. Rubenstein devoted a long section, amounting to forty-two items, to the Kelabit. Of these items just two appear to be prayers, both addressed to a vague rice spirit. The Kelabit are now heavily involved in fundamental Protestantism, and it is very possible that prior to their mass conversion in the 1940s, prayer was a feature of the Kelabit religion. At any rate, these two items display some of the metrical features typical of Berawan prayer.

As for the rest of the island, no such claim can be made confidently. For the peoples to the north, in what is now the Malaysian state of Sabah, the best source on ritual language is I. H. N. Evans's account of the religion of the Tempasuk Dusun (1953). It contains seventeen items, each a complete text with invaluable line-by-line translation. It also contains a brief glossary of words peculiar to ritual speech, with indication of their origins. They display features of parallel language, rhyme, and alliteration similar to Berawan prayer, but it is not clear how comparable they are in terms of religious function. Evans's chants are all collected from female ritual specialists whom he refers to as "priestesses." Like Maori **karakia,** the matter that the texts contain seems "foreign to the subject under treatment," and it may be that they are better compared to the songs of Berawan shaman than to Berawan prayers. Whether the Dusun also have a style of direct invocation is a moot point. A single item recorded by J. Staal (1927) does not resolve this issue.

Much more material bearing on ritual languages exists for the peoples of the southern half of the island. These ethnic groups have much larger populations—running into the hundreds of thousands—and were studied at an early date by both Dutch and German scholars. It would not be useful to attempt a full inventory of sources, so I will mention only the important ones. The single most obvious source is Hans Schärer's (1966) extensive compilation of myths and their embodiment in elaborate cycles of songs that are performed by special priests throughout extended mortuary rituals (**tiwah**). There are several other sources that examine these priestly songs. R. Brandsetter (1928) refers to his texts as "hymnen," while J. Mallinckrodt and L. Mallinckrodt-Djata (1928) describe their texts as "priesterzang." A. Hardeland's texts are appended to a dictionary (1858) containing hundreds of words peculiar to Ngaju ritual language. D. Dunselmann, in several publications (e.g., 1954, 1959a, 1959b) provides cosmological myths that appear in ritual chants of the Mualang and Kendayan peoples of southwest Borneo. What is striking about this textual material, much of it recorded long ago, is that almost none of it could by any definition be classified as prayer. In place of direct invocation in free composition, the emphasis is on the precise recitation of fixed texts that unfold some variety of mythic narrative. Whatever their metrical structure, they constitute different kinds of religious activity. There are then two possibilities: either prayer per se has been passed over in the literature on southern Borneo, a situation not inconceivable in view of Tambiah's observations, with which I started, or, alternatively, it may be that prayer is in reality a "core ritual" of the religions of central northern Borneo, where it is not in the south. The contrast, however, is unlikely to be absolute. For one thing, Berawan religion does possess texts that require precise recitation, namely the death songs, which I discuss in detail elsewhere.

The Iban of western Borneo seem to provide another tradition of prayer. In his useful summary of Iban verbal styles, Erik Jensen includes the following:

> **Sampi** are invocationary prayers used on virtually all ritual occasions. They begin with the cry "Oha" repeated three times, as a summons to the spirits, and almost invariably continue by describing the favour or assistance which the relevant spirit(s) is asked to give . . . **sampi** are poetical in form: they employ repetition, alliteration, and decorative wording with no real meaning. (Jensen 1974:67–68)

This sounds much like Berawan prayer. But a few lines later he tells us that an officiant needs only the ability to memorize prayers for a majority of heads of households in the village in which he worked could recite short prayers for everyday purposes, and that only a few could recite the longer invocations. This emphasis on rote is in contrast to Berawan prayer.

Prayer in the Performative Context

As a criterion of the presence or absence of prayer in other Bornean religions, I have utilized a test of function, the invocation and supplication of spirits. But this is not how Berawan identify prayer. They know that a prayer is in progress when they hear the style of language described at the outset, the style they call **píat**.

This style defines a particular verbal genre. There are others that have different conventions, and that are heard in different contexts, in gatherings large and small, serious and playful. Three genres that are named are: **tekena'**, **buwan**, and **gu**. **Tekena'** are stories that invariably deal with a glorious military history. **Tekena'** are not told in connection with ritual, but purely as entertainment. The locale is usually a family apartment in the evening, and the story teller is rewarded with drinks provided by the small crowd of listeners. Many old people are liable to tell **tekena'**, but only half a dozen in the longhouse are sought out because of their artful styles, which in turn identify a definite genre. **Buwan** have much the same subject matter as **tekena'**, and they are heard under similar circumstances. They are, however, performed differently because **buwan** are sung. A common tune is called **suket**, which has regular verses of four lines. The first three are sung by the lead, and display a fixed rhythm and pattern of rhyming. A fourth line is sung with the chorus (**nerang**), which includes all those in the audience skilled enough to participate. There is a fixed repertoire of these final lines (**ípet**), which are keyed by alliteration. The form of **suket** is also sometimes used to sing a welcome to a guest at a ritual such as a wedding, and it will contain compliments and expressions of pleasure at the visit. At the end of the song, its recipient must drink the full glass of rice wine that is offered, and he may then respond in kind.

Gu are also songs, but very different in impact from **buwan**. They are not for entertainment; on the contrary they form the sacred core of the mortuary rites, providing the vehicle by which the ancestors are summoned to the longhouse of the living. There are many songs, some required, some optional, each with its own rhythm. Most require a chorus, but not all, and they are sung on every evening that the rites are in progress. They are absolutely prohibited at any other time (Metcalf 1982a:190–231).

Another kind of singing that occurs in a sacred context is the songs of **daíyung**, or shamans. There is no separate name for these songs that identify them as a particular genre, perhaps because the behavior of shamans is unpredictable and unconventional, the result of inspiration by unaccountable spirit agencies. Consequently, shamans have no stable genre of their own. On the other hand, shamans are expected to sing— Berawan say that the spirits play in her body—and they may choose to pass along any useful information in this manner.

In all these types of performance—**tekena'**, **buwan**, **gu**, **daíyung**—women figure about as prominently as men. The most admired singer of **suket** at Long Teru is a woman named Bilo (widow) Kase, who was married to the most important leader of the community in recent times. She had a self-assured manner, and thought of herself as a repository of traditional culture. The majority of shamans are women. Several older men and women vied for excellence of story-telling, but there is one genre that is restricted to men, and that is **píat**.

I.

Píat—The Style of Prayer

When a Berawan prays, he employs the style of language called **píat**.[1] The social occasions on which **píat** is liable to be heard, and the individuals that are liable to speak it, are well defined. But **píat** is recognizable aside from its social context. It is a style that is marked by several linguistic features, including a free use of parallelism, segmentation into tone groups, alliteration, and other rhythmic devices. The aim of this chapter is to show how these features combine to produce the peculiar quality of **píat**.

A Controlled Comparison

This aim is best served by comparing **píat** with other ritual languages of island Southeast Asia. Given the integrity of the region as a culture area, it comes as no surprise that, in all their variants and localized manifestations, the languages share a clear family resemblance. Consequently, there are sufficient similarities to allow close comparison, and sufficient differences to point up the contrast.

In particular, it is the parallel verse of Eastern Indonesia that provides my principal comparative case. This is partly because it is the best described form of ritual language in the region, having recently been the subject of a series of papers by James J. Fox (1971, 1974, 1975, 1977, 1982), and now a collection including the work of several authors (Fox 1988). But I choose this case for a more substantial reason than simply availability of data. It is likely that **píat** provides an example of a style of ritual language characteristic of large areas of island Southeast Asia, and that it has a complementary distribution with the style that Fox describes.

The main features of the latter are now well attested. They involve what Roman Jakobson (1966:403) refers to as "canonical, pervasive parallelism." Fox's examples come from the island of Roti, near the western tip of Timor in the Lesser Sundas:

> Rotinese ritual language is a form of oral poetry characterized by the required coupling of virtually all semantic elements. The language is formal, formulaic, and parallelistic. Semantic elements comprise prescribed dyadic sets; these sets are structured in formulaic phrases; and as a result, composition generally consists in the production of parallel poetic lines. While simple in structure, elements of this language are of sufficient number, variety and complexity to allow considerable scope for stylistic elaboration but little scope—if any at all—for individual improvisation. (Fox 1971:215)

With local variations, oral poetry of very much the same kind is to be found throughout the islands of Eastern Indonesia. The articles in the collection cited above, all focused directly on this topic, support the generalization by providing instances from various parts of Sumba and Flores.

For the rest of island Southeast Asia, no such specialized studies exist. There are any number of texts available for study, both fragments and whole works, ranging from court histories and epic poems to folk genres of all types. In fact, the literature on them is vast, dating back over a hundred years, with translations and commentary in all the languages of western Europe. Yet, there has been no development of ethnopoetics for the region, and few, if any, analyses of the metrical structures of particular genres.[2]

The present study can only make a beginning on a large project of collection and analysis of texts. It identifies a previously undescribed style of ritual language in Southeast Asia, one that stands in contrast to the style that predominates in Eastern Indonesia. To specify the features that characterize this style, I begin by partially inverting Fox's description.

Loose Structure

Given a familiarity with Fox's work, the characteristic of **píat** texts (and others like them) that most immediately stands out is an absence or weakening of features that he describes. While parallel language is certainly found in them, there is no "required coupling of virtually all semantic elements," and dyadic sets are not prescribed. In that sense, the poetry is less "formal." The temptation under these circumstances is to speak of a metrical structure that is by comparison "loose," and it was in these terms that I first approached the analysis of **píat**. [3]

The notion of loose structure, however, has several inherent difficulties. First, it is something of an oxymoron. It is salutary to remind ourselves that the notion was mobilized during the 1950s to describe societies that lacked unilineal descent groups. With the wisdom of hindsight, it is apparent that the implied deficiency was evidence only of a rigidification in theory. Structure is not quantifiable; a society with less structure is like a day with less weather. Worse, the negativity of the notion directs our attention away from discovering the structures that are in fact present. The point should be that the same set of procedures or mode of analysis reveals two different structures.

In rejecting the notion of loose structure, we are led back to the fundamentals of analysis. What is fundamental here is the general principle of equivalence developed by Roman Jakobson in his essay "Linguistics and Poetics," which was published in 1960. The principle is applicable to a wide range of linguistic features. The manner in which they enter into equivalence and mark it, and the kinds of relationships involved, may differ greatly. All that is required is that sequences are counted as equivalent in some way. Such comprehensiveness allows Jakobson to equate effectively poetry with parallelism, broadly defined as the "bringing together of two elements" (1973:21).

The "informality" of **píat** and genres like it, though significant, should not deter analysis. That it need not is shown by what is the largest and oldest body of literature in existence on the topic of parallelism, which concerns ancient Hebrew poetry. Beginning in the eighteenth century, it continues to grow, in the writings of Robert Alter (1985), Adele Berlin (1985), James Kugel (1981), Wilfred Watson (1984), and others. They have elaborated classifications of modes of parallelism and a large technical vocabulary. Yet Hebrew poetry is not characterized by canonical parallelism.

Now that I have invoked the imposing edifice of Hebraic scholarship as an antidote to the notion of loose structure, I can return to my comparisons. First, I discuss the social contexts of ritual language. Then, I contrast the manner in which dyads are made and used. Next, I examine larger structures, including formulae, lists, and figures, and finally, versification.

Social Character

To begin with a point of similarity, it is apparent that all the ritual languages discussed below are socially embedded; all are spoken on public occasions, and they embody the full range of collective representations, above and beyond those concerning style of expression.

Prayer for the Berawan is inherently a group activity. They would have no understanding of the Biblical injunction:

> And when thou prayest, thou shalt not be as the hypocrites are: for they love to pray standing in the synagogues and in the corners of the streets, that they may be seen of men. Verily I say unto you, they have their reward. But thou, when thou prayest, enter into thy closet, and when thou hast shut thy door, pray to thy Father which is in secret; and thy Father which seest in secret shall reward thee openly. (Matthew 6:5–6; AV)

On the contrary, it is hardly possible to pray alone; prayer requires an audience.[4]

It follows that prayer is an aspect of ritual. If there is **píat** then there is **papì'**, which we may gloss either as prayer or as ritual since the one implies the other. By the same token, there is no utility to the notion of "silent prayer," as described by Gladys Reichard in her study of Navaho prayer: the "ritualistic act of pollen strewing is a prayer for well-being whether accompanied by words or not." There is no Berawan equivalent, no action by which invocation may occur. It is difficult to imagine how there could be, since the premise of the Navaho action is not met, that "thought is the same, or has the same potentiality, as word" (Reichard 1934:9).[5]

A further consequence is that Berawan prayer is indeed capable of hypocrisy, of being directed more at a human than a spirit audience. A

particularly blatant example is provided in prayer four, in which the ambitious Uking goads his rivals without allowing them the opportunity to
respond. Such cases are rare, and Uking was subject to criticism for his
boorishness. Yet, this extreme case reveals a general truth. The performer
of **pı́at** is always aware of his audience, and they have expectations of what
he will say. Prayer is always to some degree a political act because it is
closely related to the social order.

Much the same is true of the ritual languages of Eastern Indonesia,
which Fox describes as the "pre-eminent vehicle of social intercourse." It
stands above ordinary, individual speech:

> Ritual language may be used to convey critical assertions of advice,
> instruction, or reprimand from the ancestors or spirits; on the other hand,
> it may be used to express the hopes, fears, rivalries, anxieties or
> grievances of particular individuals that might otherwise not be openly
> divulged. Thus ritual language constitutes an elevated mode of discourse
> that is able to give public voice to what might otherwise be unspeakable.
> As a consequence, poetic compositions in ritual language are concerned
> with revelation and disclosure. (Fox 1988)

But here a difference in emphasis emerges. Although both **pı́at** and the
ritual languages of which Fox speaks are responsive to social dynamics, it is
noticeable that he emphasizes disclosure where I spoke of hypocrisy. This
is no random choice of words, but a reflection of differences in the way that
the attribute of speech is viewed.

Voice and Status

In Eastern Indonesia, ritual language is widely regarded as the "words of
the ancestors." To speak them is an act of boldness, because mis-speaking
them may have serious consequences. In indigenous conceptions, the
aptitude for correct speech comes only secondarily from learning:

> Young chanters acquire their knowledge of ritual language not by study
> or by memorizing chants but by receiving their knowledge of the
> language . . . in a single flash of insight and understanding when, it is
> said they . . . "receive the tongue and take the voice" of their ancestors'
> knowledge. Thereafter . . . they can add to that knowledge the skills of
> performance that come from practice and from hearing the performances
> of other experienced chanters. (Fox 1988:13–14)

The speaker's performance is seen not as a personally creative act, more or
less successful, but as a receptivity to inspiration. In this respect, the
chanter resembles a shaman.

The situation is different with regard to **píat.** No one ever suggested to me that proficiency in it is acquired either mystically or instantaneously, even though inspiration from dreams is frequently claimed in connection with other aptitudes. Berawan are eager to note that some speakers are clever and that others are inept; the consequences of a poor performance are ridicule at worst. At the festival of Prayers of the House, described in chapter three, I once saw an old man, far gone in his cups, launch into prayer before carefully prepared offerings. Gesturing too exuberantly, he staggered and fell among them, knocking everything askew. This performance was greeted with delighted cackles.

Paradoxically, the weightiness of ritual language in Eastern Indonesia goes hand-in-hand with its irrelevance for the social hierarchy. Acquiring the impersonal "voice" of the ancestors does not, Fox tells us, in itself confer high status. An expert gains respect, and his services may be in high demand, but he does not advance his social standing. Many of the best chanters are of common descent, rather than belonging to elite lineages. Again, in this respect, the status of the chanter resembles that of the shaman in many societies.

The social logic of **píat** works in just the reverse way. A man of any social prominence may be assumed to have some skill at making prayers, acquired simply by practice in the course of carrying out the responsibilities of his status. Consequently, there is a direct correlation with the social order: the more important the man, the more frequent his opportunity to hone his personal style. Indeed, the correlation is often made into a premise. As we shall see in the comparison of the styles of Tama Jok and Tama Aweng in chapter three, a prominent man's **píat** will almost invariably be judged more polished than that of a lesser man.

It is worth pointing out, however, that Berawan society is far more egalitarian than many of those in Eastern Indonesia. Since they lack corporate descent groups, there is no place for elite lineages.[6] The social field is smaller since, prior to the turn of the century, longhouse communities numbering only a few hundred were autonomous. Political specialization was only emergent, and there was no word in Berawan that might be glossed as "chief." All this is in contrast to the small states of Roti and Sumba, with their systems of rank.

Just who are the prominent men of Berawan society can be briefly described for present purposes. We can think of them in two groups. The heads of households constitute the first group. As we saw in the introduction, a longhouse contains apartments (**ukuk**) whose coresidents share a farm and a hearth. The eldest male in it is automatically its head, and he will be called upon to make prayers during small family rites. The agricultural cycle furnishes several such rites—for instance, when the family gathers to sample the first of the new rice. On this private occasion, a chicken is slaughtered and prayers are said over the rice before all sit down to eat and drink. But some elders never become very proficient at **píat**. On public occasions involving more than the close family, they hang back and let others take the lead. These men lack ambition. The second group comprises those who would be forward in community affairs, including rituals. They are the ones that polish their skills at **píat** by frequent practice, and vie with one another for recognition. Some men begin this competition with the advantage of noble birth, that is, they are closely related—agnatically, consanguineously, or affinally, it hardly matters which—to acknowledged leaders of past generations, figures like those whose names are recited by Tama Jok at the beginning of prayer one. But even with the advantage of birth, a man must still show himself to be of the right timber if he wishes to follow suit. A son or a brother of a great man gains reflected glory, but cannot transmit it to his own children if he is retiring in public and in ritual matters. The most prominent men of the community, men of unsullied lineage and commanding mien, are expected to be correspondingly fluent in **píat**.

It is the political overtones of **píat** that make it inappropriate for women. There are, I suspect, a number of senior women, widows perhaps and heads of household by default, who can and do pray perfectly well. Yet, they would not do so at a large gathering. This should not mislead us into believing that women are politically unimportant. There are, and apparently always have been, some who wield considerable influence. Rather it is a matter of etiquette: women should not appear forward.

To sum up the contrasting relationships of voice and status: in Eastern Indonesia, effectiveness in speaking a ritual language requires precision. Errors are noticeable, and reproved, and "required couplings" must be memorized. Yet at the same time, the skill is said to be acquired by inspiration. This paradox makes sense in terms of a social order in which chanters are like shaman. They speak with voices that are not their own; who they are does not matter. Meanwhile, high class individuals need not risk making a certifiable public error. In the more egalitarian Berawan society, **píat** is perceived as less mystical. It has its conventions, to be sure, but little about it is rigidly fixed. The speaker has no voice but his own. On that, as on other aspects of social standing, he is liable to both favorable or disparaging comparison with his peers.[7]

Parallel Lines and Parallel Words
In the case of **píat** it is particularly plain why it is appropriate to speak of a ritual language rather than ritual speech. Participants evidently assess individual utterances, such as those set out against some shared standard. Next, we will focus our attention on that standard, beginning with the formal parallelism of line and word that Fox emphasizes.

Much of the terminology in this area comes from Robert Austerlitz's classic study of *Ob-Ugric Metrics* (1958). He begins with the issue of segmentation:

> The purpose of segmentation is to cut the linear sequence of the text and to reveal its internal organization. It will be seen that this process of inspection (rather than the application of *a priori* notions) is more efficacious and enables us to isolate those imminent features which are decisive at a later stage of analysis. (Austerlitz 1958:32)

In the event, his criteria of segmentation are syntactical, and justified by their results in revealing parallel structures.

The bulk of his study is a classification of the types of lines produced. According to Austerlitz, parallelism occurs because of incomplete repetition. Two lines cohere if they share words in common but differ in others. Parallel lines are schematically illustrated in the following examples:

    Example one: XA
                   XB
    Example two: AX
                   BX
    Example three: XAY
                   XBY

A and B are then parallel words, and the lines form a couplet. Other forms of coherence include echoes and terraces. They have the following shapes:

    Echo: AX
             X
    Terrace: AX
             XY

If neighboring lines display coherence, they constitute a parallel structure of more or less complexity. Austerlitz discovered lines embedded in this structure that do not cohere with any others nearby. These he called isolated lines. Sometimes they are repetitious exclamations or introductory phrases. Such standard interjections he calls anacrustic lines. Isolated lines lacking this repetitive feature he calls orphan lines. As the name implies, isolated lines are relatively rare.

Since the ritual languages of Eastern Indonesia are similarly formal, much of this terminology and mode of analysis can be borrowed to discover the structure in them. However, the Ob-Ugric are a people of Asian Russia, far removed from Southeast Asia, and consequently it is not surprising that some modifications are necessary in the process. In particular, the negative characterization of parallelism as incomplete repetition is inappropriate. A brief poem from Roti will serve to show the problem. The translation on the left is followed by letters indicating the pattern of parallel words. The reader should note that Fox employs superscript numbers to indicate the words of a dyadic set ($a^1 // a^2$). I shall not employ his system in the Berawan texts set out in subsequent chapters, but let us follow it for the moment:

All the great ones	a^1 b
All you superior ones	a^2 b
Do you remember this	$c(x^1 d^1)$
Do you bear this in mind	$c(x^2 d^2)$
Orphans are the froth of palmsyrup	e^1 f^1 g^1
And widows are the heads of palmstalks	e^2 f^2 g^2
Palm froth spills over twice	f^1 g^1 h^1 i^1
The spills you gather for them	i^1 j^1 k
And a palmstalk's head droops thrice	f^2 g^2 h^2 i^2
The drooping head you grasp for them	i^1 j^2 k
Leaving orphans still intact	e^1 l m^1
And leaving widows still in order	e^2 l m^2
Intact like a thick wood	m^1 n^1 o^1
Intact for a long time	m^1 p^1 q^1
And in order like a dense forest	m^2 n^2 o^2
Ordered for an age.	m^2 p^2 q^2

Note that lines five and six share no words in common at all, yet we would surely want to describe them as parallel since each word is paired both conventionally and semantically with a word in the adjacent line. This pairing is what constitutes the structure. The poem is composed of fourteen parallel words, thirteen of which (a, d, e, f, g, h, i, j, m, n, o, p, q) are semantic pairs, and one (x) that is a verbal prefix. Since Rotinese (like Berawan) is a relatively uninflected language, most parallel words are lexical elements. In addition to connectives, there are only four repeated forms (b, c, k, l). One couplet has only one pair of parallel words, another four, and two have two pairs. But the most common arrangement, in this poem and throughout Rotinese verse, is three pairs per couplet (Fox 1977:76–77).

So tightly organized is this verse that one's first impression is that it must allow little room for creativity. Yet poems are not learned rote, or reproduced whole. Adepts can vary the pattern of interlacing of lines. Moreover, not all words are restricted to one parallel usage. Fox estimates that in his dictionary of some fourteen hundred semantic elements that about one third are limited in their pairing to one other term only. Another third may appear with two to four other elements, and the remainder with as many as ten. A mispairing constitutes a clear error, but it is still possible to generate an almost infinite number of different structures (Fox 1977:79–80).

Tone Groups and Dyadic Sets

There are also difficulties in applying Austerlitz's terminology to Berawan **píat,** and these difficulties surface at the first step of analysis. As noted above, Austerlitz relies exclusively on syntactical features in cutting his text into lines, and he does not take into account any phonological features. This is no doubt appropriate to his material, but he also had no other choice since he worked from written sources. As he himself points out, some do not even distinguish between texts that were sung, and those that were dictated piecemeal (Austerlitz (1958:13–14).

To apply the same technique to **píat** is unreasonable because it would suppress one of its most characteristic features. It is a feature that is obvious even to someone who has not heard **píat** before, and as a result, the Berawan can recognize prayer immediately even above the din of a crowded longhouse veranda. The opening paragraph of the introduction describes the general effect, but in technical terms, it consists of a crisp segmentation into tone groups. It is tone groups that comprise the individual lines of the prayers in this analysis. For the most part, the lines are short, about a half dozen words or less. But some speakers, especially Sadi Pejong in prayer seven, are inclined to produce long lines. Where these cannot fit on the single page, continuity is shown by three ellipsis points, and a lack of punctuation at the end of the corresponding English translation. Presenting the Berawan text in this way preserves the data, and enables the reader to gain a better idea of the original performance.

Although tone groups do provide the primary criterion of segmentation, it does not mean that lines have no correspondence with the types of syntactical phrases that define lines for Austerlitz. It is only that the former are not deducible from the latter. For example, in line 22 of prayer one, Tama Jok requests:

> mulong jìn mulong genín   a good life, a cool life.

From Austerlitz's point of view, this is two lines:

> mulong jìn
> mulong genín

with the form: XA
               XB

To avoid confusion about the two senses of the word "line," I shall refrain from talking about parallel lines. In the following discussions, a line of **píat** means the tonal segments noted above. Since the parts of a couplet may not be displayed graphically in parallel, I also avoid the term parallel words. Instead, I use the term preferred by Fox, that is, a dyadic set. The words **jìn//genín** form a dyadic set. The label parallelism, to describe the whole phenomenon, can be retained without confusion.

Other terms used by Austerlitz present no problems. Parallel structures of all kinds appear in **píat,** including terraces, often elaborated, and the occasional echo. A simple example of a parallel structure is provided by the line following the one quoted above:

> mulong jìn mulong genín   a good life, a cool life,
> mulong mída mulong luya   a slow life, a tame life.

Note that, in formal terms, **jìn//mída** and **genín//luya**, not to mention **jìn//luya** and **genín//mída**, are dyadic sets just as much as **jìn//genín** and **mída//luya**. However, there is clearly something special about the last two sets, and that draws our attention to the nature of dyads in **píat.**

Dyads and Loan Words

In contrast to the ritual languages of Eastern Indonesia, dyadic sets in **píat** are not prescribed. In Sumba, a chanter may be fined for errors in performance (Kuipers 1980:2), but no such sanction inhibits a Berawan. There are words that are frequently heard together, but one of them may occur in a novel pairing without exciting comment. A list might be made of the dyadic sets occurring in a sample of texts, but it would not constitute a definitive dictionary of the kind that Fox made for Rotinese poetry that shows all permissible combinations. In that sense, **píat** displays a less structured use of parallelism.

This freedom does not, of course, imply that the choice of new pairings is random. There are standard ways in which dyads are formed. One common technique, familiar in parallel speech worldwide, is to borrow words from the languages of neighboring peoples. In Roti, minor variations in dialect between the two ends of the islands are exploited for this purpose (Fox 1971:234). But the extraordinary ethnic diversity of central northern Borneo, only hinted at in the brief description in the introduction, provides a richer field for the borrowing. Adepts at **píat** love to show off their knowledge of other languages of the Baram watershed, and the cosmopolitan sophistication that it implies.

The borrowed words are usually synonyms of the Berawan ones for which they furnish a pair. For example, when the ancestors are invoked in prayer, the following phrase is often employed:

> **bílì' vì' bílì' sadì**
>
> **bílì' ukun bílì' dupun**

The parallel structure here is identical to that in the previous example. I gloss the repeated word **bílì'** as "spirits." **Sadì'** is the only other word used in everyday, conversational Berawan. It means "grandparents," but the term has a wider application than its English gloss, effectively including all consanguineous or affinal relatives of the second or more ascending generation. Its use after the word **bílì'** clearly implies "ancestors," since living people are not spirits (Metcalf 1982:46–50). **Ukun** is perhaps borrowed from Sebop, or from the Long Wat dialect of Kenyah (Urquhart 1956:39), where it has the same denotation. It might also be borrowed from Western Penan **ukun**, which means "forebear" (Needham: personal communication), and there is a Berawan cognate **ukong**, which means "great grandparent" or "forebear." **Dupun** is probably a Berawanized variant of **tepun**, a word found in Eastern Penan (Needham: personal communication), and in Uma Bem Kenyah (Stort 1912:13), which again has the same meaning as **sadì'**. **Vì'** is a little different, however; it is probably a modified form of **vé'** (Lepo Tau Kenyah, Galvin 1967:105), or **vueh** (Ulu Kelame Penan, Urquhart 1956:41), both of which are glossed as either "uncle" or "aunt."

We may be confident that the range of persons included covers all relatives of the preceding generation, excluding parents.

What is the impact of this multiple reference? I remarked that borrowed words are usually synonymous with a paired Berawan term. But that is not true of **vì'**, and it is only true of **ukun** and **dupun** if we pay attention only to denotation. The words take on a different flavor because they are borrowed; they sound strange to the ear, grander perhaps than the homely Berawan. This phenomenon is not unfamiliar to speakers of English, for whom related words of Romance and Germanic etymologies often have differing connotations. In this context, one may speak of the radiation of synonyms (Pei 1966:227).

These differences of meaning are subtle, however. It is unlikely that a non-native speaker would have a firm grasp of them, and even less likely that a series of glosses could be found that would render these nuances into English. Consequently, a translation such as:

> spirits of uncles, spirits of grandparents,
> spirits of ancestors, spirits of forebears,

is misleading because the assigned differences in meaning are unrelated to whatever differences are felt by a Berawan speaker. On the other hand, to offer but a single gloss:

> spirits of grandparents,

truncates the translation, giving it a shape unlike the Berawan original. Consequently, in the translations of the prayers set out below, I employ a numbering system suggested to me by Dell Hymes, as follows:

> spirits of grandparents$_1$ spirits of grandparents$_2$
> spirits of grandparents$_3$ spirits of grandparents$_4$

The subscripts indicate synonyms, or near synonyms. If other synonyms occur later in the same prayer, they are numbered in the same sequence. In prayer six, for example, there are eight terms, some familiar, some obscure, that are used to denote the act of "calling," which is the subject of the prayer. The first time that a new synonym occurs in any given prayer, its etymology is explained in an endnote (indicated, as usual, by a superscript). No punctuation is used after a subscript, even if followed by a superscript, because it might be mistaken for another digit.[8]

In this example, the one term that is not a synonym, vì', has been incorporated in the sequence, in order to preserve the parallel structure. This is not always advantageous, however. Where the words in a dyad have distinct meanings—and this is likely to be the case if both are drawn from everyday Berawan—there is no reason to avoid different glosses.

Píat-*words and Blind Dyads*

In his translations of Rotinese verse, as in the specimen quoted above, Fox always employs different glosses for the elements of a dyad. Some present real contrasts, for instance in the set $e^1//e^2$, "orphans//widows." But others appear to be near synonyms, as in $o^1//o^2$, "dense//thick," and we might expect this where words are borrowed from other dialects. Yet, even in this case, Fox prefers to search out English equivalents because of a theory that:

> The brain's processing of visual information is of the same form as its processing of auditory information. The analogy of linguistic parallelism with visual stereoscopy, a fusion of separate images, is by no means strained. (Fox 1975:127–28)

The extensive use in **píat** of virtual synonyms borrowed from other languages somewhat undermines this notion, although there is room for a subtle divergence of connotation, as we have seen.

A more serious challenge comes from the practice of inventing words *de novo* for use in dyadic sets. I call such concocted elements **píat**-words. Some of them achieve a certain currency in the repertoires of exponents. Others are used only once, and casually discarded. They all share the feature that they are not recognizable outside narrowly defined environments within **píat**. Outside these environments, they are meaningless. Even within them, their meaning can only be deduced from the word in everyday Berawan that accompanies them. For the most part that is how my informants themselves arrived at their intended meanings, which can only be identical. Where this occurs, we may speak of—continuing the optical analogy—blind dyads.

Since the glosses are of necessity the same, the system of subscript numbers devised for synonymous loan words can also be used for blind dyads. Indeed, there is a gray area between the two. I assume that a word in a dyad is a **píat**-word if it is not used in everyday Berawan, and has no known etymology, but negative proofs are difficult. Presumably, my informants would not make a mistake with regard to the first condition. However, being younger men, they might well have less knowledge of other Baram languages than their seniors who did the praying. Moreover, those languages are not well studied. There are word lists for several Kenyah dialects to which reference has already been made, but they certainly do not provide complete coverage. Consequently, there is room for a loan word to slip through the net, and be declared a **píat**-word. Another source of haziness is the familiar tendency to alter the pronunciation of a word in the process of borrowing it. How much alteration is required to convert a loan into an invention?[9]

A few examples will show the fine gradations possible. In line 31 of prayer two, we find Tama Aweng appealing to:

bíli' ca bíli' lía

As usual, the translation takes up more space:

spirits of the community$_1$ spirits of the community$_2$

Lía is a word commonly heard in conversational Berawan, often in contexts comparing "us," our kinship group, our village, even our ethnic group, to some contrasting "them." To use **ca** in such a context would draw blank stares. If the speaker were an outsider—the hapless anthropologist, for instance—the audience might guess what was meant, so common is the dyad **ca//lía** in prayers, and respond with laughter. But the usage would not be allowed to pass; it is not everyday Berawan. Meanwhile, no one suggested that it is borrowed, and it does not occur on any of my word lists. I conclude that **ca** is a **píat**-word. In the glossary, such words are shown with an asterisk and with the other element of the dyad, in parentheses after the gloss: **ca** community (* **lía**). These entries provide a complete listing for this sample of texts.

A superficially similar dyad turns out to have different origins. At line 120 of prayer one, Tama Jok is waving a chicken around by its legs, and announcing:

tu díek la díek líwa
this is the chicken sacrificed$_1$ the chicken sacrificed$_2$

This line is found in almost every prayer, but the everyday Berawan for "sacrifice" (nominal or verbal form) is **mekì**. I discovered that **la** is borrowed from Kenyah—probably in many dialects, but certainly in Lepo Tau (Galvin 1967:30). It was then easy to conclude that **líwa** is a concocted pair. In fact, it is a cognate form found, for instance, in Eastern Penan (Needham: personal communication; compare also **éwa,** Kenyah, Long Nawang). Here both elements of a dyad are almost certainly borrowed, both are very familiar within a context of **píat,** but neither element is used outside it. In the glossary, borrowed words are recognizable by the notation of origin (limited to one word) in parentheses after the gloss, for example: **la** sacrifice (Kenyah). Words borrowed from other languages of central northern Borneo are written as pronounced in Berawan. Malay loan words, many of which are used in everyday speech, follow the standard Malay orthography.

A less clear-cut case of borrowing occurs in another common dyad (e.g., prayer two line 80) which requests:

ulong tanyít ulong la'ít   a healthy$_1$ life, a healthy$_2$ life.

Tanyít is used in everyday speech, but **la'ít** is unfamiliar. Meanwhile there is a word in Lepo Tau Kenyah, **laya',** which Galvin glosses as "well, good, fine" (1967:32). Is **la'ít** a modified form of **laya'?** Is there another Kenyah dialect, better known perhaps to the Berawan, that has the word **la'ít?** Because I lack the definitive knowledge on the latter question, I treat **la'ít** as a **píat**-word especially as it is modified and in a characteristic way.

Few cases are such close calls. In lines 34 and 35 of prayer one, Tama Jok asks that the blood of his chicken enter:

lum da lum uma   into your house$_1$ into your house$_2$
lum lírín lum lamín   into your house$_3$ into your house$_4$

Uma is a word common to many Austronesian languages. It is the Kayan word for a "longhouse" (Rousseau 1978:80), and a variant, **uma',** has a similar meaning in most Kenyah dialects (Whittier 1978:99). **Lamín** is the common Kenyah word for a "longhouse apartment" or "its residents" (Whittier 1978:104). The Berawan term for that is **ukuk,** but a cognate of **lamín** is used to refer to the whole house (**lamèng**). The remaining two words are not part of everyday Berawan, are not known to occur in Kayan or Kenyah, and probably do not occur since we know the words for "house" that are widely used in those languages. A strong case exists to conclude that both are **píat**-words.

More examples of this are discussed in the next section. But to conclude here, I present an extreme case from prayer six, lines 124 and 125, just to make the point:

kaam bíli' plaké ma   you spirits of eagles,
nyí rapulé nyí ramulé   cure$_1$ him, cure$_2$ him.

The set **rapulé//ramulé** stumped my helpers. Neither word means anything in everyday speech, nor do they sound like any familiar word. No Kayan or Kenyah etymology could be discovered, which was unlikely even at first sight because words beginning with **r** are rare in those languages. My informants had no doubt that Tama Aweng had made both of them up on the spur of the moment, and they do not occur anywhere else in the corpus of prayers. If **la** and **líwa**, and perhaps **ca**, seem at times to be near-words because of their familiarity in **píat**, then **rapulé** and **ramulé** are zero-words, because neither is matched, even temporarily, with anything recognizable. The gloss assigned in the translation is nothing but a guess based on the thrust of Tama Aweng's appeal. In the glossary, each is listed as a pair of the other. Such meaningless dyadic sets are rare, but this example is not unique.[10]

Rhyme and Alliteration
A feature of blind dyads that must have become obvious even from the few examples cited above is that they invariably involve rhyme and alliteration. This is significant because it is lacking in, indeed alien to, the ritual languages of Eastern Indonesia. This is then a positive distinguishing feature of styles like **píat**.

Rhyming is generally within lines, rather than between lines.[11] It is a feature of dyadic sets. Even where these sets do not contain a **píat**-word, the preference for rhyme and alliteration persists, and constitutes a restraint on the free selection of pair words. We have already noted two such examples in the phrase used in summoning the ancestors. Both lines contain a rhyming dyadic set, **vì'//sadì'** in the first, **ukun//dupun** in the second. Another example is provided by all the dyads that can be placed in the parallel structure:

mulong X mulong Y   an X life, a Y life,

of which we have seen three so far, all rhyming: **jìn//genín** (good//cool), **mída//luya** (slow//calm), and **tanyít//la'ít**. There are yet more: **ketan//kapan** (deep//thick) and **tína//tava** (happy//laughing). Only one of these words, **la'ít,** is a **píat**-word, or perhaps a modified loan. The rest are everyday Berawan, as is perhaps appropriate in talking about so elemental a desire as life.

However, in blind dyads it is much easier to arrange for rhyming, and they invariably do rhyme. All that is necessary is to retain in the **píat**-word the final vowel, or vowel and following consonant, of the intended pair. As for the rest of it, there are various design principles that may be observed at work, and these seem to apply whether the word has achieved some currency or is entirely ephemeral. These principles are not by any means always followed, and they are not explicit. They are deduced from the dyads themselves, and from the reactions of my informants as they assisted me in transcription. They had ready opinions about which lines were good and which were bad, turning them around in their mouths to assess the possibilities of cadence. But their criteria were intuitive; they could not say why they preferred one line over another. The same applies to the adepts themselves, who, in contrast to the chanters of Eastern Indonesia, need not expect to be interrupted or corrected. The only coaching that a man receives in **píat** is the general reaction of approval or disapproval in his audience. Consequently, I cannot explain these principles of design, beyond saying that they evidently produce words that are pleasing to Berawan ears.

The principles involve inflection of the intended pair word, the one of the set that is in everyday Berawan, or is borrowed from another language, and which I shall for brevity call the base. It is advantageous to put the base first in a set, so as to tip off the audience to the meaning of the **píat**-word in advance. At the same time, the longer word in a dyad should go in second place. Consequently, **píat**-words are often one syllable longer than their bases, up to a limit of three syllables. There are very few four-syllable words in Berawan, and a **píat**-word of that length sounds clumsy. An easy way to provide this lengthening is with an epenthetic syllable, which ensures alliteration at the same time. But few words are made quite so mechanically; they evidently sound too much like their bases, too close to repetition. The consonants of the base must then be modified in some way, and a neat solution is to reverse their order. The resulting consonants, with either a suitable infix or a prefix, produce a pleasant lilt. This device reproduces a tendency toward metathesis noticeable in other contexts.[12]

Alternatively, one consonant may be dropped, loosening the alliteration but also the predictability of word making. The creative options are reduced if the **píat**-word for some reason goes first.

Some examples will illustrate the possibilities, without attempting to be exhaustive. First, a few that we have looked at already: in the set **vì'//sadì'** (grandparents$_1$//grandparents$_2$), the length principle applies, even though neither is a **píat**-word. However, at the beginning of prayer one, Tama Jok reverses them, presumably so as to put the homely Berawan term first. Most adepts find this unnecessary since the phrase is so familiar. In **la//líwa** (sacrifice$_1$//sacrifice$_2$) the two loan words are ordered as we expect, and the extra epenthetic syllable is just what one would expect of a **píat**-word. That is what led me to conclude overhastily that it is a **píat**-word. Line 129 of prayer one has a dyad, **nat//jat** (bad$_1$//bad$_2$) in which alliterative opportunities are lost because the **píat**-word is placed first, and simply varies the initial consonant of the base. It occurs nowhere else in the corpus. When the base has two syllables, more interesting possibilities are present. Line 38 of prayer one consists of the dyad **nakaan//kenumaan** (feed$_1$//feed$_2$), the former being the base. The **píat**-word retains the initial and medial consonants, but reverses their order. It acquires a new vowel and a consonant, so as to become a syllable longer, to produce a pair that is pleasing enough to be used in several other places.[13] But things do not always work so neatly. In the set **pírèng//ngelírèng** (shelter$_1$//shelter$_2$), the medial and final consonants of the base **pírèng** are left in place and the initial consonant disappears so that two new ones are required. However, one of the two serves another purpose. Verbal forms in Berawan often begin with **ng**, so that the speaker manages to suggest a verbal usage of the base, which means literally the "gable end of a house." This device is commonly used, but it is the only example of a way in which **píat**-words can be constructed so as to suggest a part of speech. If a two-syllable base gets put second in a dyad, the **píat**-word may contract. In the set **da//uma** (house$_1$//house$_2$) noted above, the **píat**-word can only retain the final vowel for rhyme, drop the initial vowel in order to contract, and vary the remaining consonant to prevent duplication. In the associated set **lírín//lamín** (house$_3$//house$_4$) the rules are broken to allow alliteration. Occasionally, alliteration can carry over from one line to another. An example is found at lines 29 and 30 of prayer one, and in several other places, where what is asked for is:

lukí melubí	luck$_1$ luck$_2$
melaí beluwaí	luck$_3$ luck$_4$

Only the first word is not a **píat**-word.

Some speakers of **píat** are more inclined than others to concoct new words in this way, but almost all do so to some extent. Sometimes this produces unforeseen results. In line 125 of prayer one, Tama Jok produces the dyad **mulong//mejong** (life$_1$//life$_2$), in which the latter is evidently a **píat**-word. But the same word appears at line 109 of prayer six, where it is not an element of a dyad. Instead it is part of a phrase borrowed entirely from Kenyah. In that context, **mejong** means "to fly." It seems that Tama Jok, in the heat of the moment, produced an accidental homonym.

The Pattern of Lines

In a discussion of synonymy, John Lyons remarks that "it is by now almost axiomatic that *absolute synonymy* . . . is extremely rare . . . at least in natural languages" (1981:50). Perhaps **píat** does not qualify as a natural language, but it does provide one of his rare cases, in the form of blind dyads. Other dyads, as we have seen, exhibit degrees of what Lyons calls partial synonymy. All of these, and there are a great number of them, partial or absolute, can be readily identified in the texts by the shared glosses and subscript numbers. The interested reader can investigate them further by following the accompanying notes, which contain more detail than can be summarized here.

It is necessary at this point, however, to broaden our view from so narrow a focus on the dyadic set for two reasons. First, **píat** is not characterized by the "required coupling of virtually all semantic elements"; the majority of words do not belong to dyadic sets, and we have had nothing as yet to say about them. Second, there are aspects of meter that go beyond the regularities of parallelism of word and line. It is on this issue that Dell Hymes criticizes Austerlitz's study in a 1960 review.

Hymes praises Austerlitz for seeking to describe the metrics of Ob-Ugric poetry in its own terms:

> Just as an unwritten language has sometimes been thought grammarless, or had its structure obscured, because conventional models did not fit, so an oral poetry . . . has sometimes been thought to be without meter, or had its metrical structure obscured. (Hymes 1960:574)

But, he argues, the results are incomplete. This is because Austerlitz's formal approach can view the whole only in terms of its parts. Austerlitz describes his method in just this way, as the segmentation of a text into its constituent units, and the description and classification of these segments (Austerlitz 1958:21). So defined, metrical analysis becomes inductive and narrow:

> There is no general description of the patterning of lines within texts as wholes, or complete analysis of the patterning of a single text. This leaves the picture of the structure of this type of poetry quite incomplete. (Hymes 1960:575)

The material with which Hymes works, mainly folk tales and narratives from American Indian communities of the Northwest Coast, would not tempt one to employ Austerlitz's formal approach. For the most part, the tales lack the "canonical, pervasive parallelism" of word and line that characterize Rotinese verse. This does not mean that they lack parallelism, but only that we have to take a wider view of parallelism. In this respect, the narratives resemble **píat**. We have already discovered one feature that comes within this wider view, namely the rhyming of dyads. Rhyming, Jakobson tells us, is only a "particular, condensed" case of parallelism (1960:368).

To describe the pattern of lines in **píat** is difficult because the pattern keeps changing, or perhaps it would be better to say that it is patterned at several levels. This is in contrast to the ritual languages of Eastern Indonesia. Consider the Rotinese poem translated earlier: each line is connected to its neighbor by one or more dyadic sets. Each line leads the listener to expect something in the next, or it fulfills an expectation. Sometimes the artful speaker keeps the audience waiting by having the second element in a dyad occur two lines later, but the texture of the lines is uniform.

By contrast, recall the sets that fit into the structure **mulong X mulong Y**, such as the one found at lines 22–25 of prayer one. To point up the contrast with Rotinese verse, I show the dyadic sets by means of superscript numbers, as employed by Fox in the sample given earlier ($a^1//a^2$):

a good life, a cool life,	$a^1\ a^2$
a slow life, a calm life,	$b^1\ b^2$
a deep life, a thick life,	$c^1\ c^2$
a happy life, a laughing life.	$d^1\ d^2$

There is no hooking together of lines here, and there is no hint in one about the next; the speaker might make a single line of the structure, or two, or more, just as he pleases, one dyad per line.

Moreover, there are many lines that contain no dyads or elements of dyads at all; they comprise what Austerlitz calls isolated lines. Both types are represented. In several of the prayers, anacrustic lines are prominent. For instance, much of the rhythmic effect of the last half of prayer six is provided by the constant repetition of **balí flakí,** "spirit of eagle." In the closing section of prayer two, the reiterated phrase is **bílì' no bíkuí,** "you spirit of the pig." In the text and the translation, anacrustic lines are indented well to the right so that they stand out prominently, just as they do in the spoken text. But anacrustic lines occur only in certain passages. Orphan lines are even more common, and, in contrast to Ob-Ugric poetry, many of them may occur one after the other.

These features taken together—the lack of dyadic connections between lines, and the frequency of orphan lines—show that **píat** does not have the uniformity of Rotinese verse. Instead, there are pieces of diverse parallel structures mixed in with sections composed of orphan lines. To use a culinary analogy, Rotinese verse has the smooth texture of pound cake. **Píat,** by contrast, is like fruit cake, with its rich and varied constituents. We have already seen some of the ingredients in **píat,** but the ones that provide the most noticeable changes in texture remain to be described. I call them formulae, figures, and lists.

Formulae, Figures, and Lists

Formulae are highly repetitive, cropping up almost identically time after time. There may be small variations from speaker to speaker, but any particular speaker habitually uses the same phrases. An example is the formula used to refer to the ancestors, with its two utterly familiar rhyming dyads.

Figures are repeated from one **píat** to another, and from one exponent to another, but lend themselves to variation each time they are used. Often they can employ any number of dyads from a selection of possible ones. An example is provided by the structure **mulong X mulong Y** (an X life, a Y life), in which there are several alternatives for X//Y. Commonly, the first dyad is **jìn//genín** (good//cool), but the order and the number of dyads after that varies. A similar figure is **belurí M belurí N** (let us have M, let us have N), and again there are a string of dyads that may be used optionally. These two figures are in fact often found together, so that we may speak of a master figure incorporating them both. In prayer one, it occurs twice, beginning at lines 22 and 87 respectively. Another master figure referring to the power of sacrificial blood turns up in many prayers, but in varying forms. This master figure is discussed in chapter two.

Figures contrast with formulae in exhibiting word variability, although some figures are more variable than others. While still recognizable, figures are relatively loose. An example is provided by another figure concerning sacrifice, in which the victim is dispatched as a messenger to the spirits. Again, this figure is described in chapter two.

Finally, there are lists, often with the structures that Austerlitz calls terraces. The most obvious examples are the lists of spirit agencies that occur in almost every prayer. Tama Avit is particularly fond of them, and in prayer three he produces two of baroque elaboration (beginning at lines 33 and 66). It is interesting to note how he relieves the tedium of a simple list by prefixing the names of some spirits with a pronoun or a connective to form a definite rhythm. Similarly, at the beginning of prayer one Tama Jok gives a list of the great men of past generations, prefacing each with the title **ke sadì'** (late grandfather). Lists can incorporate formulae, as when the ancestors are invoked in a list of supernatural agencies. These lists are of particular interest in the next chapter.

Some exponents make a rich **píat**, full of formulae, figures, and lists, and spiced with any number of dyadic sets, both within these devices and outside them. A few experiment with new ingredients, making up novel parallel structures, or expanding on familiar forms. Tama Aweng experiments in this way at several points in prayer two, sometimes successfully, sometimes not. Yet even the stylists who make an effort to produce elegant **píat** leave orphan lines here and there, and sometimes a succession of them. Often these passages are explanatory in nature, laying out the special circumstances of the prayer. For example, both prayers three and six are concerned with the recurrent illness of the same little boy, and both contain passages describing his symptoms and the anxieties of his parents. These are not topics adequately covered in conventionalized phrases. Explanatory sections do not entirely lack alliteration and rhyme, but these features are less conspicuous.

Other speakers hardly bother to enrich their **píat** at all. The most extreme example of this tendency among the texts set out below is by Uking (prayer four), though Lian Yang (prayer five) is hardly better. Sadi Pejong (prayer seven) is perhaps a special case since he is already an innovator in religious matters, and less concerned with exemplifying traditional forms.

Nevertheless, we can contrast these people with the highly effective Tama Jok (prayer one), Tama Aweng (prayers two and six), and Tama Avit (prayer three). In this particular group—and I make no claims of representativeness—we have a neat split of three and three.

What is involved in this split is not alternative styles available within **píat**, but a difference in competence. I make my argument for this *ad hominem*. As described in the prefatory remarks to prayer five, Lian Yang is a retiring man who does not often put himself in a situation where he must make **píat**, at least for an audience larger than his own household. He had to be cajoled into saying this prayer, on the grounds that no other suitable person was present. Uking's temperament is quite the reverse, and no one would accuse him of being retiring. He is noisily forward in ritual matters, and on that basis one might expect him to be polished in his **píat**. But Uking's influence, one might almost say his charisma, has little to do with the status hierarchy of the community. Uking's powers lay in another direction, that of shaman, and shamanistic power is not based on routinized skills like **píat**. When his prayer was recorded, he was in an excitable mood, and he jumped up uninvited by his hosts. His motives in making the prayer were not those that usually apply, as is explained in chapter five. In short, there is no reason to believe that Uking sought or achieved much ability in **píat**. The unique circumstances surrounding Sadi Pejong have already been mentioned, and details of his new religion are provided in chapter eight.

By discounting the competence of Lian Yang, Uking, and Sadi Pejong, I emphasize the concept of **píat** as a ritual language, rather than ritual speech. The fact remains, however, that even those with lesser abilities encountered no difficulty in having their prayers accepted as fully valid. This being so, one might well wonder whether it is possible to say anything, anything at all, and make it sound like **píat**. To this I reply, cautiously, in the affirmative. Given that there are tight social restraints on who makes prayer and when, it is made minimally recognizable and acceptable by features of intonation.

Intonation

The subject of intonation is a complex one, and there can be no question here of discussing intonation in Berawan generally, or even fully analyzing intonation in **píat** (Cruttenden 1986; Waugh and van Schooneveld 1980). However, its function in making **píat** recognizable calls for some account.

To put it another way, the act of praying has a radical effect on intonation. It is not that other intonation patterns are erased, only that they are modified. In Dwight Bolinger's metaphor:

> The surface of the ocean responds to the forces that act upon it in movements resembling the ups and downs of the human voice. If our vision could take it all in at once, we would discern several types of motion, involving a greater and greater expanse of sea and volume of water: ripples, waves, swells and tides. It would be more accurate to say ripples *on* waves *on* swells *on* tides, because each larger movement carries the smaller ones on its back. (Bolinger 1972:19)

The major effect of **píat** is to flatten out the ups and downs of speech in segments that I have already described as tone groups.

The first aspect of this is that tone groups are separated from one another. Sometimes there is a definite pause, with an intake of breath; but even in very rapid speech, where the lines come tumbling out apace, there is still an audible catch between one line and the next. It is significant that the individuals singled out above as less competent are the very ones who chop their **píat** into short, explosive segments, as if to compensate for the relative lack of parallelism. In the preface to Uking's prayer, I describe his delivery as like a machine gun, the words spat out in short bursts. The effect is only slightly less marked in Lian Yang's prayer, reflecting the man's temperament, and more important perhaps, the fact that he was not competing with a noisy crowd to make himself heard. In this, as in other things, Sadi Pejong has his own way of doing things, but marked disjunction remains a feature of even his overlong lines.

The second aspect of the intonation signature of **píat** is that changes in pitch, loudness, and speed occur most noticeably at these disjunctions between segments. Within segments, the intonations of normal speech, or of rhetoric, or whatever—Bolinger's waves and tides—are noticeably flattened. Intonation in **píat** is not used to make either syntactical or emotional distinctions; the effect is uniformly declamatory without a hint of questioning or surprise. As we noted at the outset, most prayers begin with a phrase that in written form might be taken for a question but is heard as a summons. In the translations of the prayers, question marks and exclamation points do not appear.[14]

On the other hand, the variation between lines *en bloc* in gross features of loudness and speed is equally characteristic. Consequently, I have devised a simple system for indicating how these changes are distributed. This system employs a symbol put at the beginning of each line of the Berawan text:

■   Voice is definitely raised; the lines are spoken slowly so individual words can be made out easily.

■   Voice is clearly audible, and in the range of loudness for normal speech. Words are clear.

◆   Line is spoken very fast, with all the words run together. Loudness is normal or low. Transcription may miss the occasional word.

▪   Line is marginally comprehensible; speaker is mumbling or whispering, sometimes garbling his words together. Transcription is not completely reliable.

It must be emphasized that this classification is only a preliminary attempt to deal with the intonation of **píat.** But even as such, it is necessary in order to display a feature that the speaker is very conscious of, in which bold shifts are used for dramatic effect. The four-point scale clearly runs together variables of pitch, loudness, and speed, and there is no inherent reason why they should covary in the manner that the scale indicates. There is no category, for instance, for either fast, loud speech, or clearly audible whispers. The justification is that these types of speech empirically do not exist in the corpus. In practice it has been found, by trial and error, that this four-part classification serves to show the shifts in which we are interested, and that gradations that were much more comprehensive or fine grained could not be reliably applied.

Versification

Intonation patterns provide the criterion for identifying lines in **píat,** but there are other levels of segmentation that may be applied to the texts, so as to further reveal their structure. A useful model is provided by Hymes's well-known analysis of the Chinookan narrative of "The Deserted Boy" (1981:142–83).

Hymes emphasizes that the process of segmentation is not mechanical, and does not depend on any single feature. Instead, it is a matter of interpretation, involving repeated experimentation until the most satisfactory arrangement is revealed. Two interdependent principles guide analysis:

> That there is a consistent structure, and that it is to be found in terms of form-meaning covariation, taking form here to be linguistic form.
> (Approaches that can recognize only one [form or meaning] are rejected.)
> (Hymes 1981:150–51)

The nature of the "form-meaning covariation" is peculiar to the genre. Nevertheless, **píat** resembles Hymes's narrative in that it lends itself to segmentation into verses.

In Chinookan narrative, initial particles play an important part in identifying verses. In his translation, they appear as phrases beginning each verse: "Now then," "Now again," or "Truly," but these openings are not, Hymes cautions, to be taken as invariantly demarcative, nor can it be known in advance which of them will be employed in any particular verse. Consequently, it is necessary to consider other features at the same time, features that contribute to the general coherence of the text, including the significance of higher level segments. Occasionally, verses have none of these particles to mark them, and this is also significant. One exceptional passage with verses of this kind comprises a climax of the tale, an "idyllic moment of union between man and woman" (Hymes 1981:152–53).

Similar circumstances apply to the verses of **píat,** except that the repetitive initial particles are not found in quite the same way. In part, this is due to differences in the basic syntactical structures of the languages. This difference results in a greater diversity of ways in which verses may be demarcated, and more reliance on overall coherence of the text in confirming those demarcations. Nevertheless, there are recurrent phrases, or more commonly recurrent constructions, that serve to signal verses. For instance, many prayers begin with a series of verses initiated by acts of invocation. The resonant sound I render (inadequately) as ooo . . . is itself a summons, and it is soon followed by a more specific one: "Where are you," and again "you spirits," and again "come." But after a few verses, the construction changes, shifting perhaps to one of supplication: "Give us," or "let us have." Precisely the same phrase is seldom used to initiate two verses in a row, though each may recur elsewhere in the same prayer. This structure is outlined in the appendix, which provides a listing of the first lines or constructions of all the verses in prayers one to six.

The identification of verses is confirmed by their internal structures, as revealed in the dyadic sets and parallel structures that we have already examined in some detail. They are displayed in the translation by indentation of lines and blocks of lines. This process is, again, interpretive, its purpose being to represent the structures that are discovered, and, as far as possible, to suggest graphically the rhythmic effect of the spoken words. Nevertheless, there are a number of conventions that are followed in most cases.

First, two or more lines that participate in a parallel structure are indented a uniform distance from the preceding line. If the first of them also initiates a verse, there is no call to indent, and the verse begins with a block of lines. But it is more common in practice that the first line of a verse is an orphan and stands alone. Subsequent parallel structures in the same verse are indented again, so that an elaborate one moves away from the left-hand margin in a series of steps. A new verse moves us back again to the left. A pair of lines that form a terrace are usually treated in the same way, but if there are three or more lines in the structure, the pattern of indentation is different: the second line is given whatever indentation is necessary in order to bring the repeated phrases of the terrace underneath each other. This makes the repetition of the words more graphically obvious. The latter technique is also used if a pair of lines forming a terrace are the last lines of a verse.[15] As already noted, anacrustic lines are deeply indented.

These procedures may sound complicated, but they are designed to be visually simple, if not self-explanatory. A reading of any of the prayers should make them familiar. Their operation is not mechanical, and exceptions do occur. These exceptions are not random, but instead indicate that some other aspect has taken precedence. The most trivial occurs because of the low redundancy of Berawan phrases. Sometimes their English translations are so long that they cannot fit on the page if indented normally. So, occasionally, a block of lines is moved back to the left of those preceding it. Other exceptions are more interesting, showing some peculiarity or irregularity of the structure.

Lines not part of a parallel structure may be interpreted in various ways. Sometimes they contain a dyadic set, and may be treated as if constituting a block of one line. But many do not, and do not qualify for indentation. Consequently, we have a pattern that is characteristic of the less skilled speakers, the ones that do not mix many parallel structures into their **píat**. Their verses often appear with the second and all the subsequent lines indented equally; a single block of undifferentiated lines. In effect, these verses are simply paragraphs in a **píat** that moves away from poetry toward prose. Of the former it retains only the segmented line, for the latter it reverses the usual convention for indicating paragraphs.

Much of Sadi Pejong's prayer seven marches along in this fashion, but even Tama Jok and Tama Aweng include similar verses, particularly in explanatory passages. Moreover, orphan lines occur here and there even in the richest **píat**, where they play an essential and creative role. This is to say no more than that **píat** is unlike the poetry of Roti. Where a verse begins with two orphan lines, the second is indented. Subsequent lines may begin a paragraph as described above, or a parallel structure may appear. Orphan lines may similarly appear in midverse, between structures.

It should be noted that the devices of indentation are applied to the English translation, and not to the Berawan text, with two exceptions. First, terraces are invariantly indicated by lining up the repeated word or words. Second, anacrustic lines are set to the right. The point about these rules is they are mechanically applied in contrast to those applied to the English translations. My intention has been to reserve interpretation for the translations, which because of their nature cannot avoid it. The Berawan texts present strictly phonological data. Like legal documents, they lack punctuation. Commas cannot be heard, they must be inferred. Capital letters are used only for words that are unambiguously proper names. The Berawan texts reflect the interpretation built into the translations only in the breaks between verses, which is necessary in order to keep lines of text and translation level with each other.

Such directness is not possible in the translation without abandoning analysis. Moreover, I have no choice but to construe sometimes obscure Berawan. Nevertheless, it is still desirable to retain as literal a gloss as possible, so as to avoid a false poeticism. This was the justification for employing subscript numbers to label synonyms, rather than ransacking the thesaurus. By the same token, I have chosen where possible the most obvious gloss of a word, rather than secondary or derived meanings. I hope in this way to preserve the directness, in places the earthiness, of the original. An example is provided by the words **vì', sadì', ukun, dupun,** which are used in the formula that collectively refers to the company of the ancestors. This is a rather grand concept; it suggests anthropological theorizing. So, I prefer the intimacy of simple "grandfather" or "grandmother."

A final point concerns the fit between intonation and versification, or rather the lack of fit. Contrary to what might be expected, it is not the case that speakers of **piat** raise their voices and enunciate clearly at the beginning of verses, and then decline into breathlessness toward the end. That finding only underlines the analytic nature of the verses in the first place. On the other hand, patterns of intonation are not random. As I have already argued, they are consciously employed for dramatic effect. Consequently, if the scoring of intonation is read along with the verses, it is possible to see where the speaker wishes to place emphasis, and which other parts he regards as routine.

Higher Levels of Segmentation

In Hymes's analysis of "The Deserted Boy," verses make up only the second level of segmentation, after lines. There are three others. Beginning with the most inclusive, they are called "acts," "scenes," and "stanzas." If the verses of **píat** bear at least a superficial resemblance to those of the Chinookan tale, these other segments cannot be matched. The reason for this is straightforward: **píat** is not narrative. Prayers do not have plots, and they do not have climaxes. Often, they hardly have even an ending to speak of, but merely break off when they seem to the speaker to have gone on long enough. Sometimes a prayer falls silent, only to revive a few moments later with renewed vigor when a sacrifice is to be made. An adept is never at a loss for a little more, as required. The nature of **píat** is not that it unfolds a drama, but that it picks up, and then drops, and then picks up again, any of a number of themes.

These themes are already apparent in the way that verses are initiated. It was noted above that a series might be initiated by repeated acts of summoning spirits; invocation is a theme. The series of verses comprise a verse group referring to that theme. Another follows it, dealing perhaps with the theme of supplication, and then another, or possibly the prayer returns to the theme of invocation. A further elaboration of the conventions of indentation is generally used to indicate verse groups. The first line of the first verse is placed on the far left-hand margin. The first lines of all subsequent verses are indented one step. Parallel structures within these verses are indented again in the standard manner.

The themes of **píat** are the characteristic mode of form-meaning covariation in Berawan prayer. We must next turn our attention to them.

2.

Papì̀—The Themes of Prayer

The themes of Berawan prayer exist as an analytical construct, and simultaneously as its content, what it is about. There is no limitation on what may be talked about in prayers. Somewhere in the examples that I have set out, just about every aspect of life is addressed: matters practical and religious, personal and communal, to do with the old life of the jungle and the new world of work and schooling, all jumbled together.

Nevertheless, there are certain themes that recur in almost every prayer, couched in familiar language of figures and formulae. They are not numerous, but they reward our attention by providing direct expression, in terms now comprehensible, of abstract concepts. Such expressions are not easy to obtain because Berawan religion is so much a matter of doing, of ritual (Metcalf 1982a:4–6).

I begin as do the prayers, with invocation.[1]

Prayer is Addressed to Spirits

In the prayers I have set out, there are some two dozen agencies that are invoked, that is, they occur in verses beginning "where are you," or "come," or similar, in verse groups concerned with the theme of invocation. There is no other context in which Berawan make lists of such agencies.

The first thing the lists reveal is that Berawan ontology is surprisingly simple, terminologically. All agencies are addressed as **bílì'**, for which a reasonably precise English gloss is "spirit" or "spirits" (since nouns do not inflect for number). There are no words that might be construed as meaning "god" or "deity," and there are no classes of demons, sprites, or whatever. All are simply spirit. In order not to overdetermine Berawan conceptions at the outset, I avoid all such terms. I use the term spirit as freely as they use **bílì'**; whenever I employ the former, then there is a Berawan phrase employing the latter.

In the Berawan view, all volitional agencies in the cosmos are **bílì'**, with one single exception. Human beings instead have **telanak**, which I gloss as "soul" (Metcalf 1982a:48–66). But prayers are not addressed to human beings.

The spirit agencies that are invoked are an odd assortment. Some are mentioned frequently, some rarely. Some are important, some hazy, and some are downright obscure. The combinations that occur in particular lists are also diverse, reflecting the circumstances of the rite and the temperaments of the speakers. Nevertheless, by aggregating the lists from our prayers we can gain some mapping of major cosmological features, provided we keep in mind that the corpus is not a representative sample, and any statistics that we draw out of it can only give a general idea of relative importance.

What the collection of names does not show is that Berawan cosmology comprises a pantheon of two dozen deities. The reality is more subtle. Two features at least disrupt so simple a view: multiple naming and taxonomic indeterminacy.

Formulaic Reference

There are just four spirit agencies that are referred to by formulae:

1) **bílì' puwong bílì' ngaputong**, "spirit(s) that hold(s) (held, shall hold), spirit(s) that create(s) (created, shall create)." The low redundancy of Berawan syntax enables this stock formula to be indeterminate in regard to

number, tense, and gender. Only the first of these is capable of resolution, or worth the bother of resolving.

Dual godheads are not unknown in Borneo. Hans Schärer (1963) describes the religion of the numerous Ngaju people of southern Borneo as pervasively dualistic. There are deities of the Upperworld and the Underworld, each associated with certain personages, colors, animals, and so on. Might not the same be true of Berawan ideas? Is there perhaps a conception of an Owner Spirit and a Creator Spirit, or a committee of each, like shareholders and directors in some celestial holding company?

What makes this idea unconvincing is the lack of thoroughgoing dualism in Berawan symbolism. Certainly it is not absent, but there is nothing to compare with the elaboration found among the Ngaju. The most obvious kind of dualism in ritual is the parallel language of **píat,** but that hardly serves as evidence of a dual godhead. On the contrary, the fact that **puwong//ngaputong** constitute a dyadic set subsumes the double reference under an aspect of meter. At best, it suggests a stereoscopic view of a unitary object. Moreover, there are everyday usages that confirm this interpretation. Outside the context of prayer, people still have an occasion to refer to this agency. They say, simply, **bílì' ngaputong.** The pronoun used to refer to this agency is the third person singular **nyí,** and the same is true even in **píat.**[2] It is for this reason that I speak of the Creator Spirit, or the Creator for short. Finally, if asked directly, most Berawan were willing to assert that the Creator is unitary. They only hesitated when they attempted to relate their cosmology to that of their neighbors.

The usual difficulty in making this relationship is the female Kenyah deity, Bungan, the consort of Bali Penyalong. She has no counterpart in Berawan cosmology, but since 1950 she has become the focus of a revivalist cult among Kayan and Kenyah folk that spread to some Berawan communities. More details of this innovation are given in chapter eight. The point for now is that it is entirely characteristic of **píat** to borrow eclectically terms and titles from neighboring languages. Does the tacit importation of Bungan prove that the Berawan Creator is male? I found it surprisingly difficult to elicit firm responses to this question. Most informants assented weakly, and I believe that Berawan conceptions of the godhead tend to be less anthropomorphic than those of their neighbors. No sentimental or dualistic logic requires them to provide the Creator with a mate, and Berawan syntax allows the gender of the Creator to remain a nonissue. The English language, however, does not allow the same indeterminacy, and I am obliged to choose between he, she, and it. Feminist hermeneutics notwithstanding, Westerners are acculturated to think of the godhead as male. Since I am unwilling to deny to the Berawan concept the dignity of our own, I conform to this usage.

As regards the tense of the verbs, it is surely not to be determined. Certainly the Creator did create; for one thing, he ordained the taboos that, if broken, bring automatic retribution. Yet he is no retiring Creator, leaving his world to its own devices. From him still issue the souls of children, and they will continue to do so. That is stated without hesitation. Moreover, his aid is still petitioned in prayer.

2) **bílì' vì' bílì' sadì' bílì' ukun bílì' dupun,** "spirits of grandparents₁ spirits of grandparents₂ spirits of grandparents₃ spirits of grandparents₄." This formula is familiar because the etymologies of its terms were discussed in chapter one. It refers to the ancestors, unambiguously collective, numerous, and of both sexes. In everyday conversation they are called simply **bílì' sadì'.**

3) **bílì'ca bílì' lía,** "spirits of the community₁ spirits of the community₂" This formula is less easy to construe. The first thing to notice about it is that ca//lía is a blind dyad. The first element is a **píat**-word, and the second is a term commonly used in everyday speech. When Berawan speak of themselves, "our people," their families, their fellow villagers, the Berawan as a whole, they say **dé kíta,** literally "they-we." **Lía** has a similar range of reference, varying by context. I choose the gloss "community" because so many of the rituals are community based.

But who or what are the "spirits of the community"? The first response to this question is invariably **bílì' sadì',** those same ancestors described in the previous formula. But these two categories do not quite collapse into one because of a certain openendedness in the former that is absent in the latter. If the question is pursued, informants—after a moment's reflection—add further categories: there are the spirits of unrelated people who lived in the area long ago, perhaps of the quasimythical Lemiting after whom the river is named. They are no more anonymous than the ancestors whose names have been lost to memory even as their tombs have sunk into decay. Their tombs lie in the same ground, unmarked to be sure, but still charged with their spiritual power. In fact, their very antiquity connotes power. The close association of these nonancestral humans with the land makes this category merge with the next: spirits of nonhuman origin that are somehow associated with natural features in the area—rivers, hills, large trees, and so on (Metcalf 1982a: 240–65).

As a cover term for this nebulous third category some informants used the phrase **bíli' atak tu** (atak means "place," tu means "this"), which also occurs in prayers. The temptation is to label this third source as "nature spirits," which is a phrase with a grand nineteenth century ring to it. But that would be misleading because the category of place spirits has the same openended quality as does that of spirits of the community. In particular, both encompass ancestral spirits. Worse, the phrase cannot but suggest an animistic view of nature, and that is false. Berawan explicitly do not believe that every rock or tree has its own animus, and they do not believe that there are species of rock spirits and tree spirits. What is evident, as far as they are concerned, from everyday experience, is that spirits have their haunts and habits. As to what the nature or appearance of these habitués might be, information is scanty.

The openendedness of the categories of spirits of the community and place spirits also applies to the last of the agencies for which a formula is found in the prayers. I put it last because it is used less frequently and is less standardized than the other formulae.

4)   **bíli' atong Bunok** / **bíli' atong luvak**, "spirits along the Bunok / spirits around the lake." **Atong** means "throughout." **Bunok** and **luvak** are geographical features that call for some explanation since they are so frequently mentioned in the prayers.

Much of the life of the people of Long Teru revolves around a large lake (**luvak**) that is unique in central northern Borneo. It is labeled on figure 2 with its Malay name Loagan (lake) Bunut. Hills encircle it to the south and to the east. Between the lake and the main river (Tinjar in Malay, Lemiting or Meliteng in Berawan) the land is swampy. Out of the lake flows a stream called Bunut in Malay, the Bunok of our formula. This stream joins a slightly larger one, called Teru in both Malay and Berawan. Long Teru is simply the place where the Teru joins the larger watercourse (**long** means "river mouth"). The ancestors of the Long Teru folk have lived around this lake for generations beyond memory. In fact, the longhouse was by the lake edge until the turn of the century (see chapter three, prayer one, note 7). The area is of great economic importance. The hills provide some of the best farmland for many miles because they are high enough not to be vulnerable to disastrous flooding. The lake, and even more so the Bunok stream, provide an abundant supply of fish (see chapter three, prayer two, note 16).

Some idea of the membership of these spirits of stream and lake can be gauged from references in the prayers. At the beginning of prayer one,

Tama Jok invokes great leaders of the past (see notes 4, 5, and 6 of this chapter), describing them as the ones

lo mígang atong luvak tu	who rule throughout this lake,
lo mígang líko' Bunok tu	who rule this river Bunok.

So, it is once again ancestral spirits that first come to mind. However, in prayer two, lines 88–91, Tama Aweng sees other agencies involved:

ní jíu ko ngan kaam bílì' belungín	That's what I say to you spirits of water dragons,
lo dukep atong Bunok tu	who rule along this Bunok river,
lo makíng atong Bunok tu	who guard this whole Bunok river.

A **belungín** is an aquatic version of the mythical **naga** that appears as a motif all over Southeast Asia and beyond. Clearly it is at the other end of the same spectrum that we observed in the spirits of the community. Later in the same prayer (lines 135–40), Tama Aweng lists **bílì' belungín** along with other watery spirits: **bílì' bíjì'**, "spirits of crocodiles," not to mention **bílì' sau** and **bílì' dacíen, sau** and **dacíen** being other mysterious water monsters. He closes his list with the appeal:

ra ní kanaí kamé ngaran	we don't even know your names,
tapí kamé tu ní'é tawa tupaan kaam	but we call all of you.

Tama Aweng specifically pleads ignorance. There are bound to be spirits of which humans know nothing, he reasons, and so he issues a catchall invocation, just to be on the safe side.

If we compare the categories of spirits of stream and lake and spirits of the community, we find that there is no difference in the range of spirit agencies that potentially could be included. Both categories are omnibus. The difference is one of emphasis, in the images that are brought to mind. The latter evokes a procession of the ancestral spirits stretching away from the longhouse until lost from view. The former brings to mind their merging with the topography. Every corner of the lake and its surroundings is familiar, and associated with names and incidents. The great leaders of the past are entombed on an island in the lake, or in a graveyard that guards access to the Bunok stream. The roofs of their tombs are decorated with a carved design—a tracery running the length of the ridge—that depicts a water dragon. Its presence marks a claim of descent from a legendary hero who emerged from a dragon's egg to found a noble line. Another hero actually created the lake by turning his magical canoe around in the Bunok stream (see chapter five, note 23). From the lake one can see the great mountain on top of which it still rests, abandoned by the hero on his way to heaven. Such heros have no graves, yet they have descendants. So they provide a bridge to spirits not of human origin, of species real and imaginary, of topography, and of natural phenomena.

To sum up, of our four spirit agencies invoked in the prayers by means of formulae, two seem distinct and basic, namely the Creator and the ancestors. The other two are more vague, in that they can potentially include all manner of spirits. Moreover, they are similar to each other, and both may incorporate ancestral spirits, though in different guises. Now let us see how frequently each is called.

Frequencies of Invocation

Table 1 shows all the agencies that are invoked, tabulated prayer by prayer, and with totals. Prayer seven is left out because it relates to the Bungan cult and not to the traditional religion. Its pattern of invocation is basically different, and it is treated separately in chapter eight.

The first comparison in frequency of invocation is between the clearly delineated agencies of Creator and ancestors. The score is eight to thirteen, a significant superiority for the latter, and one that runs counter to a common assertion by my informants that all prayer is primarily to the Creator. My sample may be the cause of this skewing, since two of the longest prayers (one and two) are taken from a longhouse festival emphasizing collective continuity. But there is another factor: the prevalence of borrowing from neighboring languages, in this case the names of supreme deities. This is often done with a cheerful disregard for cosmological niceties. All the proper names listed after the Creator in table 1 are instances of such borrowing and may be added to the total for the godhead. The origins of most of the titles are explained later in the text, and also in the notes to the prayers. The inventory includes the female Kenyah deity Bungan, already noted, and even Tama Aweng's eccentric call to Allah.

At the same time, however, alternate references to the ancestors need to be included as well. I score for each great man of the past summoned by name, and also for each use of our third formula—spirits of the

Table 1. Frequencies of invocation by prayer.

Agencies	Prayers							
	One	*Two*	*Three*	*Four*	*Five*	*Six*	*Subtotals*	*Totals*
Creator		5		3			8	
Tenangan		4	4				8	
Penyalong		2					2	
Pesalong			3				3	
Bungan	3	4	1				8	
Allah		1					1	30
ancestors	3	6	2	1		1	13	
great men	4			5	4		13	
community		3	2			1	6	
hero				1			1	33
stream/lake	2	6	2				10	
mountains			1				1	
land			1				1	12
belungín		2	1				3	
crocodile		1					1	
sau		1	2				3	
dacíen		1	3				4	11
tapo'	1		1			3	5	
kaju unong	1						1	
daren			1			2	3	
bíto' tíloí			1			1	2	
síkíp			2				2	13
aman	1	3	1			1	6	
moon/sun			1				1	
dreams			1				1	

community—since it predominantly focuses on the ancestors. (However, I include the spirits of stream and lake elsewhere.) I also put the lone invocation of the hero that made the lake here. This brings the final totals to a close thirty to thirty-three. A reasonable conclusion is that the Creator and the ancestors figure about equally in prayer.

No other agency or reasonable grouping of agencies comes close to them in frequency. Nevertheless, there are significant blocs that may be distinguished. None of these necessarily implies a category of Berawan thought. There are no cover terms for these blocs. They are interpretive in nature, perhaps helping us to see how Berawan attribute spirit influences in their world.

The first of these blocs shown in the table relate to place spirits, and is mainly composed of the spirits of stream and lake. I demarcate them because of their geographical specificity, the earthiness of the entombed dead, and the greater evocation of spirits of nonhuman origin. A couple of other references can be included. Each occurs only once, and hence cannot be counted as a formula, despite the incorporation of a dyadic set, but they interestingly confirm the concept of place spirits. The first is **bílì' junyang bílì' tukung** (**junyang** means "to guide," **tukung** means "mountain"), "spirit guides, spirits of the mountains." **Junyang** refers to the notion that individuals who are skilled in tracking receive advice from spirits in the form of intuitions. The second is **bílì' dita' bílì' tanaa** (**dita** means "plain," **tanaa** means "land"), "spirits of the plain, spirits of the land."

The next bloc is made up of creatures; one a real species, the others mythical. Together they are invoked eleven times, or about as frequently as the agencies in the previous bloc. So we can make out two secondary blocs, neither as important nor as clearly delineated as the first pair, but still significant.

But other aggregations are possible, and it might be more true to the character of Berawan cosmology to allow blocs to overlap. Perhaps the spirits of stream and lake might be included with the ancestral bloc, and conversely the spirits of the community could be added to the bloc of place spirits. Then there would be forty-three invocations of the former, and eighteen of the latter, producing no significant change in relative importance.

Or the bloc of place spirits could be bracketed with the aquatic species that have such significance for the riverine Berawan. Together, their two dozen odd instances of invocation approach in frequency those of the ancestors and the Creator. Indeed, we could go further. There is a myth that tells of a man who was tricked into eating his own children, and so turned into a crocodile. His descendants live in longhouses at the bottom of the river, so it is said, kinsmen in an inverted, watery world. Conversely, the water dragon appears as an ancestor in other stories. So perhaps all of the last three blocs should be seen standing together against the only clearly delineated one, the first, in which case they jointly outweigh it.

Suggestive as these considerations may be, however, no amount of juggling will reveal fixed categories of spirits, even of a polythetic type. What we find is—excepting the Creator—a continuum ranging from spirits of remembered ancestors to spirits of natural species and features. Or perhaps there are several continua, varying in anthropomorphism, geographical specificity, or mythicality, each marked out in spirit agencies that intersect adjacent ones.

A final bloc remains to be discussed. As indicated by the figures in table 1, this bloc has about as much prominence in the prayers as the previous two. The first agency in the bloc is the spirits of the **tapo'**. A **tapo'** is a structure in front of which prayers are made, and I will describe it in some detail later. **Kaju unong, daren,** and **bíto' tíloí** are parts of the structure, or things often associated with it. The last are a kind of magical stones and so are **síkíp,** though not necessarily found near a **tapo'**. If we now ask what manner of spirits are associated with these objects, it comes as no surprise to discover that there is no simple answer. **Tapo'** are not animated by a class of spirits that are called into existence at their construction, but they provide a locus for the gathering of spirits—presumably by the very act of invocation. Many **tapo'** are made in front of the longhouse, and then the spirits summoned to them may be assumed to be much the same as the spirits of the community. Others made near the lake may draw more of those associated with that location, but the difference is hardly radical.

Three agencies that do not seem easily to aggregate with others are shown near the end of table 1. Of these, the spirits of the omen creatures (**aman**) are significant. These spirits are discussed below. The remaining two are eccentric notions of Tama Avit (prayer three). This observation directs attention to another feature that is obvious in the table: the great differences in number and in variety of spirit agencies invoked in each prayer. These differences reflect the competence of different speakers in making **píat** and the circumstances of the prayer. Tama Avit shows the most fondness for elaborate lists, closely followed by Tama Aweng in prayer two. But Tama Aweng's other prayer (prayer six) is much less elaborate in this regard. The reason is that his attention is focused on a special act of invocation. Lian Yang (prayer five) goes to the other extreme. He is not much skilled at **píat,** and his prayer is narrowly addressed to a single spirit agency. I will leave the discussion of these special circumstances to the descriptions that preface each prayer.

Finally, it is worth drawing attention to agencies that are missing from the prayers. Many accounts of Bornean cosmologies emphasize the role of departmental deities that control one or another aspect of its working, but there are no such deities in this inventory. In fact, the only one that I heard mentioned frequently in any context was **bílì' gau** (**gau** means "thunder"), the "spirit of thunder." This spirit is associated with various stones, to which are attributed mystical origins and powers. At the turn of the century, Alfred Cort Haddon discovered similar charms in longhouses on the Tinjar River, where both Kenyah and Berawan informants identified them as the "toenails of Baling Go, the thunder god" that had fallen to earth (1901:370). Indeed, W. J. Perry cites examples from all over Southeast Asia to support his grand diffusionary theory (1923). But the point for the present is that **bílì' gau** is only mentioned when these charms are brought out for some reason, and that is not often.

Even less conspicuous is **bílì' menalí. Menalí** is a word borrowed from Kenyah, meaning "to twist" (Galvin 1967:45). This spirit is credited with causing landslides, and it was mentioned to me a couple of times by an elderly informant who enjoyed displaying his knowledge. On one occasion he offered the opinion that **bílì' gau** and **bílì' menalí** are brothers, but then he paused, and added: "or maybe cousins, how should we know?" Such agnosticism with regard to minor spirit agencies is typical of Berawan cosmology.

An Overview of Berawan Cosmology

Berawan notions of spirit resist taxonomy. This finding is consistent with their view that the worlds of spirits are vast and unknowable, and that they intersect mysteriously with our own.

On one occasion, a large, utilitarian jar of the type called **gusí** began to exhibit strange behavior. It emitted groaning sounds, so it was said, and moved about of its own accord. Immediately, people spoke of **bílì' gusí,** but the phrase was a neologism. No one thought that jars have spirits, or that this jar had itself become animated, or that there was some new jar spirit abroad. All that they meant was that some spirit was somehow involved. When I asked what spirit, they replied, predictably: "how should we know?" Later, however, a shaman was able to discover its identity and its purpose in manifesting itself, by using his own spirit familiars as intermediaries. He was even able to recruit it as an ally.

Berawan cosmology is not entirely static. Tidbits of information about minor spirits are constantly supplied through shamanism and through dreams. Occasionally, such insights become significant in the life of the community if the shaman acquires significant new powers or if the dreamer is inspired to promote some ritual innovation. Neighboring communities, both Berawan and Kenyah, may also be sources of new information. Although Berawan are usually skeptical of the supposed revelations of those that they do not know and trust, there is no fundamental objection. The premise that human knowledge of spirit worlds is incomplete permits novelty. The language of **píat** manifests that openness by invoking spirit agencies whose membership is unlimited and by borrowing the titles of deities from neighboring peoples.

Moreover, the spirit of thunder and his mysterious stones provide an example of the sort of minor cult that permeates central northern Borneo. This cult is the result of a diffusionary process in the distant past, and enjoys occasional revivals of enthusiasm; Haddon himself triggered such a revival. The first stone that he was shown turned out to be a ground adze blade, and this evidence of neolithic activity in an area that had known the use of iron for centuries naturally interested him. But his efforts to purchase it, and similar specimens elsewhere, only confirmed the value the owners had placed on them. Three quarters of a century later, people at Long Teru still remembered the Westerner who had been so anxious to acquire their coveted charms (Haddon 1901:369–70).

It would be a mistake, however, to conclude from these examples that Berawan cosmology is vague or unstable. On the contrary, for all its openendedness, it is centered squarely on two agencies that stand above the others, however numerous: the Creator and the ancestors.

Contrast with Iban and Kayan Cosmology

It is worth emphasizing that the cosmology of the Berawan is not the same as that of other peoples of central Borneo, if only to dispel a notion propagated by a century of indifferent travel literature that the cultures of the region are uniform in all but detail. Paradoxically, this notion came about precisely because there is such ethnic fragmentation. Faced with a bewildering array of group names it is easier to lump them all together under a cover term such as Dayak. Even a brief comparison of cosmologies will show how much is liable to be swept under the rug in the process.

Contrast, for instance, the spare notion of the Creator Spirit with the baroque elaboration of deities observed by the Iban, a numerous people whose main centers of population are to the south of the Berawan:

> The Iban are a polytheistic people whose pantheon contains scores of named gods and goddesses. The most important of them is Singalong

Burong, whose main concern is with conquest and the arts of war. (Freeman 1960:76)

There are deities that are associated with augury employing the appearance and behavior of certain species of birds:

> The seven main augural gods are believed to live in the same celestial longhouse as Singalong Burong, and five of them—Ketupong, Embuas, Beragai, Papau, and Bejampong—are married to his daughters. It is thus usual for the Iban to refer to their augural birds as **menantu Lang,** or the sons-in-law of Singalong Burong. All the principal gods of the Iban are anthropomorphic, and live in a society that has a structure identical with that of the Iban themselves. The genealogies of these gods are known and remembered by **lemambang,** or religious experts, who make use of their knowledge in the invocations (**timang**) which are chanted at Iban rituals, or **gawai.** All seven of the augural gods have siblings, parents, and grandparents, all named, who are important in the Iban pantheon. For example, Apai Embuas (the father of Embuas), whose full name is Bujang Bungah Jajingah Tinggi Serukong, lives beneath the immense buttresses of a mythical **plai** tree (*Alstonia sp.*); his special task is the safeguarding of the **bedilang** (the hearth stones over which enemy heads are smoked), the manufacture of rattan casings (**ringka**) in which these heads are secured, and of the circular framework (**bengkong**) from which they are suspended. (Freeman 1960:76–77)

All of this detail, of sons-in-law and genealogies, of special functions of deities, microscopically specified, is alien to Berawan thinking.

The Iban and the Berawan, although neighbors, are not closely related linguistically or ethnologically, at least from an insular viewpoint. Yet the Kayan are supposed to be first cousins in Leach's Kayan-Kenyah-Kajang complex (Leach 1950:46). Here is the list of Kayan deities supplied by Hose and McDougall:

> The Kayans recognize a number of gods that preside over great departments of their lives and interests. The more important of these are the god of war, Toh Bulu; three gods of life, **Laki Ju Urip, Laki Makatan Urip,** and **Laki Kelasai Urip,** of whom the first is the most important; the god of thunder and storms, **Laki Belari** and his wife **Obeng Doh;** the god of fire, **Laki Pesong;** gods of the harvest, **Anyi Lawang** and **Laki Ivong;** a god of the lakes and rivers, **Urai Uka; Balanan,** the god of madness; **Toh Kiho,** the god of fear; **Laki Ketira Murei** and **Laki Jup Urip,** who conduct the souls of the dead to Hades. Beside or above all these is **Laki Tenangan,** a god more powerful than all the rest, to whom are assigned

no special or departmental functions. He seems to preside or rule over
the company of lesser gods, much as Zeus and Jupiter ruled over the
lesser gods of the ancient Greeks and Romans. (Hose and McDougall
1912, 2:5)

The Kayan pantheon is less complex than the Iban, but still much more
elaborate than the Berawan.[3] In fact, it is straining the term to talk of a
Berawan pantheon at all. There are virtually no departmental deities, other
than **bílì' gau,** the thunder spirit, who was not significant enough to be
mentioned in any of six prayers.

Given the anthropomorphic nature of Kayan deities, it is not surprising
that Laki Tenangan has a wife, Doh Tenangan. The Kenyah have a
similar range of departmental deities, and their supreme deity, Bali Penyalong, has a consort (or, in some accounts, a daughter) called Bungan,
whose acquaintance we have already made. Her appearance in the prayers
is an illustration of the kind of borrowing described in the previous section,
but in this case the borrowing occurs at two levels. In the first six prayers,
the borrowing is trivial, a matter of names, but in the seventh, it is profound, an expression of a new cult with major modifications of previous
ritual forms.

There is more to be said about the comparison between Kayan and
Berawan cosmology. For instance, the prefix **laki** in the names of male
gods is also the "title of respect given to old men who are grandfathers,"
hinting at a parallel between Kayan deities and Berawan ancestors. There
is also a wide range of other spirits in the Kayan world, and Hose and
McDougall's unconvincing attempt at a classification system suggests another parallel (Hose and McDougall 1912, 2:4–10). For present purposes,
however, the point is made that Berawan cosmology is markedly different
from their neighbors'.

Supplication

Inevitably, the first theme of a prayer is invocation. For the second, there is
more flexibility. A frequent choice is supplication. It is a theme that is easy
to grasp, and it is often expressed in figures that have already been noted in
the previous chapter.

One figure concerns itself with desirable qualities of life, spelled out in a
string of dyadic sets. Let us have, it says, a life that is good and cool, slow
and calm, deep and thick, healthy, happy, and laughing. These adjectives

are literal glosses of Berawan words, which have their own unique connotations. Nevertheless, it is not difficult to imagine what a Berawan means by a life that is "deep" or "thick," even if we are not accustomed to using those metaphors ourselves. The reader's intuitive understanding is probably as good as any elaborate explanation. This situation accords nicely with A. M. Hocart's celebrated theory of the nature of ritual. We understand because ritual everywhere is fundamentally about the same thing: the procurement of life (Hocart 1952:46–52).

A second figure is more materialistic. It says, "give us," (**kícung**), or "let us have," (**belurí**), and then there follows a number of dyadic sets. Yet in almost every case there are just two things asked for, over and over again: rice and money.

A final figure often tacked onto the second is even simpler. In blind dyads, it says simply: luck.

Beyond these three figures, the things requested of the spirits are endless, and each speaker has his own priorities. Beginning at line 85 in prayer one, Tama Jok employs all of the common figures, but there two more verses in the group. The last is:

> You spirits shield$_1$ us, shield$_2$ us,
>> against those who would throw us down$_1$ throw us down$_2$
>> would disturb us, would kill us,
>>> you see it, you throw it away, you turn it back,
>>> you shield$_3$ us,
>>> you shield$_2$ us.

The wording contains two parallel structures and several dyadic sets, and might qualify as a figure were it repeated elsewhere. In lines 87–89 of prayer three, Tama Avit's wording is simpler, his request more specific. He says of the sick child Ukat:

> May little Ukat live,
> until his head is white,
> his nails curly with age.

An equally direct, if darker, supplication is addressed by Lian Yang to the ghost of the man whose bones are about to be moved from the graveyard at the village of Batu Belah to one at Long Teru (prayer five, lines 62–65):

That's what I say to you, Tama Suleng,
   don't disturb₁ disturb₂ Batu Belah,
   don't disturb₁ disturb₂ Long Teru,
      those that care for you.

When the dead "disturb" the living, the result is death. In all these acts of supplication, various as they are, it is easy to detect the common objective that Hocart pointed out.

Offering: Tapo' and Pakaan

The themes of invocation and supplication are inherent since I employ them as defining features of prayer in the introduction. Other themes are not essential in this way. However, the presentation of offerings is a type of ritual action that is a frequent adjunct of prayer. In the Berawan case, the association is invariant: ritual requires both prayer and offerings. So, it is not surprising that the topic is often mentioned in **píat**. In fact, it is no less pervasive than are invocation and supplication, and it furnishes two distinct themes. The first of these I deal with under the general heading of offering to distinguish it from another that speaks exclusively about blood sacrifice.

The simplest offering is an egg. Moreover, eggs are the most appropriate offering that can be made to the Creator. This collective representation draws on a symbolism that is sufficiently widespread that the nineteenth century scholar J. J. Bachofen could see in it a universal: "In religion, the egg is a symbol of the material source of all things, of the . . . beginning of creation" ([1859] 1967:25). The symbolism of the egg, so powerfully representing the attributes of containment, wholeness, and generation, serves to confirm the previous assessment of the nature of **bílì' puwong bílì' ngaputong.**

An offering of eggs is the usual accompaniment of prayer, and it is often made in a formal manner that is peculiar to Berawan ritual. It involves the construction of a **tapo'. Tapo'** are not found among any of the neighbors of the Berawan, although, inevitably, there are echoes of it throughout the culture area of central northern Borneo. What is unique about **tapo'** is the prescribed orderliness of the structure.

There are four essential elements in the construction of a **tapo'**. First, there are the uprights that hold the eggs, and they are also called **tapo'**. To make them, straight sticks are selected that are about five feet long and two inches thick, and that have white sapwood. After the bark is stripped off, the stick is decorated with one or several bands of ruffs that are made by running a sharp knife up the surface of the stick so as to lift up shavings, called **pegerok**, which are left attached at their top ends and allowed to curl. Once the appropriate spot is selected, the sticks are set up in a neat row, all the same height, and equally spaced about a foot apart. There must be either four or eight of them. The use of eight sticks indicates a grand occasion, and the decision must be made to use either two rows of four sticks or one row of eight. No other arrangements are permissible.[4] Two cuts are made in the top end of each stick at right angles to one another, so that the splits can be pried open to hold the egg.

Three or five long, willowy wands are required next. These are cut from some fast-growing shrub, and should be reasonably straight, with some leaves attached at the top end. They are not stripped of their bark but thrust directly into the ground. The longer they are the better; the average is about seven feet in length. One is set up at each end of a row of **tapo'**, for a total of two or four, and these are called **penusu**.[5] Berawan say spirits descend to the **tapo'** along the **penusu**. The remaining leafy wand stands at the center of the row or rows of **tapo'**, and has a special name: **kaju unong. Kaju** means simply "wood" or "stick." **Unong** is derived from **mulong**, which means "life" or "to live." The **kaju unong** is consequently another form of the Tree of Life, a motif found throughout Borneo.

Finally a short, sharpened stick is required to spike the head of the sacrificial animal. The stick is called **spak kaju** (**spak** means "branch," **kaju** means "wood"). It is set up somewhere in front of the **tapo'**.

The **tapo'** sticks, the **penusu**, the **kaju unong**, and the **spak kaju** make up the structure called **tapo'**. When one is prepared, it is exclusively for the purpose of making prayers. Several speakers may make **pìat** in front of it on one occasion, but it is not reused on another. Once the rite is over, a **tapo'** is left to fall into ruin. **Tapo'** are not demolished, but people do not hold them or their sites in awe. Children play around them, and if the sticks are knocked over in the process, no one pays any attention. These features make it inappropriate to describe **tapo'** as a kind of altar, which is the term that Charles Hose used to describe a less orderly Kayan variant (Hose and McDougall 1912, 2:8). The gloss "shrine" presents an additional distraction because it has, in the anthropological literature, a special usage in Africa. Consequently, I refer to **tapo'** as "prayer stations," an expression that may seem somewhat colorless, but at least is not encumbered with misleading connotations.

Figure 3.   An adept makes a prayer before a **tapo'** (prayer
station) outside a new longhouse. He holds a chicken,
which he will sacrifice at the end of the prayer. There
are, in fact, two **tapo'** in front of him—the one on the
right has eight sticks, each holding an egg, and the
irregular one on the left has only two sticks. The latter
was made incomplete on purpose to evade certain
proscriptions (see chapter two, note 4 for details).

Prayer does not have to be made in front of **tapo'**. Many rites are
conducted inside the longhouse, and nothing prevents a senior man from
launching into prayer on the veranda, or inside a family apartment, if the
affair is small. Even outdoors, prayers may sometimes have to be made in a
hurried way because there is no time to construct a proper prayer station.
This is the case, for instance, when a work party enters a graveyard to

prepare a new tomb. Fearing the wrath of those already entombed there, they make **píat** loudly as they slash through the undergrowth. Yet most rites of any consequence do manage at some point to include prayers before a **tapo'**. At the family occasion described in chapter four, most of the activities, including prayer, went on inside the house. But at one point, the small crowd of kin traipsed outside to hear Tama Avit speak before his newly completed prayer station.

When prayers are not made in front of **tapo'** it does not mean that they go unaccompanied by offerings. There is an alternative, and equally common, mode of presenting offerings, called **pakaan**. The term is a nominal form of **nakaan**, "to feed." As the name implies, a **pakaan** is made up of various kinds of comestibles, usually presented on a tray. The tray may be grand or utilitarian. Some families take the opportunity to show off valuable heirlooms, pieces of brassware imported in the last century from the coastal sultanate of Brunei. The trays are raised on graceful pedestals, and pierced with filigree work. If several are required, cheap, modern enamelware ones will serve equally well. A host of small items are loaded on them, often arranged in pleasing designs and decorated with flowers. One essential item is eggs, in this case hard-boiled, and often peeled. Other items may include small packets of savory rice, tied up in strips of banana leaf (**kelupé**), candy and biscuits bought from the Chinese stores, small glasses of rice wine (**borèk**) or its distilled liquor (**arak**), cigarettes both of local manufacture and store-bought, and small coins. Sometimes **pakaan** are very simple; small, loosely woven baskets containing a single egg and a handful of cooked rice that are hung under the eaves to placate some minor spirit that is suspected of malicious potential. I gloss **pakaan** as "offering tray."

Tapo' and **pakaan** are both fundamentally offerings of eggs, but there are important differences between them. The former are used only for making prayers. The latter appear in other contexts as well, particularly as offerings to the spirit familiars of a shaman. Shamanistic performances involve various kinds of vocalization: some sing, often in one or another Kenyah dialect, others mutter in esoteric languages not comprehensible to humans. Yet none of them employ the declamatory, measured language of **píat**, nor do they begin a performance by the direct invocation of their familiars, as in prayer (Metcalf 1982a:60–63).

Sometimes a **pakaan** is hung in the rafters after the shaman has finished his or her performance so that the spirits may feed at leisure. But it is equally common for the audience to pick at them casually, and they offer the familiar rationalization, heard worldwide, that the spirits have "eaten already." This includes the eggs, which are cooked for consumption by the minor spirits that are the shamans' allies, or by humans, or both. Yet no shaman has the Creator as a familiar. The eggs on a **tapo'** are raw, and no one would dream of eating them. That is not because they are sacred, in the sense of reverenced in themselves. It is because of their powerful symbolism of the cosmos and the Creator. Berawan assert that all **tapo'** are made, first and foremost, for the Creator. This is true regardless of how many times he is mentioned in the accompanying prayers, or if he is mentioned at all. As proof of their assertion, they point to the row of whole, raw eggs.

This implicit relationship makes **tapo'** the centerpiece of Berawan ritual. At the most important festivals, the prayers made for the welfare of the entire community are made in front of prayer stations. This is the case in the first two recorded prayers, and they may stand as patterns from which the others are more specialized variants. The third prayer was made at a small family gathering, but was nevertheless spoken before a **tapo'**. The remaining prayers were made in special circumstances, having been selected to illustrate the range of prayers possible. Prayer four was made inside the house, and in too impromptu a manner to allow much preparation. Atypical as Uking's prayer may be, it does not, and could not, lack something to be offered to the spirits. In his closing verses, he finally gets around to mentioning the chicken that will later be immolated. Prayer five is made while entering a graveyard to remove an occupant—weighty work that cannot be accomplished without placating the dead with at least a donation of rice wine (verse beginning line 66), the typical offering at a tomb. Prayer six was spoken outdoors, and careful preparations had been made. But it was addressed predominantly to one spirit, and that spirit was not the Creator. Hence a prayer station was inappropriate, and a **pakaan** was used instead. The final prayer belongs to Sadi Pejong's version of the Bungan cult, which has abolished **tapo'**. In its place, a table is used, covered with small offerings. It is a solution that manages simultaneously to suggest both a **pakaan** and a Christian altar.

Tapo' and **pakaan** may be seen as alternatives, as ways of making an offering of eggs appropriate to different contexts, but they are also used together. At the rear of a row of **tapo'** sticks, or slightly to the side, there is frequently a short post (**tapeng**) designed to support a **pakaan**. The tray used may be an heirloom, if the prayer station is made adjacent to the longhouse, but it will be removed within a day. More likely, a small basket is used, and the **tapeng** is split open at its upper end to hold it, just like the **tapo'** sticks.

This use of offering trays is one example of the way in which prayer stations attract all manner of other ritual apparatus. A common addition is a strip of softwood, perhaps a foot long, mounted atop a stick at the height of the **tapo'**. Eight crudely carved stick figures are stuck into this strip, and the little structure is called **along Anak Tau** (**along** means "canoe," **anak** means "child," **tau** means "orphan"). It refers to the same hero who dug out the lake (**luvak**) by turning around his canoe in the Bunok stream. The eight sticks represent Anak Tau and his crew of animal helpers, the original omen creatures, who are thereby enlisted with the spirits of **tapo'**.

If a prayer station is set up where others have been before, then there is sure to be planted nearby a particular shrub, with large, succulent leaves tinged with red; **daren,** as the Berawan call it, is most likely from the genus *Dracoena*, or it may be the red croton *Colodracon jacquinii* (Hose and McDougall 1912, 2:15; Whittier 1973:245). The red leaves of **daren** provide a striking record of former prayer stations long after they themselves have disappeared and are suggestive of the blood shed there in sacrifice. Such locations occur in the Bunok stream, where prayers are made annually for success in fishing. Others are found near the farmland at the southern end of the lake. Since the land is swampy and naturally irrigated, it is used year after year.

The most frequently used location, however, is in front of the longhouse, especially outside the apartments of the most august family. Here prayer stations are constructed at least once a year for the festival of **papì' lamèng** (see chapter three), and often at other times as well. The **daren** plants are closely packed, and some have grown tall with age—a veritable sacred grove. Between the bushes are the remains of many **tapo'**, some still erect, with shiny, white sapwood showing, others graying and knocked askew, yet others half rotted on the ground. A close inspection reveals other artifacts. A large round stone, worn smooth in the riverbed may be seen near a new prayer station. Others are obscured under detritus nearby, or buried under the bushes for safekeeping. These stones are mystically acquired by their owners, like those of **bílì' gau,** and they are the focus of their own cult. They are supposed to grow over the years, if rubbed with blood of sacrifices, and to exert a benevolent influence on the entire community. They are called **bíto' tíloí** (**bíto'** means "stone," for **tíloí** I could elicit no meaning). The "house stones," as I call them, are kept where prayer stations are frequently made so that they can be smeared with blood, and participate in the invocation, both contributing their own spirit contingent and benefiting from others summoned there. The same logic applies to other items of ritual paraphernalia, and it is for that reason that prayer stations act as magnets for them. Near the house stones at Long Teru, I once uncovered a pair of crudely carved statuettes that were about a foot tall, one male, one female. They were not wholly unfamiliar; smaller versions are used in death rites (1982a:81), and similar figures were formerly carved by the Kenyah (Hose and McDougall 1912, 2:plates 148, 149). These were old, and no one could, or would, tell me anything about them. In all probability, they were made either on the instructions of a shaman, or as a result of dream inspiration. Whatever their motivation or use had been, they had ended up among the **daren** in front of the longhouse.

Prayer stations and offering trays provide a physical form for offerings, but the theme of offering in the texts seldom speaks of them directly. As we have seen, the spirits of **tapo'** and **daren** are usually mentioned in verses dealing with the theme of invocation. Verses dealing with offering begin with a phrase of the type: "Come . . . eat" or "This . . . we give." For example, beginning at line 17 of prayer one, Tama Jok invites the spirits that he has previously invoked to:

vaí la tekelo'	Come all of you,
kumaan tíku tu	eat these eggs,
kumaan angaan	eat this food$_1$
kumaan jakaan	eat this food$_2$
kumaan banyak tu	eat all of this.

The eggs mentioned in the second line stand synecdochically for the entire **tapo'**, including the **pakaan** that is a part of it. But so do the objects named in the third and fourth lines, by a metaphor that is hard to render briefly in English. **Angaan** and **jakaan** are types of stands used to hold cooking pots above the coals of a fire. So the terms imply food. In addition, the sticks of the **tapo'** are like the legs of the stands, a comparison with several possible implications: that the prayer stations feed the spirits as the hearth feeds the people; that the former will ensure the latter; and that oblation is a type of cooking.

In the theme of offering, eggs often stand for the entire prayer stations. The same kind of synecdoche applies to rice wine. In prayer five, it provides the minimal offering, which is hastily splashed over the posts of a temporary tomb. In other cases, rice wine is supplemental. In prayer three,

Tama Avit speaks in front of a prayer station complete with offering tray. He pauses in the middle to pour liberal amounts of rice wine over the **tapo'** sticks, and four times announces:

This is the rice wine we give to you,

before launching into liets of spirit agencies. In addition, there were small cups, simply carved from a node of bamboo, inserted between the stick figures in the structure representing the canoe of the Orphan Child, and these too were filled. Sometimes a large diameter bamboo is used to make a cup that is spiked into the ground by an offering tray.

Verses concerned with offering describe food and drink, often in a short list. Yet as a theme, offering is not conspicuous in the prayers. It is crowded out by another theme that is concerned with a special type of offering: blood sacrifice.

Sacrifice

Sacrifice occurred in association with all seven of the selected prayers. Indeed, it is only under exceptional circumstances that this is not so. Once, while traveling upriver, we passed a graveyard belonging to a long-house that had been abandoned generations ago. I wanted to go into it to look at the ancient tombs, but we had not made provision for the intrusion. My companions made **píat** loudly as they slashed through the under-growth, and a little rice wine was found to pour on the posts of the tallest tomb. Even so, they felt compelled to sacrifice a chicken with further prayers when we finally arrived home.

In four of the prayers, including the three made in front of prayer stations, the theme of sacrifice takes up a substantial part. These verses provide insight into the Berawan view of sacrifice, and this is intriguing because it is a hoary problem in the anthropology of religion, and one that is now receiving renewed attention. All the classical paradigms of sacrifice, those of Edward Burnett Tylor, William Robertson Smith, Henri Hubert, and Marcel Mauss, can in some measure be made out in the Berawan words, but none fits them well. Luc de Heusch has recently attacked them all as ethnocentric, too much influenced by the Judeo-Christian tradition. At the same time, he wonders whether it is possible to restore objectivity by comparative studies, or whether there is no unity to the phenomenon at all, a "sacrificial illusion" to go with Claude Levi-Strauss's "totemic illusion." He concludes that answers to these questions must be postponed, and that in the meantime we "must listen patiently to the ideological speeches of a multitude of sacrificers, in the most diverse societies" (de Heusch 1982:23).

To that multitude we may now add the half dozen whose speeches are recorded here. It is no simple matter, however, to discover their ideologies of sacrifice, in part because their speech is couched in the language of **píat.** Lists and formulae are not much in evidence in verses on the theme of sacrifice, but there are several figures—some variable, some repeated rote—that constantly recur. Each has its own emphasis.

One loose figure treats the sacrificial animal exclusively as messenger. Beginning at line 179 of prayer two, we find Tama Aweng squatting beside a trussed pig, and instructing it as follows:

> There is a reason why I call$_1$
> why I call$_2$ spirit of the pig:
>> don't wander away,
>>> you spirit of the pig,
>> don't get lost,
>>> you spirit of the pig,
>> listen to what I say,
>> to the prayer I speak for you,
>>> you spirit of the pig,
>> you go,
>>> you spirit of the pig,
>> go to Bungan Tenangan,
>>> you spirit of the pig.

Tama Aweng unambiguously commands the pig to listen to him, and then to seek out the Creator—here described under a fanciful title that hyphenates Kayan and Kenyah deities of opposite sexes. Pigs are the most valuable sacrifices, reserved for major rituals. At line 204 Tama Aweng continues his instructions:

> go,
>> you spirit of the pig,
> to the spirit that holds, the spirit that creates,

>   you spirit of the pig,
> say to Bungan Penyalong,
> to grandmother Bungan,
> the reason you come,
>   you spirit of the pig,
> is because you are asked by the community of Long Teru,
> to request a good life.

It is clear that the spirit of the pig is expected to deliver a message. If one asks why the pig must be killed, the answer is readily forthcoming: to loose the spirit from the animal so that it can travel to the Creator. Pigs do not make such expeditions in their physical bodies anymore than men do, but there is a contrast in their immaterial nature. Human beings, uniquely, possess souls, **telanak**. For them, dying is a long process of metamorphosis into ancestral spirits, a process that underlies the long and complex series of death rites. Animals, however, are already spirit. Death for them is evanescence, and they are free to make cosmic journeys. If we put it the other way around, this concept of sacrifice, this constant appeal to the spirit of the pig, is evidence that Berawan conceive of animals in this way.

In prayer seven, starting at line 119, Sadi Pejong gives more details of the cosmic journey that he expects the spirit of his sacrificial animal to make directly after immolation. In this case the animal is a chicken, a less valuable sacrifice, and the only other one that is permissible:

> You spirit of the chicken travel$_1$ travel$_2$
> across the plain$_1$ across the plain$_2$
> follow$_1$ follow$_2$ the path
>   that is clear$_1$ that is clear$_2$
>   that is bright$_1$ that is bright$_2$
>   that's where you walk$_1$ where you walk$_2$
>   don't get lost$_1$ don't get lost$_2$

> Walk$_3$ walk$_1$ spirit of the chicken.

> Whenever there is a path that is wet, that is overgrown
> that is bad, that is made all to the left,
> watch out$_1$ watch out$_2$

that is the path of the dead,
don't take that path.

Where is the path
    that is clear$_1$ that is clear$_2$
    that is bright$_1$ that is bright$_2$ truly,
        that's the path to walk$_3$ walk$_1$
        spirit of chicken.

Walk$_3$ walk$_1$ spirit of the chicken,
follow$_1$ follow$_2$ the path that is bright$_1$ that is bright$_2$

When you next espy$_1$ espy$_2$ a house,
a bright$_1$ house, a bright$_2$ house,
that house of brass, that is the house of the Creator
that's where you go.

There follow equally lengthy instructions about what the spirit of the chicken is to do and to say at the house of the Creator.

This notion of the sacrificial victim as messenger seems so plain, so straightforward, that it comes as a surprise to find that it is central to none of the extant theories of sacrifice. It can be read into them, but it is not emphasized. For instance, one reading of the classic schema of Hubert and Mauss implies transition. "The model that came to their minds," de Heusch argues, "was that of rites of passage. The 'consecration' of the victim, its passage from one state to another, takes place in an isolated zone, cut off from the rest of the world" (1982:3). De Heusch does not explain how Van Gennep's notion of the rite of passage, set out in a 1909 essay, could have been the model for Hubert and Mauss, writing in 1898. Nevertheless, we can accept that the latter conceived of sacrifice in terms of a movement between sacred and profane. Levi-Strauss's description also employs the language of motion. The object of sacrifice, he says:

> is to bring to pass the fulfillment of human prayers by a distant deity. It claims to achieve this by first bringing together the two domains through a sacralized victim . . . and then eliminating this connecting term. The sacrifice thus creates a lack of contiguity, and by the purposive nature of the prayer, it induces . . . a compensating continuity to arise on the plane where the initial deficiency experienced by the sacrificer traced the path which leads to the deity (Levi-Strauss 1966:226).

It is interesting that Levi-Strauss makes so close an association between prayer and sacrifice, an association that is apt for the Berawan case. When he discusses the sacrifice itself, he speaks of the "path traced" to the deity, just as de Heusch talks of the "passage" of the victim between states, but these metaphors are, if not dead, at least very tired. They hardly match up to the colorful language employed by Sadi Pejong.

In his recent study of sacrifice and kingship in Hawaii, Valerio Valeri lists four "theses" that are found in different combinations in the various theories of sacrifice, old and new. They are:

1. Sacrifice is a gift to the gods and is part of a process of exchange between gods and humans;
2. Sacrifice is a communion between man and god through a meal;
3. Sacrifice is efficacious representation;
4. Sacrifice is a cathartic act. (Valeri 1985:62)

The notion of the victim as messenger is irrelevant to the last three and at best marginal to the first.

If one stops to wonder why this simple idea should occur so readily to the Berawan when it has apparently evaded the theorists, there is an answer thats suggest itself. It is hinted at in the quote from Sadi Pejong, and it concerns a model provided by another phase of Berawan ritual. The single most important festival of Berawan religion, in terms of scale and sacredness, is called **nulang**. It is a rite of secondary treatment of the dead that is performed for a few select individuals a year or more after death. It is also the occasion for renewal of the links between the communities of the living and the dead. Its core is a sequence of songs (**gu**), which have the formidable power to confer life and death. The key song takes the dead person, now at last transformed into spirit, on the journey to the land of the dead. The journey takes some hours to sing, and recounts the itinerary in detail. Moreover, the death songs are more than just a model because the newly dead are also a kind of sacrifice. They also are destroyed in this world, though involuntarily, so that they can be reconstituted in the beyond, and they also provide an avenue of communication with spirit worlds, although a slow one (Metcalf 1982a:107–10, 213–31).

The language of journeys does not exhaust the ways that Berawan talk about sacrifice. There are in addition a trio of figures that are constantly reiterated in very similar words. Together they make up a master figure, connected by the word **sema,** "blood." In prayer one, Tama Jok moves rapidly to these figures after he invoked the ancestors and requested of them "a good life." I give them in the same order that he does, though elsewhere the order is different. The first, beginning at line 32, is:

nak kíjì' butí selí pun
sema díek tu masak
lum da lum uma
lum lírín lum lamín

which I translate as:

Even if only a drop as small as a seed of grass,
let the blood of this chicken enter,
into your house$_1$ into your house$_2$
into your house$_3$ into your house$_4$

Butí means a scrap or a grain. It is often used to refer to the grains that drop from the fingers when eating rice. Selí is a variety of grass, though its seeds are far too small to collect for food. Together they emphasize that the merest speck of blood is sufficient to consummate the sacrifice. But how or why it should "enter the house" of the ancestors is unclear. Some variation of wording occurs. In other places in the prayers, it is the "house" of the Creator that is specified, without otherwise changing the figure. Also the structure lum X lum Y can employ other dyads than those used here. Their etymologies are explained in the endnotes to the prayers.

The second figure is yet more mystical:

tu la píléo telang sa'an
telang kenumaan
telang wat
telang tabat kaam

It is difficult to translate. The word-by-word gloss given in the introduction does not read in a connected way. The most literal translation I can manage that is readable is as follows:

Charge it with power to convey,
power to nourish,

power to satisfy,
power to heal, you.

The key words are **píléo telang**. **Píléo** is a verb connoting spiritual transformation. It is used, for instance, to speak of human souls in their transformation into ancestral spirits. **Telang** means "power," or perhaps "efficacy." Sa'an means literally "to carry on the shoulder," **kenumaan**, "to feed," **wat**, "guts," and **tabat**, just as it is rendered, "to heal." Of the four terms appearing after **telang**, not all occur invariably, or in this order. But sa'an is often the first, and it echoes the idea of transmission expressed in the first figure. **Kenumaan** is plain enough and suggests the gloss for **wat**, which is effectively "stomach power." **Tabat** is straightforward, but the second person plural pronoun tacked on after it is misleading. It seems to imply that it is the spirits themselves that will be healed or nourished, but other uses of the figure do not insert **kaam** at the end. Moreover, it is a device of emphasis in Berawan to hold the subject of a verb until the close of the phrase. This is indicated by the comma. **Kaam** is the subject of the verb **píléo**, and **tu**, "this," is its object. Elsewhere, two other words occur after **telang**: **jo**, which also means "guts" and is glossed as "to satisfy," and **sío**, which is a word borrowed from Kenyah, meaning "life giving force" (Galvin 1967:90), and which I gloss as "to give life" (see chapter three, prayer one, note 42). In summary, the figure requests that whatever spirits are invoked—usually the ancestors or the Creator—will give the sacrificial blood profound mystical powers.

Tama Jok next repeats (line 46) a truncated version of the first figure, before producing the third:

apan kaam wong ketí wong balí
   wong langèt wong sarèt
   wong pejong wong tulong

The translation is quite literal:

You take it to be charm, to be spirit,
   to be feverish, to be quivering,
   to be lifted up, to be help.

The first and second lines of this figure hardly vary at all. **Kaam** has the same referent as before. **Ketí** covers a range of objects felt to have the power to protect their owners in some way. Examples that we have already met are the stones of **bílì' gau**, and the **síkíp** that are hung onto scabbards of fighting blades (**belílík takèng**). The latter are anthropomorphically-shaped pieces of stone or fossilized tree resin, wrapped in a small bundle decorated with the tusks of wild boar. Some have the power to make the sword jump from its sheath if danger is near, while others can make their owners invisible at critical moments. Charms are also hung under the eaves of the house to ward off various malign influences. In each case, the utility of the object is revealed in a dream or by a shaman. Some Berawan keep all manner of charms secreted away, hoarding objects dating back to their grandparents' generation. But others are skeptical, arguing that it is unlikely that the effects will persist long after the original revelation. As a class, they represent another instance of the mysterious, and ultimately unknowable, intersection of human and spirit worlds. The word with which **ketí** is paired requires less explanation. **Balí** is a Kenyah term cognate with **bílì'**, and presumably has much the same connotations as the Berawan term. The thrust of the first line of the figure is a plea that the blood of the sacrificial animal (**sema díek** in line 44 is the direct object of **apan**) acquire supernatural power.

The dyadic set in the second line suggests the nature of that power. **Langèt** describes the feeling that a person might have when running a temperature; not so much ill as in an altered state of consciousness. Significantly, shaman in a trance are often said to be "feverish." Similarly, **sarèt** refers to the trembling of anticipation rather than fear. These metaphors project a kind of power that is no mere abstraction, but something that the participants will experience physically. Other lines are sometimes tagged on to these two, but they are less significant. Tama Jok's third line reinforces the notion that the power of sacrifice is beneficial.

These three figures are among the most common in the texts, but their very repetitiveness makes them resistant to exegesis. When I quizzed Berawan about one of them, the standard response was, in effect, to repeat the wording of another, or to fall back on the homely language of messengers and journeys. It is plain that the figures have their own power, a power of allusion and evocation that cannot be translated without distortion into a mechanical account of just how sacrifice is supposed to work.

Nevertheless, it is possible to explore some of the allusions. When a chicken is sacrificed, it typically happens in this way: during the prayer, the speaker paces about holding the chicken in the crook of his arm. Occasionally, he takes it by the legs and waves it over the top of the prayer station, as if it were an object. The chicken squawks and flaps its wings desperately, but no one takes any notice. This particularly occurs when the speakers introduce the chicken, often with the formula:

tu díek la díek líwa
kaam bílì'

This is the sacrificial₁ chicken, the sacrificial₂ chicken,
  for you spirits.

A list of spirit agencies usually follows. When the speaker nears the end of his remarks, he pins the chicken under his left elbow, holding its neck out with his left hand. Then, with his right hand, he draws his **parang**, hooks it under the chicken's head, and unhurriedly saws the head off. Without pausing in his **píat**, he lifts his elbow to let the carcass fall to the ground. He holds on to the head, and walks around the congregation dabbing blood onto the backs of their right hands, held out for this purpose—all the time continuing his invocation and supplication. Alternatively, he can use the flat of the bloody blade. Once the crowd received the sacrament, they drift away. Later, someone will pick up the carcass, and take it off to the kitchen to be cleaned and cooked.⁶

On grand occasions when a pig is sacrificed, it is left trussed on the ground. Sometimes the speaker sits on its side, nudging it gently, while briefing it with messages for the Creator or an ancestor. For a large male pig, the efforts of two men may be required to sever its head. There is one rite that now occurs as part of the death ritual sequence—formerly it was a great festival in its own right—that celebrates military values and inducts boys into their first grade of warrior status (Metcalf 1982a:121–23). The pigs sacrificed at the time are picked up bodily by the adult men, and blood is poured copiously over the initiates in a show of blood lust. This is extraordinary behavior, however, since normally, a dab of the bloody blade is sufficient. At the other end of the spectrum, the sacrificial animal may be nothing more than a tiny chick, left on a **pakaan** until immolated and barely sufficient for a small crowd of onlookers.

The application of blood is clearly a sacrament in the sense that it allows or ensures the participation of the onlookers in the rite, both prayer and sacrifice. In the Judeo-Christian tradition, which, as de Heusch points out, has conditioned all our theorizing on sacrifice, sacraments are an aspect of communion. The other aspects commonly specified are sharing and communication. The sharing of food with the deity is one of Valeri's "theses," and it is an almost inescapable feature of sacrifice. Among the Berawan also, the immolated creature is given to the spirits, and then eaten by humans. Moreover, **pakaan** are explicitly offerings of delicacies to spirits. In lines 75–76 of prayer one (and elsewhere) Tama Jok refers specifically to the ancestors:

that we have so often fed$_1$
so often fed$_2$
   at this lake.

Just before these lines, Tama Jok has pointed out the offerings of food and rice wine, but it is significant that he makes no mention of the meat of the sacrificial animals. In fact, only one such reference occurs in all the prayers, and then in an ironic way. In prayer four (lines 99–103), the eccentric Uking says:

Its not because we want
to eat your thighs, eat your wings, eat your skin,
you spirit of the chicken,
but to make prayers and sacrifice for all of us in this community.

This disclaimer only underlines the point that, in sharp contrast to the theme of offering, sacrifice is not talked about in terms of food. The emphasis is elsewhere, and it surely does not imply that the spirits drink blood.

Moreover, the offerings made to the Creator, as opposed to the **pakaan** offered to minor spirits, do not much suggest feeding. The raw eggs atop their **tapo'** are offered more as recognition than alimentation.

On the other hand, the final aspect of communion, that of communication, does strike a chord because of the imagery of the victim as messenger. Moreover, it accords well with the close association in Berawan ritual between prayer and sacrifice. They are nearly synonymous because each occurs in association with the other. So the question becomes: how does sacrifice augment the communicative process of prayer? This is the core of the mystical power of sacrifice and of sacrificial blood. It has the power to "enter the house" of the ancestors and the Creator. It has the power somehow to conduct positive energy from those sources to humans, energy that can be felt by humans, who ground this energy. The electrical analogy that I employ here is not one that is likely to occur to Berawan. But in several discussions, informants fumbling for words to describe sacrifice likened it to a rope. Similarly, people sometimes describe the connection between humans and their life-giving souls in terms of a filament (Metcalf 1982a:58–66).

An act that is visually suggestive of the same notion occurs when a pig is to be sacrificed. At line 170 of prayer two, we find Tama Aweng hunkered down beside a trussed pig. He takes out his cigarette lighter and singes the coarse bristles on the back of the pig's neck. The released smoke is dark, and it can be clearly made out, rising in a wispy column toward the jungle canopy. Tama Aweng calls softly, renewing his prayer, and begins:

> This smell, this odor of singed pig,
>
> let it ascend to Bungan Malan,
>
> let it ascend to the spirit that holds, the spirit that creates.

What also ascends to the Creator is, of course, the words of the prayer.

The communicative emphasis in these figures serves to temper our understanding of the occult power of sacrificial blood. There is a temptation to place an Old Testament coloring on it: "Only be sure that you do not eat the blood, for blood is life" (Deuteronomy 12:23). As a counterbalance, it is worth noting that the figures are not exclusively used to talk about blood. Occasionally, they are adapted to other contexts. Beginning at line 34 of prayer two, it is the whole chicken that is "to be charm, to be spirit." In lines 71–74 of prayer one, it is rice wine that is to "enter the house$_1$ enter the house$_2$" of the ancestors. Finally, around line 160 of prayer two, we find Tama Aweng speaking in flattering terms about the official role of Gumbang, scion of a noble family, who just happens to be standing at his elbow:

> Make whatever he says effective,
>
> make it as a charm, as spirit,
>
> make it feverish, make it quiver,
>
> make it so, you spirits.

The phraseology is probably somewhat excessive. Nevertheless, it is here words themselves are invested with the enigmatic "power to convey."

I argue that the two ways in which sacrifice is portrayed in **píat** converge in notions of communion, but it remains the case that one is remarkably direct, the other mystical, and they are weighted differently by different speakers. In prayer one, Tama Jok returns insistently to the power of blood. In contrast, Sadi Pejong seems unwilling to deal with the deeper connotations of sacrifice. Perhaps he is influenced in this by the aversion of Christian missionaries. In any event, he concludes his itinerary for the sacrificial chicken as follows:

> although no bigger than a tailorbird,
>
> not as big as a black hornbill,
>
> not as big as a rhinoceros hornbill,
>
> > yet big as charm, as spirit,
>
> > with strength$_1$ with strength$_2$
>
> You carry these offerings,
>
> you carry all,
>
> the cooked food, savory rice, betel, tobacco,
>
> carry the food,
>
> this rice wine,
>
> these things
>
> > to meet at the place$_1$ to meet at the place$_2$
>
> > to meet the persons$_1$ to meet the persons$_2$
>
> > of the Creator Spirit and grandmother Bungan.

The "strength" of the poor chicken is no more than that required to carry a tableful of offerings. Sadi Pejong has reduced the sacrificial animal to a cosmic busboy. Nevertheless, it is plain that there is an ideology of sacrifice in native central northern Borneo for which current theories do not adequately account.

Anacrusis

One last aspect of the treatment of sacrifice in the prayers requires comment. In some sections, the sacrificial animal is addressed directly and repeatedly. If these instances were counted as acts of invocation, then the spirit of the pig and the spirit of the chicken would swamp all the spirit agencies listed in table 1. This does not happen because these instances do not occur in verses concerned with the theme of invocation. This distinction is a formal one, but even a casual inspection of the texts shows that the sacrificial animals are addressed in ways different from spirits that are properly invoked. The devices that are employed involve the anacrustic line and the imperative mood.

In chapter one, the anacrustic line was defined as a kind of isolated line involving "repetitious exclamations or introductory phrases." An example is provided above in the first extract used to illustrate the theme of sacrifice. It comprises a part of the last thirty-two lines of prayer two. Twelve of those lines consist of the words **bílì' no bíkuí,** "you spirit of the pig." Occurring every second or third line, these words provide a uniform rhythm for the whole section, which is spoken rapidly (◆) with the occasional loud line (■). The lines sandwiched between the anacrustic lines offer rapid-fire advice to the sacrificial animal: "go," "don't get lost," "listen to what I say." I render all thirty-two lines as one verse dealing with the theme of sacrifice. As we have seen, the themes of **píat** do not lend themselves to any natural climax or denouement. If one is desired, it has to be generated, and such overlength verses are the result. Usually these verses occur just before a sacrifice is made, and other speakers join in, adding their voices to the crescendo.

An alternative type of anacrusis is also found. In prayer three, Tama Avit displays a particular fondness for the device, managing to use it in most verses. His most characteristic introductory phrase is: "Tell them this, spirit of the chicken," and then he follows with a verse that may have to do with any of several themes and not just with sacrifice. In fact, in one place where the phrase does introduce this theme (line 43), the effect is inappropriate:

Tell them this, spirit of the chicken:

This is the sacrificial$_1$ chicken, the sacrificial$_2$ chicken,
   for you grandfather Penyalong (with this pig,
                    wherever that pig is just now).

To put the formula **tu díek la díek líwa,** itself introductory, into the chicken's mouth is ludicrous, an impression heightened by the absentminded aside about the missing pig. Since the imperative does not condition what follows, I discount such lines for the purpose of segmental analysis. They are set apart like one line verses, with a colon to indicate their connections to the following ones.

This analysis is confirmed by the presence of another introductory phrase. Four times between lines 60 and 80, Tama Avit repeats the line, "This is the rice wine we give to you." In three cases, the line is followed by a verse, and none of them concerns the theme of offering. The first two concern invocation and furnish the long lists of spirit agencies analyzed in table 1. The theme of the third is discussed later.

Sadi Pejong is another aficionado of the introductory phrase. In fact, the last two-thirds of prayer seven is presented as messages that the sacrificial chicken is to repeat to the Creator and Bungan. Sadi Pejong must attribute considerable powers of memory, as well as strength, to his chicken because he covers many different topics. In fact, they are complicated enough that he himself loses track of his device, so that he muddles personal pronouns. In some places he refers to "them," being the Berawan folk as described by the chicken, and at other times he says "we." These two prayers, however, do not exhaust the cases of anacrusis in the prayers.

Divination

The most conspicuous example of repeated exclamations occurs in prayer six, where the same anacrustic line (or very slight variants of it) accounts for no less than 47 out of 155 lines, or almost one line in three throughout all but the opening section of a lengthy prayer. The line is marked all the more by employing wording borrowed from Kenyah, **balí plakí**, rather than the Berawan **bílì' plaké**, "spirit of eagle."

The spirit of eagle is addressed directly and repeatedly, and it is called to attend. But this is an act of invocation that is unlike the others because the spirit of eagle is expected to appear in physical form. This calling of an omen creature is unique to the eagle **plaké**, which is the one especially associated with the Creator. How this calling is accomplished and how the omens are interpreted are explained in chapter seven. But the point for the present is that divination must be acknowledged as another theme of prayer. The verses that pertain to the theme of divination are various so it is not easy to list the opening lines that signal them. Some verses explain the ways omens are to be read, others describe the desirable features of the augural bird, others encourage a rapid response, and so on. But they are readily recognizable because they incorporate multiple uses of the anacrustic line **balí plakí**.

Calling the major omen bird is a serious business, not undertaken lightly or casually because of the awesome power that the bird represents. The whole of prayer six is focused on it, and it is consequently not surprising that many—although not all—of its verses concern the theme of divination. By the same token, it does not crop up in any of the other prayers. The theme has its own figures and formulae, but they need not be discussed in detail here, because they are all found within the one prayer that has its own chapter.

Minor Themes

This brings us to the end of the major themes of prayer—those that contribute many verses to the corpus or are represented in most of the prayers. In addition to these major themes, there are a number of minor themes that represent personal foibles of the speaker or special circumstances of the rite. They are bound to exist in view of the ability of **píat**, which was pointed out at the beginning of the chapter, to address any aspect of Berawan life.

Explanation

One minor theme concerns explanation—the rationale or purpose of the rite, set out in forthright fashion. By the nature of the theme, verses concerned with explanation do not lend themselves to the use of figures or formulae, and do not have standardized opening lines. They are not found in the first two prayers, which address the welfare of the entire community, but they are found in prayers three and four, which have a much narrower focus. For example, line 75 of prayer three is an anacrustic line, followed by a succinct explanation:

> This is the rice wine we give to you:
>> Because we said if he lived,
>> because we said if little Ukat were safe,
>>> we would give one large jar of rice wine,
>>> that's what we said that night.

The night in question saw the child named Ukat pass the climax of his illness. During that night, pledges were made that are redeemed in the current rite. Explanation is an even more conspicuous theme in prayer five, where Lian Yang is anxious to have the recently deceased Tama Suleng understand exactly what he and his companions in the graveyard have in mind:

This is why I'm,
talking to you,
    because you are going to be moved,
    because you are going to be brought,
      back to your own apartment,
      to your own longhouse,
    to bring you together with Lawai,
    to bring you together with Tama Julan Tinggang,
        at the lake.

Subsequent verses elaborate the explanation.

Identity

Another minor theme that crops up briefly in the first two prayers concerns identity. In both of them, the speaker wants to lay claim to the protection of the spirit agencies of the locality, including the ancestral spirits. Beginning at line 80 of prayer one, Tama Jok claims:

We the Lelak people living here,
    are not outsiders here,
  all of us,
      you see$_1$ you see$_2$
      everything, you spirits.

Tama Aweng echoes the theme, in a verse that makes a statement about the whole nature of ritual (**adèd**):

We your children, your grandchildren,
  the origin of ritual,

from grandparents$_1$ from grandparents$_2$
from grandparents$_3$ from grandparents$_4$
    of ours long ago,
  who lived on this land,
        this plain,
        this soil.

Other Minor Themes

Finally, there are occasional verses that do not pertain to any of the themes identified above, and they do not resemble any other verse in the corpus. They fall into a miscellaneous category that is inherent in the nature of prayer, however many themes are named. For example, at line 127 of prayer two, Tama Aweng makes the following plaint:

We human beings,
  truly we stare with big eyes,
  truly we appear big,
  but we have no name,
    no house$_1$ no house$_2$
    no secure place$_1$ no secure place$_2$
    no room, no path.

Tama Aweng seems to be striking a note of humility, but the wording is unique—not to say obscure—and hardly justifies a theme to itself. A little later he has a verse about the special duties of the man in charge of the fishing in the Bunok river, and again the sentiments and wording are unique.

Finally, there is one verse in the corpus that is truly anomalous. It is spoken by Uking, beginning at line 67 of prayer four, who pontificates:

All you women and men,
  don't you mistrust what Kajan says,
  don't you mistrust what the committee says,
  that is deputy to Kajan,
  in this community.

As it happens, this piece of advice was not welcome, but the verse does violence to the form of **píat** in a more fundamental way. The verse is directly addressed to the audience; prayer is addressed to spirits.

These are the themes of Berawan prayer. No two prayers employ the same combination. Each is unique, and it is possible to compare them by means of a tabulation. This type of analysis, however, is best postponed until the examples have been presented.

3.
Papì˘ Lamèng—Prayers of the House

The annual festival of **papì˘ lamèng** (**papì˘** means "prayer" or "rite," **lamèng** means "house") is the only Berawan ritual named for the act of praying. It is also the only calendrical rite that involves the entire longhouse community. The prayers said at the festival are intended to secure the welfare of the village as a whole throughout the coming year. Prayers made at other times are more specific, either in terms of the people represented, or in terms of the benevolence sought, or both. In this sense, the Prayers of the House provide a model from which others are more specialized variants. Consequently, it is appropriate to begin with them.

Nature of the Festival

Papì˘ lamèng is held soon after the rice year is completed. However, Berawan do not think of it as a harvest festival. It is simply held at a time

98

when food supplies are high since hospitality is the order of the day. **Papì'**
lamèng initiates an informal ritual season, when weddings and parties
follow one another. The very fact that people are gathered for one rite
makes it easier to organize the next. Formal litigation, involving an assembly of the entire community, also tends to occur at this time.

The activities of **papì' lamèng** itself are two: first, the sharing of food and
wine; and second, the making of prayers and sacrifice.

The festival is, above all else, a rite of commensality. The production of
food in Berawan society is organized around the social unit called **ukuk,**
that is, the coresidents of a longhouse apartment (**ukuk** means both the
"room" and the "inhabitants of the room"). This group of people, related
by blood and marriage, shares one farm, one hearth, and one common
store of rice. Strict rules of etiquette prescribe hospitality; for instance, no
one would dream of not offering food to anyone who walked in on them
while they were eating. Indeed, this is not just a matter of etiquette, for
supernatural perils await those who fail to offer food and those who fail to
receive it. But contrary to the impression that these niceties convey,
Berawan do not as a rule share food beyond the **ukuk** group. Toward the
end of the rice year, when one family runs out of rice, their neighbors will
not offer to help. Some will go hungry, while others have ample supplies.

This is not a cause for pity; those who perennially have a poor rice crop
are looked down on. Their failure is attributed to laziness or ineptness, and
their respectability erodes. Some heads of households do indeed sell off too
much of their crop for ready cash each year, frittering away the proceeds on
luxuries and leaving their families hungry at the end of the year.

These harsh realities are inverted at **papì' lamèng.** Now everyone has
rice, and it is consumed joyously and communally, but still not corpo-
rately. Each family cooks ample supplies of food—rice, fish, whatever
meat is available. Each family prepares stocks of rice wine, a fermented
liquor prepared from cooked rice. The agenda throughout the days of the
festival is to pay visits back and forth along the veranda of the longhouse,
sampling the new rice and the brew from each room. In the evenings,
there are parties on the veranda, with dancing and games. Lamps burn
well into the night. Groups of friends, a gaggle of teenage girls here, a pair
of middle-aged men there, saunter down the veranda arm-in-arm and
wander into whatever room attracts them with sounds of laughter and
conversation. There is always someone at home to bring out more food
and drink, and presently the company will disperse and new groups will
form elsewhere, so that no one family's stocks are depleted.

At such times, longhouse solidarity and identity are palpable. They are equally in evidence in the other phase of **papì' lamèng,** the prayers and the sacrifices. As the examples below illustrate, the wording of prayers constantly reiterates the same themes: the collectivity of all the ancestors, shared by and peculiar to the people of the village of Long Teru; particular named ancestors, leaders of the past who shaped the community and whose names bring to mind eras in its history; and the intimate relation between these ancestral spirits and features of local geography, particularly the all-important lake and farmlands nearby (see chapter one, prayer one, note 7). It is well to keep in mind that the constant references to "spirits of (or in, or at) the lake" (**bílì' lum luvak**) mean primarily the ancestral spirits. It is their tombs that lie in and around the lake, and their spiritual presence that is most felt (see chapter two).

The locations of major sacrifices further emphasize these themes. Every year a pig is sacrificed, with appropriate prayers, either on the banks of the lake itself, or near the mouth of the Bunok stream where it joins the Teru River. Both lake and stream are economically important, and both have ancient graveyards adjacent to them.

Prayer and sacrifice at the longhouse are organized room by room. Any family that cares to may erect a **tapo'** (prayer station; see chapter two) on the riverbank in front of their apartment. The prayers can be said by the head of the household, or he may invite a person more skilled at **píat** than himself to make them, or several people may offer prayers. In any given year, perhaps half a dozen of the thirty or so rooms at Long Teru will prepare **tapo',** and a shifting crowd of people will go from one to the next all morning, with individuals falling out for a drink and rejoining later. Just which rooms choose to sponsor **tapo'** is determined by complex social factors, but generally it is sponsored by families that wish to restate or advance claims to superior social standing and concern for the public welfare. Whenever animals are sacrificed—certainly a chicken or two, and perhaps a pig—they provide meat for the food that is offered to visitors inside the rooms. The biggest pig is always sacrificed outside the most important **ukuk** in the longhouse, the one that furnished the last important leader of the community and houses the man regarded as his most obvious successor. Outside this room the new **tapo'** is erected amidst the tumbled remains of those of former years, and the sacrifices of **papì' lamèng** reach their climax in impassioned prayers by several experts. In this way, the social order is made manifest. Characteristically, attention is focused both on the collective interests of the entire community, and on the preeminence of particular families.

June 1, 1972

In 1972, the people of Long Teru decided to coordinate **papì' lamèng** with a state-wide public holiday called Gawai Dayak, which is intended to honor interior folk. There is, of course, no reason why upriver farmers should concern themselves with a bank holiday, but there was a desire to participate, however indirectly, in a national event. In subsequent years, the coordination has not been repeated, indicating a progressive disenchantment with state politics.

The prayers in this chapter were made on the previous day, near the mouth of the Bunok stream. After some confusion, with people changing their minds about whether to come or not, a canoe set out with a dozen passengers, including Tama Jok and Tama Aweng, our prayer makers, and Gumbang Lawai, who is the son-in-law of the last major leader of the Long Teru community, Oyang Ajang, and the son of the leader before him, Penghulu Lawai. Gumbang Lawai is the obvious person to emerge as the next major leader of Long Teru, but he spends much of his time away earning money in the lumber camps. Nevertheless, he is the man entrusted with supervising the fishing operations in Bunok (see chapter three, prayer two, note 51). The canoe also contained provisions for the event.

When we arrived at the chosen spot at about noon, a prayer station was rapidly constructed. Tama Aweng was the first to make **píat**, but his prayer was split into two parts. First he prayed, waving a chicken around. Then Tama Jok spoke, using the same chicken. When Tama Aweng finally immolated the bird, he began his prayer anew over a pig that lay trussed at his feet. This passage begins at line 169 of prayer two, but the transcription breaks off after line 213 because Tama Aweng's voice cannot be made out on the recording. This is because almost everybody present joins in, producing a veritable crescendo of **píat** in the moments before the pig was decapitated. Its blood was splashed on the sticks of the prayer station, augmented with that of a couple more chickens, and dabbed onto the participants.

After this climax, the tensions evaporated. A fire was lit so the pig could be roasted on the spot. Unfortunately, it began to rain while the cooking was in progress, and we made a rather miserable picnic of half-cooked pork and pungent rice wine. On the way back, Gumbang stopped at several fishing sites along the Bunok to see if all was well. One or two showed evidence of illegal manipulation of the river bed to increase catches at other peoples' expense. Gumbang waded around in the river, pulling out driftwood that may or may not have been stuck into the riverbed on purpose. There was a lot of joking directed at those suspected of cheating, but I was warned not to say anything about this back at the longhouse. An unsupported charge would cause much bad feeling. We arrived back at the longhouse after sundown to find festivities in full swing.

On the next day, perhaps a dozen men made prayers in front of different **tapo'**. The contents of their prayers were entirely similar to those offered at Long Bunok, and all displayed skill at **pìat**. The recordings are hard to make out, however, because of the noisy, excited crowds that surrounded every speaker. At some stations, old swords and shields and other military equipment were stacked and sprinkled with blood, so as to gain further strength from the spirits. At climactic moments, women brought water to splash on the crowd. This piece of liminal symbolism (Metcalf 1982a:142–46) caused more uproar.

While all this was in progress outside, a crowd inside, mostly women, took this auspicious opportunity to chase malign influences from the long-house. They began at the downriver end of the house, standing shoulder to shoulder in a line, each person armed with a canoe paddle or a rice pounder. At a signal, they advanced in a phalanx, pounding furiously on the raised wooden floor of the house. As they passed by each room, a contingent would fall out to sweep through it too, and then rejoin the main body. This numbing din is intended to scare away all evil spirits. Three times they swept up and down the veranda.

The last sacrifice occurred outside the room of Gumbang Lawai at about noon. The victim was of the most valuable kind, a large black pig. Several voices were raised in **pìat,** and a general splashing of water followed. When the final climax was over, people drifted away to resume drinking in one or another room of the longhouse.

Prayer One

Speaker: Tama Jok

Time: Approximately four minutes

Summary: Tama Jok begins by appealing to the company of the ancestors as a category, relating them immediately to the terrain that contains the farms and fishing grounds of the community. In lines 6–14 he names specific leaders whose spirits may be expected to be as influential in death as in life. This is a political statement, presenting in effect a digest of the history of the community. Each name is associated with particular epochs and events. This summary is appropriate to the festival of **papi' lamèng,** which is focused on the corporate existence of the village.

In lines 16–20, Tama Jok points out that the **tapo'** carries offerings of several kinds, and launches into a list of the things the people of Long Teru expect to receive from the ancestors. It has been argued that, among other Bornean peoples, the ancestors can only act as emissaries to the gods and not independently (Schärer 1963:153). This passage demonstrates force-fully that the Berawan see the ancestral spirits as able to intervene directly on the behalf of the living, and perhaps as the supernatural agency to be relied on most in this respect.

Lines 32–48 talk about the nature of sacrifice and its effectiveness, and include two esoteric passages that have been untangled in chapter one. In lines 49–62 there is a special appeal made for the safety and success of the young men who have left the community and gone off to seek advance-ment in the towns on the coast. While Long Teru was not particularly active in promoting schooling among its children, some had gone for higher education and everyone hoped they would secure good jobs and be

Figure 4. Tama Jok says the prayer set out in chapter three on a bank of the Bunok stream while waving the sacrificial chicken over the **tapo'** (prayer station). In the middle of the **tapo'** sticks is a tray holding small offerings (**pakaan**). At the edge of the river below stands one of the large fish cages described in prayer two, note 16.

able to send money back home to their families. Other young men had gone to work in lumber camps, where they rubbed shoulders with people from all over the country.

The next section (lines 63–106) repeats the themes of lines 16–31. In the midst of it, Tama Jok hears the call of an omen bird and breaks off immediately to address it (line 107). Lines 108–17 repeat the images of lines 32–48, and then Tama Jok closes for the moment with a standard formula.

After a pause, during which he consults with people standing nearby, Tama Jok decides to go ahead and kill his sacrificial chicken. Lines 120–38 are his hurried dedication.

---

ooo . . .

- ▪ a kaam pì'
- ▪ bílì' sadì' bílì' vì'
- ◆ bílì' ukun bílì' dupun kamé
- ▪ lo mígang atong
- ▪   mígang tanaa tu

- ▪ ke³ sadì' Ajan Tama Langet
- ▪ ke sadì' Tama Julan Tínggang
- ▪ ke sadì' Lawaí
- ▪ lo mígang atong luvak tu   10
- ▪ lo mígang líko' Bunok tu

- ▪ bílì' ke sadì' Orang Kaya Luwak
- ▪ lo adang suken atong líko' tu
- ◆   suken tanaa tu
- ◆   suken díta' tu

Style: Tama Jok is said to have a good style. Not coincidentally, he is a man of solid standing in the community. His father, Tama Ukat Sageng, was a widely known and much respected shaman. Though Tama Jok is not himself a shaman, he is well versed in ritual matters. His delivery in **píat** is more subdued than Tama Aweng's, but my informants claimed that his wording is more elegant. Occasionally he mumbles, and that, combined with a slug of betel nut in his mouth, makes some sections hard to hear.

Note: For an explanation of the conventions of notation, see chapter one. A synopsis of these conventions is provided on the last printed page of the book.

Calling noise

Where are you all,

 spirits of grandparents$_1$ spirits of grandparents$_2$

 spirits of grandparents$_3$ spirits of grandparents$_4$[1]

  who rule[2] over all,

  rule over this land.

 Grandfather Ajan Tama Langet,[4]

 grandfather Tama Julan Tinggang,[5]

 grandfather Lawai,[6]

10 who rule throughout this lake,[7]

  who rule along this river Bunok.

 Spirit of grandfather Orang Kaya Luwak,[8]

 who actually supports the whole of this watershed,

  supports this land,

  supports this plain.

- vaí la⁹ tekelo'
- kumaan tíku tu
- kumaan angaan
- kumaan jakaan
- kumaan banyak tu   20

- kícung kamé lía Long Teru tu
- mulong jìn mulong genín
- mulong mída mulong luya
- mulong ketan mulong kapan
- mulong tína' mulong tava'
- kamé utan kaam

- belurí wang belurí paraí
- belurí lígìt belurí duít
- lukí melubí
- melaí beluwaí   30
- kaam sínyu nyadu

- nak kíjì' butí selí pun¹⁶
- sema díek tu masak
- lum da lum uma
- lum lírín lum lamín
- kaam bílì' vì' bílì' sadì'
- lo malaí
- nakaan kenumaan
- kamé lum luvak

- tu la píléo telang sa'an   40
  -             telang kenumaan

verse continues uninterrupted

Come all of you,

    eat these eggs,

    eat this food$_1$

    eat this food$_2$[10]

20   eat all of this.

Give us at this community of Long Teru,[11]

    a good life, a cool life,

    a slow life, a calm life,[12]

    a deep life, a thick life,[13]

    a happy life, a laughing life,

      grant us this.

Let us have money, let us have rice,

let us have dollars, let us have cash,

    luck$_1$ luck$_2$

30   luck$_3$ luck$_3$[14]

      you push$_1$ push$_2$ to us.[15]

Even if only a drop as small as a seed of grass,

    let the blood of this chicken enter,

      into your house$_1$ into your house$_2$[17]

      into your house$_3$ into your house$_4$[18]

    you spirits of grandparents$_1$ spirits of grandparents$_2$

    whom we are accustomed,

      to feed$_1$ to feed$_2$

        here in this lake.

40   Charge it with power to convey,

      power to nourish,

verse continues uninterrupted

◆　　　telang wat

◆　　　telang tabat kaam

▪ sema díek ko tu masak

◆ lum tílong lum padong kaam

◆ apan kaam wong ketí wong balí

◆　　　wong langèt wong sarèt

◆　　　wong pejong wong tulong

▪ vaí tílé matelo' lo anyam

◆　　　matelo' lo anak co^{24} ubín tu　　　50

■ kara' tílo' lo kellèjjé pelíta

◆ ra ko kanaí ngaran tílo' ngapato tílo'

▪ kaam bílì' lum luvak tílé

▪ kaam bílì' lum luvak tu nulong tilo'

▪ mejong tílo'

■ a'an ngayan lakau

◆　　　ngayan urau ngayan usau tílo'

▪　　　ngayan uma ngayan da tílo'

▪ ílaan orang putéé

◆ ílaan ka'é ka'é bangsa　　　60

◆ lutok ngaran tílo' serong dé utan kaam

◆ bísa' telang jíu tílo'

▪ tu sema díek

▪ bípì mekì

▪ kaam bílì'

verse continues uninterrupted

power to satisfy,

power to heal, you.[19]

Let the blood of this chicken of mine enter,

into your fastness$_1$ into your fastness$_2$[20]

you take it to be charm, to be spirit,[21]

to be feverish, to be quivering,[22]

to be lifted up, to be help.[23]

Come look at us your grandchildren,

50   we children, your descendants.[25]

All those who work for the government,

I do not know their names or titles,

you spirits of the lake, look out for them,

you spirits of the lake, help them,

lift them up.[26]

Wherever they go,

wherever they stay$_1$ wherever they stay$_2$[27]

wherever they settle$_1$ wherever they settle$_2$

whether among white men,

60   whether among any other race,

let their names float among them,

let their words be powerful.[28]

This blood of the chicken,

is a sacrifice$_1$ a sacrifice$_2$[29]

to you spirits,

verse continues uninterrupted

- co matelo' melì
◆ co matelo' kappì

▪ tu angaan jakaan
◆ peno' ma peno' naga
◆ peno' mang peno' lagang   70

▪ burèk matelo' tu
◆ masak lum da lum uma kaam
◆ bílì' ukun bílì' dupun
◆ bílì' vì' bílì' sadì'
▪ lo malaí nakaan
▪   malaí kenumaan
▪ co luvak tu
▪ atong Bunok tu
▪ atong Teru tu

▪ kamé lo bangsa Lelak tu mulong ato'   80
◆ ra wong dé lo accì ato'
◆ kamé tu
▪ kaam tilé kaam ngelaté
◆ tupaan kaam bílì'

▪ tupaan lamèng Long Teru selamat pì' kamé
▪ díccu anak
◆ mulong jìn mulong genín
◆ mulong mída mulong luya
· mulong tanyít mulong la'ít
· kamé utan kaam   90

that we use to buy,

that we use to ask.[30]

This is the prepared food, cooked food,[31]

full indeed$_1$ full indeed$_2$

70 full again$_1$ full again$_2$[32]

Let this rice wine of ours,

enter your house$_1$ enter your house$_2$

spirits of grandparents$_3$ spirits of grandparents$_4$

spirits of grandparents$_1$ spirits of grandparents$_2$

whom we are accustomed to feed$_1$

accustomed to feed$_2$

at this lake,

along this Bunok river,

along this Teru river.

80 We the Lelak[33] people living here,

are not outsiders here,

all of us,

you see$_1$ you see$_2$[34]

everything, you spirits.

Let us all of the Long Teru house be secure,

women and children,

a good life, a cool life,

a slow life, a calm life,

a healthy$_1$ life, a healthy$_2$ life,[35]

90 grant us this.

- belurí paraí belurí síju
- belurí wang
- belurí lígìt belurí duít
- melaí beluwaí
◆ lukí melubí

◆ kaam kícung bílì' pujì bílì' kelawí
◆   bílì' yan bílì' pelukan
■ ngan lía Long Teru tu
- díccu laké anak umí
■ ra wong kena na kena tusaa   100

- kaam bílì' ngelatang ngelalang
◆ wong nyí lo ka mapat ka mímat
         ka ngacau ka peleta' kamé
◆ kaam tílé kaam katé kaam puléí
· kaam ngelatang
· kaam ngelalang

■ kelo' bílì' kutèk ní

- tu sema díek ko
◆ na'a masak lum lírín
·   masak lum lamín   110
·   masak lum jalan kelo'

◆ píléo telang sa'an telang kenumaan
◆   telang jo telang sío
·   telang wat telang tabat
· kelo' rè na'a

Let us have rice, let us have fish,

let us have money,

let us have dollars, let us have cash,

    $luck_3$ $luck_4$

    $luck_1$ $luck_2$[36]

You give the spirit of reputation, spirit of fame,

spirit of $name_1$ spirit of $name_2$[37]

    to the community of Long Teru,

    the women, the men, the small children,

100   will not strike $difficulties_1$ strike $difficulties_2$[38]

You spirits $shield_1$ us, $shield_2$ us,[39]

    against those who would throw us $down_1$ throw us $down_2$

    would disturb us, would kill us,[40]

        you see it, you throw it away, you turn it back,

        you $shield_3$ us,

        you $shield_2$ us.

You spirit of the tailorbird there.[41]

This blood of my chicken,

    let it afterwards enter your $house_3$

110   enter your $house_4$

        enter your path.

Charge it with the power to convey, power to nourish,

        power to satisfy, power to give life,

        power to fill, power to heal,

    you, afterwards.[42]

- apan kelo' wong ketí wong balí
- ◆ wong pejong wong tolong

◆ rè jíu ní

Pause

ooo . . .

- tu díek la díek líwa   120
- kaam bílì' atong Bunok
- ◆ bílì' atong luvak
- tu na'a

- telang matang kaam
- ◆ mulong mejong
- anak lía Long Teru tu umí kíjì'

- kaam bílì' kaju unong
- bílì' tapo' tu
- píon bílì' nat bílì' jat

◆ tu sema díek ko   130
◆ na'a masak lum da
- lum uma kaam na'a

◆ pílέɔ telang sa'an telang kenumaan
◆ telang jo telang sío
- telang wat telang tabat
- kelo' bílì' na'a

◆ apan kelo' telang matang
◆ apan kelo' wong ketí wong balí

You make it as a charm, as spirit,

to help$_1$ us, to help$_2$ us.

That's what I say.

Pause

Calling noise

120 This is the chicken sacrificed$_1$ the chicken sacrificed$_2$[43]

   for you spirits of the Bunok,

     spirits of the lake,

    here afterwards.

  Make it powerful, effective,

  to give life$_1$ life$_2$[44]

  to the children of Long Teru, big and small.

You spirits of the **kaju unong**,

  spirits of this prayer station,[45]

    challenge bad$_1$ spirits, bad$_2$ spirits.[46]

130 This is the blood of my chicken,

    let it enter your house$_1$

      your house$_2$ afterwards.

  Charge it with power to sustain, power to nourish,

      power to satisfy, power to give life,

      power to heal$_1$ power to heal$_2$

    you spirits, afterwards.

  Make it powerful, effective,

  make it as a charm, as spirit.

Prayer Two

Speaker: Tama Aweng

Time: Approximately eight minutes

Summary: This prayer is in two parts. The first part addresses topics similar to those in Tama Jok's prayer, with the addition of some novel stylistic flourishes. The second part is mainly in the form of a set of instructions directed to the spirit of the pig.

The first part opens, as usual, with a roster of supernatural agencies. But Tama Aweng is unusual because he selects the omen creatures (see chapter three, prayer two, note 1). He calls and shouts to them in a formula that he repeats several times, in one form or another. From line 15 on, he returns to more familiar deities: the ancestors and the spirits of the lake—classes that overlap. Lines 34–43 talk about the sacrifice that is going to be made, and lines 44–59 spell out what is requested in return, including a colorful plea for success at fishing (see chapter three, prayer two, note 16). Lines 60–90 reprise the now familiar themes of appeal to spirits, offer of sacrifice, and request of boon. There are more original phrases in lines 91–116, some which are successful, and some that are not. A justification of the use of chickens is followed by a grand image of the power of sacrifice. A request for favors in lines 117–21 begins with a colorful evocation of the vigor of youth, likened to the leap of a tiger. Lines 127–33 are a statement of humility not often found in **piat**: humans think they are big, says Tama Aweng, but in fact they are powerless. Now that Tama Aweng is ready to close, he pulls together another roster of spirit agencies, typically beginning with relatively insignificant ones and working up to the ancestors (lines 134–47). Then he thinks of another theme he wants to cover that is appropriate to the occasion and location: Gumbang's role as supervisor of fishing operations in the Bunok stream (see chapter three, prayer two, note 49). This is spelled out in terms that are flattering to Gumbang (lines 148–63). A final burst of similarly structured phrases appeals to the major spirit agencies.

The second part is spoken over a small pig that lies trussed at his feet. As the moment of sacrifice approaches, other speakers join in, and the tape recording becomes impossible to decipher. Consequently the transcription breaks off at this point.

This second section.has a false start. Tama Aweng is singeing the hairs on the back of the pig's neck with a cigarette lighter, causing a pungent

Figure 5. Tama Aweng makes the prayer set out in chapter three. He is standing before the same **tapo'** (prayer station) shown in figure 4. He wears a jacket because of the rain and the chill.

smoke to rise, and simultaneously he calls on both Bungan and the Creator. After a pause, Tama Aweng starts off again more forcefully, soon addressing the spirit of the pig directly and repeatedly. The pig is told to listen to the prayers that are offered, and then to carry them to the supreme deity, referred to under various sobriquets.

Style: Tama Aweng's style is more showy than Tama Jok's, and this is consistent with his social standing. Tama Aweng is not closely related to any important leaders of the community, and he has had more than his share of misfortune, including poor crops and illness in his family. Nevertheless, he tries to be in the forefront in community affairs. He speaks up at the gatherings that administer traditional **adat**-law, and he is on the **komíti** that nominally run these events, though that implies more formality than is in fact in evidence at them. He tries also to be prominent in ritual matters, although his efforts are sometimes denigrated behind his back.

In these prayers, there is evidence of this striving. He raises his voice more frequently than Tama Jok. He risks using novel material in his **píat**, where more sober souls stick for the most part to familiar themes and formulae. He uses more Malay words than other exponents, partly because he is hunting around for new phrases rather than sticking to traditional ones. Malay is the lingua franca of Baram District and often supplies words for new and unfamiliar concepts. Nevertheless, Tama Aweng's prayer shows considerable technical control and a full use of the resources of the medium. The reasons for the lower evaluation of Tama Aweng's **pìat** as compared to Tama Jok's have more to do with social standing than competence. Poor Tama Aweng cannot succeed for trying.

Two small points are worth noticing. First, Tama Aweng has a tendency to raise his voice on the last syllable of a line, which makes him sound at times like an English sergeant major at drill. Second, the final thirty-four

---

ooo . . .

- ■ a kaam bílì' aman
- ■ a kaam lurok ketu'o
- ■ a kaam penguwèk ketu'o
- ▪   sírèk ketu'o
- ▪   lukíng ketu'o
- ◆   asé ketu'o
- ◆   nyawan ketu'o

- ■ tu kamé ngajoí
- ▪ tu kamé ngaluroí   10
- ▪ tu kamé ngeluwok
- ▪ tu kamé ngelíok
- ▪ tu kamé nyíkí
- ▪ tu kamé ngelagí
- ■ kaam bílì' Long Bunok
- ▪ kaam bílì' lum luvak

lines are not broken up into verses. This reflects the hectic speed with which they are tumbling out, without any development of themes beyond a line or two. The phonetic impact of the passage is mainly the result of the appeal **bílì' no bíkuí,** "you spirit of the pig," repeated time after time between almost every line. The effect is similar to, and may be patterned on, the constant calling to the omen-giving eagle, as in the latter half of prayer six.

Note: For an explanation of the conventions of notation, see chapter one. A synopsis of these conventions is provided on the last printed page of the book.

Calling noise

Where are you spirits of the omen creatures,

where are you trogon on the right side,

where are you trogon on the right side,

    woodpecker on the right side,

    omen bird on the right side,

    kingfisher on the right side,

    snake on the right side.[1]

We call$_1$ thus,

10   we call$_2$ thus,

    we shout$_1$ thus,

    we shout$_2$ thus,

      we rouse$_1$ thus,

      we rouse$_2$ thus,[2]

        you spirits of Long Bunok,

        you spirits of the lake.[3]

◆ urok barang tu

◆ bukan tu tenebí

◆ kamé lo anak lo anyam

▪ andang tu adèd   20

▪ tekun vì' tekun sadì'

◆ tekun dupun tekun ukun

· kamé uní

◆ mulong co[7] tanaa

◆   co díta'

◆   co dísa

▪ tu ko ngajoí tu ko ngaluroí

▪ tu ko ngeluwok tu ko ngelíok

◆ tu ko nyíkí tu ko ngelagí

◆ kaam bílì' vì' bílì' sadì'   30

◆   bílì' ca bílì lía

▪ kaam bílì' aman

■ kaam bílì lum luvak

▪ tu díek co[9] ko melaí

▪   co ko melígaí

◆   co ko papì'

◆   co ko mekì

◆   co ko pemata

◆   co ko boya

◆   co ko pelana usaa   40

▪ apan kaam wong ketí wong balí

▪ apan kaam wong langèt wong sarèt

◆ apan kaam wong kata wong tua

Because this thing,

is not unfamiliar to you:[4]

    we your children, your grandchildren,

20   the origin of ritual,[5]

        from $grandparents_1$ from $grandparents_2$

        from $grandparents_3$ from $grandparents_4$[6]

           of ours long ago,

                who lived on this land,

                    this plain,

                    this soil.

Thus I $call_1$ thus I $call_2$

thus I $shout_1$ thus I $shout_2$

thus I $rouse_1$ thus I $rouse_2$

30   you spirits of $grandparents_1$ spirits of $grandparents_2$

           spirits of the $community_1$ spirits of the $community_2$[8]

        you spirits of the omen creatures,

        you spirits of the lake.

This chicken I use for a $spirit-house_1$

                I use for a $spirit-house_2$[10]

                I use for prayer,

                I use for sacrifice,

                I use for an $offering_1$

                I use for an $offering_2$

40   I use to preserve health[11]

Take it to be charm, to be spirit[12]

take it to be feverish, to be quivering,

take it to speak, to be lucky.[13]

♦ tubor nyasí lía Long Teru

▪ kappì pejong kappì tulong

▪ umí kíjì' lía Long Teru tu

▪ makípík pì' pì'

▪ wong ngaran pì' pì'

◾ mano' lírèk lía Long Teru tu

▪ belurí uraí belurí paraí   50

▪ belurí wang

♦ belurí lígìt belurí duít

◾ nak acì' dapat lít pukat

▪ lamulong lum luvak

◾ nak acì' urak lít labau

▪ lamulong atong Bunok

▪ ma kedíín lo sínyu senadu síju

▪ masak lum pukat

▪ masak lum labau

◾ tu díek la díek líwa   60

♦ co kappì ketí kappí balí

♦   kappì langèt kappí sarèt

◾ tupaan kaam bílì' vì' bílì' sadì'

▪   kaam bílì' aman

▪   kaam bílì' puwong bílì' ngaputong

♦ kamé lum luvak tu

♦ kamé atong Bunok tu

Take care of, look after, the community of Long Teru,

we ask for help$_1$ we ask for help$_2$[14]

for the people of Long Teru, big and small,

support them all,

give name to them all.

When the people of Long Teru make farms,

50   let them have rice$_1$ let them have rice$_2$[15]

let them have money,

let them have dollars, let them have cash.

Even if their nets are only one fathom long,

the people at the lake,

even if their seines are only a hand's width,

the people along the Bunok,

anyway push, cram, fish,

into their nets,

into their seines.[16]

60   This is the chicken sacrificed$_1$ the chicken sacrificed$_2$[17]

to ask for power, to ask for spirit,

to ask for inspiration, to ask for energy,[18]

all you spirits of grandparents$_1$ spirits of grandparents$_2$

you spirits of omen creatures,

you spirit that holds, spirit that created,

us in this lake,

us along this Bunok stream.

- ■ tu ko ngajoí
- ■ tu ko ngaluroí
- ◆ tu ko ngeluwok   70
- ◆ tu ko ngelíok

- ■ tawa bukan tu acì' ko
- ◆ tawa lía Long Teru
- ■ Kajan Gumbang Mítang Lejau dé tu

- ■ kícung kaam bílì' lum luvak tu
- ■ cukup tau místí
- ◆ kaam nakaan kamé
- ■ kappì ulong jìn ulong genín
- ◆   ulong mída ulong luya
- ◆   ulong tanyít ulong la'ít   80

- ◆ ní lo nappì lo nelì
- ◆ kappì kamé belurí wang belurí paraí
- ■   belurí lígìt belurí duít

- ◆ ní lo kenajoí lo kelaroí
- ■ ngan kaam bílì' lum luvak tu
- ■ ngan kaam bílì' ca bílì' lía
- ■ ngan no bílì' puwong bílì' ngaputong

- ■ ní jíu ko ngan kaam bílì' belungín
- ■ lo dukep atong Bunok tu
- ■ lo makíng atong Bunok tu   90

- ■ tu raan tiku ícung ngan kaam
- ◆ tu raan pakaan ícung ngan kaam

This is what I'm calling$_1$

this is what I'm calling$_2$

70   this is what I'm shouting$_1$

this is what I'm shouting$_2$

It is not me alone that is calling;

the community of Long Teru is calling:

Kajan, Gumbang, Mitang, Lejau, all of them.

Give us, you spirits in the lake,

enough for our needs for the year,

so that we can make offerings to you;[19]

we ask for a good life, a cool life,

a slow life, a calm life,

80   a healthy$_1$ life, a healthy$_2$ life,[20]

These are the things we ask for, we seek,[21]

we ask to get money, we ask to get rice,

we ask to get dollars, we ask to get cash.

That's what I call$_1$ that's what I call$_2$[22]

to you, spirits of the lake,

to you, spirits of the community$_1$ spirits of the community$_2$ 2

to you, spirit that holds, spirit that creates.

That's what I say to you spirits of water dragons,[23]

who rule along this Bunok river,[24]

90   who guard this whole Bunok river.[25]

See here the eggs we give to you,

see here the offering tray we give to you.[26]

- tu díek la díek líwa
- ◆ díek turíp díek takíp tekelo'

- aroo pun[28] temenggang
- aroo pun tepíon
- ◆ ra ní co kamé bulu mulong
- ◆ urok ní bukan jíu tudu
- ◆ bílì' puwong bílì' ngaputong
- · jíu tudu   100
- · Allah Ta'ala
- · lo adang mutong
- ·   mutong síko'
- ·   mutong líèk
- · kamé   bulu mulong

- nak umí pun díek
- · kíjì' ka sepèk kíjì' lasulèk pun díek
- bukan kíjì' temenggang keda awang
- ◆ tapí nyí kíjì' ketí kíjì' balí nyí
- ◆ píon bílì' lebang bílì' latang   110
- ◆   bílì' amat bílì' angat
- lo ka ngímaí lo ka ngalaí kamé

- · kíjì' keta'un keda abun
- · kíjì' ketí kíjì' balí
- co nyí pírèng ngelírèng kamé
- lía Long Teru tu

- mo kedíin luro' upo' luro' maccì
- dínak lía Long Teru tu

verse continues uninterrupted

This is the sacrificial$_1$ chicken, the sacrificial$_2$ chicken,

the chicken of life$_1$ the chicken of life$_2$ for them.[27]

Many are the black hornbills,

many are the rhinoceros hornbills,[29]

but they are not what we humans use,[30]

because it is not the will,

of the spirit that holds, the spirit that creates,

100   not the will,

of Allah,[31]

who actually shapes,[32]

shapes the elbows,

shapes the knees,

of us human beings.[33]

However small is our chicken,

no bigger than a sparrow$_1$ no bigger than a sparrow$_2$[34]

no bigger than a hornbill up in the sky,[35]

yet it has great power, it has great spirit,

110   to challenge evil$_1$ spirits, evil$_2$ spirits,

bad$_1$ spirits, bad$_2$ spirits,[36]

that try to scatter$_1$ try to scatter$_2$ us.[37]

As huge as a mass of clouds in the sky,

let its power be, let its spirit be,

that it may shelter$_1$ may shelter$_2$ us,[38]

of the community of Long Teru.[39]

Like the leap of a tiger, the leap of a lynx,[40]

let the young people of Long Teru be,

verse continues uninterrupted

- lukí melubí melaí meluwaí
- mala wang mala barang   120
- mala duít mala lígìt

- ní jiu attéé ko
- ngan kaam bílì' atong Bunok
- ngan kaam bílì' lum luvak
-       bílì' lo kenajíu
-         lo kelaríu rè ní'è

- kamé bulu mulong tu
- tu'o kamé kíjì' kulong matta
- tu'o kamé kíjì' raan kita'
- ra ngaran   130
- ra da ra uma
- ra dong ra padong
- ra lamín ra jalan

- kaam bílì' lum luvak
- kaam bílì' bíjì' bílì' belungín
- bílì' sau bílì' dacíen
- ra ní kanaí kamé ngaran
- tapí kamé tu ní'è tawa tupaan kaam
- tupaan kaam
- bilì' vì' bílì' sadì'   140
- bilì' ukun bílì' dupun

- a bílì' lo nakaan kenumaan
- uvì' sadì' ukun dupun
- lo mukong telíèk

verse continues uninterrupted

lucky$_1$ lucky$_2$ lucky$_3$ lucky$_4$[41]

120   to get money, to get goods,

          to get cash, to get dollars.[42]

This is what I say,

        to you spirits along the Bunok,

        to you spirits in the lake,

                spirits that I addressed$_1$

                        that I addressed$_2$ just now:[43]

We human beings,

        truly we stare with big eyes,

        truly we appear big,

130   but we have no name,

                no house$_1$ no house$_2$[44]

                no secure place$_1$ no secure place$_2$[45]

                        no room, no path.[46]

You spirits of the lake,

        you spirits of crocodiles, spirits of river dragons,

        spirits of water monsters, spirits of water creatures,[47]

                we don't even know your names,

                but we call all of you,

                all of you,

140   spirits of our grandparents$_1$ spirits of our grandparents$_2$

          spirits of our grandparents$_3$ spirits of our grandparents$_4$

        Where are the spirits that we have fed$_1$ we have fed$_2$

        grandparents$_1$ grandparents$_2$ grandparents$_3$ grandparents$_4$[48]

                that have received from old times,

verse continues uninterrupted

- sema díek sema bíkuí
- uvì' sadì' kamé uní atak tu
◆ lo ko ngajoí ngaluroí

- kamé lo anak lo anyam
■ tu Gumbang mang
- lo dukep atong Bunok tu   150
- kena íjìn lía Long Teru
- lo suken atong Bunok tu
- bíra lía Long Teru tu
◆ lo jaga kedíín co ngelabau
◆ lo jaga kedíín lum liko' tu

- íno attéé nyí
- ngan lía kíng lía kraí
◆ íno jíu nyí
◆ muléí ngan matelo'
- muléí ngan lo síngala bísa attéé nyí   160

◆ ano' íno rè síngala bísa
■ ano' ketí ano' balí
■ ano' langet ano' sarèt

■ ano' kaam bílì' lum luvak
■ ano' kaam bílì' ca bílì' lía
■ ano' kaam bílì' puwong bílì' ngaputong
■ ano' kaam bílì' vì' bílì' sadì'
■ ano' kaam bílì' ukun bílì' dupun

Pause

blood of the chicken, blood of the pig,

    our ancestors from long ago in this place,

    its you I'm calling$_1$ I'm calling$_2$

We are your children, your grandchildren,

    this is Gumbang,

150   who controls the Bunok river,

        given that right by the community of Long Teru,[49]

    who maintains the Bunok river,

        at the request of the community of Long Teru,

    who watches out for how people fish,[50]

    who watches out for the condition of the river.

Whatever he says,

    to the people downriver, the people upriver,

    whatever he says,

        returning to us,

160   returning to the many, let his words be effective.[51]

Make whatever he says effective,

    make it as a charm, as spirit,

    make it feverish, make it quiver.[52]

Make it so, you spirits of the lake,

make it so, you spirits of community$_1$ spirits of community$_2$

make it so, you spirit that holds, spirit that creates,

make it so, you spirits of grandparents$_1$ spirits of grandparents$_2$

make it so, you spirits of grandparents$_3$ spirits of grandparents$_4$

Pause

aaa . . .

◆ tu bí'o suro leto' bíkuí   170

▪ sakí ngan Bugan Malan

▪ sakí ngan bílì' puwong bílì' ngaputong

Asides

ooo . . .

▪ ra ko ngajoí

▪ ra ko ngaluroí

▪ kaam bílì' lum luvak

▪ ngan no bílì' bíkuí

▪ tu sebareng

◆ puku a'an[56] ko ngajoí

◆   a'an ko ngaluroí bílì' bíkuí   180

◆ kaa no selawan kellajjì'

◆   bílì' no bíkuí

◆ kaa no pabé

◆   bílì' no bíkuí

◆ atan no nalinga jíu ko

◆ píat jíu ko pattéé ngan no

◆   bílì' no bíkuí

▪ cì'[58] no

▪   bílì' no bíkuí

▪ pulo Bungan Tenangan   190

▪   bílì' no bíkuí

verse continues uninterrupted

Soft calling noise

170   This smell, this odor of singed pig,[53]

       Let it ascend to Bungan Malan,[54]

       Let it ascend to the spirit that holds, the spirit that creates.

Asides

Calling noise

I'm not calling$_1$

I'm not calling$_2$

    to you, spirits of the lake,

    to you, spirit of the pig,[55]

       carelessly.

    There is a reason why I call$_1$

180   why I call$_2$ spirit of the pig:

       don't wander away,[57]

              you spirit of the pig,

       don't get lost,

              you spirit of the pig,

       listen to what I say,

       to the prayer I speak for you,

               you spirit of the pig,

       you go,

              you spirit of the pig,

190   go to Bungan Tenangan,[59]

              you spirit of the pig,

verse continues uninterrupted

- no Bungan Tenangan
- nangan udíp nangan típ
-      bílì' no bíkuí
- kamé bulu mulong
-      bílì' no bíkuí
- níat pulo pattéé
- ngan Bungan Penyalong
-      bílì' no bíkuí
- ngan uko pa Bungan   200
- nyí lo tubor sebang bulu du'an
-      bílì' no bíkuí
- pulo
-      bílì' no bíkuí
- ngan bílì' puwong bílì' ngaputong
-      bílì' no bíkuí
- jíu no ngan Bungan Penyalong
-      ngan uko Bungan
- níat no sakí
-      bílì' no bíkuí   210
- yo no bíra lía Long Teru
- kappì mulong jìn mulong genín
-      mulong mída mulong luya

you it is Bungan Tenangan,

who preserves life$_1$ preserves life$_2$[60]

> you spirit of the pig,

of us human beings,

> you spirit of the pig,

your purpose is to go and talk,

with Bungan Penyalong,[61]

> you spirit of the pig,

200 with grandmother Bungan,[62]

she who cares for the world of the living,[63]

> you spirit of the pig,

go,

> you spirit of the pig,

to the spirit that holds, the spirit that creates,

> you spirit of the pig,

say to Bungan Penyalong,

to grandmother Bungan,

the reason you come,

210 > you spirit of the pig,

is because you are asked by the community of Long Teru,

to request a good life, a cool life,

> a slow life, a calm life.

4.

Kumaan Selamat—A Prayer for a Sick Child

The Prayers of the House that we looked at in chapter three are concerned with the general welfare of the entire community. The prayer set out in this chapter is at the other end of the scale; its entire concern is the health of one small boy.

A Child's Illness and the Parents' Response

At the time of the ritual, the sickly child was about one year old. For the parents, this represented an important milestone because infant mortality is tragically high. Some are lost in childbirth, but more die of viral infections and stomach disorders in their first year. An active infant suddenly

136

may run a high temperature, and the next morning he or she is dead. The situation is similar elsewhere in interior Borneo. Improved hygiene and medical care are slowly bringing improvement, but the Berawan are painfully aware that the first year of life is the most dangerous. Parents anxiously watch throughout for signs of waning vigor, which warrant immediate response. Probably over half of all shamanistic performances are for sick infants.

In addition to these healing practices, there are usages that are designed to deflect the malice of evil spirits from the vulnerable infants. If a pregnant woman accidentally stumbles onto a decaying carcass in the jungle, or if a birth occurs in a manner that the Berawan regard as irregular (**sangakam**), or if any of a host of other bad omens occurs, then the parents will consider giving the child away in adoption (Metcalf 1974). If they choose to ignore the omen and then the child becomes ill, they will rush to find a new home for the infant. This is not so wrenching as it may sound because the adopting parents are likely to be close relatives of the mother, and she has only to go a few doors down the longhouse veranda to visit or to feed the child. A shaman may seek to discover where the child will be best off, and a location nearby is usually chosen. As much as twenty percent of adult Berawan were at least partly raised by foster parents. The objective of this maneuver is to give the slip to the evil influences that follow the child. If the new surroundings do not produce better luck for the infant, another move may be in order.

The same notion of evasion lies behind the practices of naming children. To give an infant a beautiful, melodious name would only serve to attract unwelcome attention. Consequently, small children are not given names at all, or to be more precise, the names that are selected in infancy—by divination or by shamans—are not used. Instead, a kind of generic name is employed: Ukat for a boy, Itang for a girl. The parents of the boy discussed in this prayer are Gumbang and Keleing. Their first child was a girl so they take a teknonym from her. Gumbang becomes Tama (father of) Itang; Keleing becomes Tina (mother of) Itang. At the time of this ritual, the girl was about three years old, and used a proper personal name. Her mother, however, continued to be referred to as Tina Itang Keleing. Her father always preferred to be known simply by his personal name, reflecting the idiosyncratic variability characteristic of the use of teknonyms (see chapter three, prayer one, note 4). Throughout the prayer, the second child of Gumbang and Keleing is referred to as Ukat, although that is not how he was addressed in everyday life. To further discourage the interest of spirits, sickly children are given unattractive, often scatological, names. This child had made it through his first year under the name Jumbun, which means, politely put, "latrine."

Jumbun had been ill repeatedly, but the crisis came a couple of months before this ritual when his parents had all but abandoned hope for him. Nevertheless he hung on, provoking intense shamanistic activity because Jumbun's father is a prominent member of the community. There are half a dozen active shamans at Long Teru, and all of them attempted to help the child. In the Berawan conception, illness may have any of several possible etiologies. Consequently, a number of treatment techniques are possible (Metcalf 1982b). In serious cases, several techniques may be used simultaneously. In the middle of one particular night, with Jumbun again running a high fever, Gumbang and Keleing made a prayer to the Creator in which they promised that, if Jumbun lived, they would arrange a feast for the spirits.

The Rite of Kumaan Selamat

When Jumbun survived his first year, the time had come to redeem that promise. The term used to describe the feast was **kumaan selamat** (**kumaan** means "to eat," **selamat** means "safe"). The word **selamat** is of Arabic origin, borrowed by the Berawan from Malay. **Kumaan** is cognate with Malay **makan** (eat), and the phrase **makan selamat** is widely understood throughout Malaysia and Indonesia to mean a "small celebration of some success obtained or crisis averted." Geertz's account of Javanese religion begins with the **slametan,** a gathering of just this kind, which he describes as a "core ritual" (Geertz 1960:11–15). The linguistic borrowing should not be taken to indicate that this rite is any less a part of the indigenous religion than any other.

The **kumaan selamat** for Jumbun was held on July 13, 1972. It involved three phases: a gathering of shamans, with offerings for their spirit familiars; the making of a prayer station, with prayers and sacrifice; and the sharing of a meal by all present.

The first phase was the most elaborate, which involves the preparation of special ritual apparatus and offerings. From early morning there was activity in the family apartment (**ukuk**) of Gumbang and Keleing, and also on the veranda outside it. In the kitchen, a group of women were organizing the food and drink, cleaning fish and game, preparing to cook lots of rice, decanting rice wine from the large jars in which it had fermented, collecting enough plates, glasses, and spoons from neighboring kitchens, and so on. In the living room, and on the veranda, youths were assembling trays of offerings (**pakaan**; see chapter two), one for each shaman that was expected to attend. The trays contained a host of small offerings: hard-boiled eggs, uncooked yellow rice for the shamans to throw over the crowd, tiny packets of cooked rice neatly wrapped in a special leaf, salt in little bowls, biscuits and candy of many types, and the like. The trays were artistically arranged and decorated with flowers and ribbons. Small valuables of one kind or another, loaned temporarily by their owners, were discreetly included in the design. For example, a new watch was the centerpiece of one tray. Special spirit houses (**melígaí**, see chapter three, prayer two, note 10) were also being prepared. The familiar spirits of the senior shaman had ordered, during a seance, that one of these special houses be created to be their new home. The spirits had specified how the **melígaí** was to be made and what to put inside it. It was a whimsical structure, carved from softwood, with representations of people and of mythical beasts standing inside it. Other spirit houses were taken down out of the rafters, dusted off, and refurbished with small offerings. At about ten in the morning, the four most respected shamans took their places among the trays and spirit houses. At Long Teru, the most active shamans, including these four, are men. This is unusual because the majority of Berawan shamans are women. The male style of Long Teru originated with Tama Ukat Sageng, the father of Tama Jok, who achieved un-paralleled fame (Metcalf 1982a:61–63, 165–68). After much jocularity, Tama Ukat Sageng blessed the crowd, and the other shamans followed suit. They muttered under their breaths, presumably addressing their familiars. Then, they took pinches of the gritty yellow rice, and threw it out over the crowd. Next, they requested music from the **sapé**, a banjolike stringed instrument, and each man in turn danced. At this point, they were supposed to be possessed of their familiars, but the dancing was restrained and there was no outward show of trance. Each shaman had on special hats and beads, to suit the fancies of his spirits. The shamans conversed, seemingly, in a language not comprehensible to the crowd, the language of spirits.

After this had gone on for some time, Tama Avit appeared. He had been putting the finishing touches on his **tapo'**, which was constructed in the familiar fashion described in chapter two. As the husband of Gumbang's prestigious mother, and a man known for his knowledge of ritual, Tama

Figure 6. Tama Avit says a prayer at the ritual described
in chapter four. The sick child, for whom this rite was
held, sits on his mother's lap as Tama Avit waves a gong
filled with yellow rice above their heads.

Avit was the appropriate person to make the main prayers at this **kumaan
selamat**. Tina Itang Keleing took her seat atop a large gong, holding
Jumbun in her arms. Tama Avit took a smaller gong containing yellow
rice, and waved it over her head. He made a short prayer for the health of
Jumbun while he sprinkled rice over the crowd. After this prayer a chicken
and a small pig were killed. Blood from the sacrificial animals was dabbed

onto the arms of all the small children in the crowd, and also onto the spirit house. On this occasion, the blood of the sacrificial chicken literally arrived "in the house" (**lum da, lum uma**) of the spirits. A glob of blood in a bowl was handed to the shamans, and they rolled it around trying to read in it an omen of success for the ritual. Meanwhile, other senior relatives of Gumbang and Keleing in turn made prayers over the mother and child.

Meanwhile, Tama Avit had already left the longhouse, and was standing outside in front of his **tapo'** below. There he made the prayer set out in this chapter. Unfortunately, there was a crush of people on the narrow stairs down from the veranda, and I was late starting my tape recorder. Consequently, the opening lines of the prayer are missing. This prayer, and the sacrifice of another chicken, completed the second phase of the **kumaan selamat**. Afterwards, people drifted away to bathe or to chat on the veranda. There was now nothing to do but wait for the meat of the sacrificed pig and chickens to be cooked, and the celebratory meal served. The feast occurred at about three in the afternoon, when dozens of people sat down to eat from trays of rice, and bowls of fish, meat, and other delicacies. Drinking and socializing continued well into the evening.

Prayer Three

Speaker: Tama Avit

Time: Three minutes

Summary: The first half of the prayer consists of specific instructions given to the spirit of the sacrificial chicken, which Tama Avit is all the while waving around by its legs. Lines 1–16 tell the spirit of the chicken to seek out the supreme deity, specified under a variety of different labels. Lines 17–31 spell out the message that the spirit of the chicken is to deliver; and that it is sent by Gumbang and Keleing, who are celebrating the recovery of their sickly child, for whom they ask continued good health and fortune. Lines 32–42 comprise the first of two long lists of spirits, here credited with having helped in the recovery of the child. They are an oddly assorted bunch, some important (the supreme deity, the ancestors), others minor but familiar (the spirits of the house stones), and some downright obscure (spirits of the mythical water creatures, **sau** and **dacíen**). One interesting item on the list is the spirits of the sun and the moon (line 41), which I do not recall hearing cited in any other **píat**.

Lines 43–53 reemphasize the mission of the chicken, to go to the supreme deity to ask for continued health for the child. Lines 54–59, however, suddenly shift to a different view of the meaning of sacrifice (see chapter two).

After line 59 there was a short pause, during which Tama Avit pours a quantity of rice wine over the base of the **tapo'**. Then, he launches into his second extended list of spirits, to whom the rice wines is offered (lines 60–74). This second list is as heterogenous as the first, with the supreme deity rubbing shoulders with fight magic and mythical fish. Again, there is an interesting and unusual item: the spirit or spirits of dreams. Berawan take dreams seriously. If a person has a vivid dream, he or she may discuss its meaning with other people, including perhaps a shaman. If it is decided that the dream portends good things, the dreamer may seek to "own" (**puwong**) the dreams by making offerings and prayers to the Creator and to whatever other spirit agencies seem appropriate. A **pakaan** (offering tray) or **tapo'** (prayer site) may be prepared. If the dream is ominous, prayers may be made to avert evil.

Lines 75–80 set out briefly the rationale for the entire rite. The amount of rice wine promised is a **sítong**, which is a jar of several gallons in capacity. In other words, the rite is to be a considerable celebration. To drive home the point, Tama Avit sloshes more wine over the bottom of the **tapo'**. He then points out the eggs and the **pakaan** also presented at the **tapo'** (lines 81–86), and closes with an appeal for the welfare and longevity of the child.

Style: Tama Avit's **píat** is generally easy to follow, with occasional bursts of rapid speech. He is considered an effective speaker, although he is sometimes mimicked because of his accent, and his use of unfamiliar lexical items, both of which are the result of having only recently moved to Long Teru.

Tama Avit spent most of his life at Long Jegan, a large Berawan community upriver from Long Teru. The ancestors of these people have inhabited the middle and upper Tinjar for dozens of generations, unlike the Berawan of Long Teru, who are recent immigrants from the Tutoh river (see chapter three, prayer one, note 33). Tama Avit is a descendant of important leaders of the past and generally has a high social standing. In the religious controversy that convulsed Long Jegan in the 1960s, Tama Avit was a conservative, strongly in favor of retaining the old religion against both Christianity and the revivalist Bungan cult. He moved to Long Teru after the majority of his community had gone over to a home-grown version of Bungan. Himself a widower, he married the long-time widow of the last great leader of the Long Teru community, Penghulu Lawai. It was a suitable marriage, and he is well respected at Long Teru.

Tama Avit's accent is noticeable. He occasionally produces diphthongs where Long Teru folk have simple vowels, and these are shown in the transcription. There are few words that are entirely different in the Long Jegan isolect, and Tama Avit usually avoids them, but occasionally he makes a slip: for instance, in lines 61–65, he repeatedly uses **kau** (you, singular) instead of **no**. A more noticeable variation in lexical items comes about because of his familiarity with Kenyah folk. He laces his **píat** with loan words that may not be known to some of his audience.

Paradoxically, given Tama Avit's aversion to the Bungan cult, he shares a tendency with Tama Aweng to refer frequently to Bungan, and also to amalgamate her with the supreme deities of traditional Kayan and Kenyah religion. But **píat** is amenable to linguistic syncretism.

The most singular feature of Tama Avit's style, however, is made apparent only by segmental analysis. To some extent, it does not fit the conventions set up in chapter one. Instead of forcing his words into a preconceived framework, I have let them dictate the shape of verses. Tama Avit's peculiarity is the framing of all verses within anacrustic lines: "Spirit of the chicken," "Tell them," "This is the rice wine." The themes of the verses that follow these isolated lines are variable, and not predictable from them. (For a list of the themes of successive verses, see table 4 in the conclusion.) In lines 43–50 he even manages to repeat this structure within a verse: first, there is the anacrustic line "tell them," then, the line "this is the sacrificial chicken" is used three times to bracket the names of spirits. The symmetry is somewhat spoiled by the absentminded aside in line 56, but there is no doubt that Tama Avit displays an interesting and original style.

Note: For an explanation of the conventions of notation, see chapter one. A synopsis of these conventions is provided on the last printed page of the book.

- bílì' díek tu

- pulo uko pa Bungan
- urok uko pa Bungan
- lo nangan lakíp nangan uríp
- kamé bulu mulong
- tusong díta' tusong tanaa tu

- bílì' díek ní

- ngayan usau ngayan lakau
- no pulo Bungan Tenangan
- kappì ulong jìn ulong genín   10
- kappì ulong tanyít ulong la'ít
-          ulong mída ulong luya
- ngan tupo' Ukat

- cí' no mang nuvang uko Tenangan
-                    uko Tenangan
- lo nangan lakíp nangan uríp kamé

- atau tílo ngan nyí

- ko tu vaí lakau vaí usau
- yo bíra Tama Itang Gumbang
-     bíra Tína Itang Keléíng   20
- kappì ulong jìn tupo' Ukat

Spirit of the chicken:

    Go to grandmother Bungan,[1]

    since grandmother Bungan,

        is the one who gives life$_1$ gives life$_2$[2]

        to us human beings,[3]

        inhabiting this plain, inhabiting this land.

Spirit of the chicken:

    Your destination, your goal,[4]

    is Bungan Tenangan,[5]

10   to ask for a good life, a cool life,

    to ask for a healthy$_1$ life, a healthy$_2$ life,

        a slow life, a calm life,

                for my grandson Ukat.[6]

    Go and meet grandfather Tenangan,

        grandfather Tenangan,

    who gives life$_1$ gives life$_2$

Tell him:

    I am coming$_1$ coming$_2$[7]

    because asked by Tama Itang Gumbang,

20   asked by Tina Itang Keleing,[8]

    to request a good life for little Ukat.

- ní tajun ko vaí tu

- nuvang no uko Tenangan

- kappì ulong jìn ulong genín

- ngan anak díséí[9]

◆ lo a'an[10] dé pava

◆   a'an dé tusaa rè malam

- mané jíu no bílì' díek

◆ urok ícío tu dé kumaan selamat

◆ ngan nyí   30

- urok nyí jìn

- urok ano' uko Tenangan

◆ urok ano' uko Bungan

◆ urok ano' uko Jalong Pesalong

- urok bílì' vì' bílì' sadì'

◆   bílì' daren bíto' tíloí

◆   bílì' ca bílì' lasaan bílì' síkíp

◆   bílì' tapo' bílì' belungín bílì' sau bílì' dacíen

- urok bílì' junyang bílì' tukung

- urok bílì' luvak   40

- urok bílì' bulíín bílì' mattacío

◆ lo napì' dé rè uní

- ní jíu no bílì' díek

- tu díek la díek líwa[20]

- no uko Jalong Penyalong[21] ngan bíkuí tu

- a'an bíkuí ní ní'è

verse continues uninterrupted

That's the reason I come,

to meet you grandfather Tenangan,

to ask for a good life, a cool life,

for the child of those two,

about whom they worried,

anxious all the night.[11]

Tell them this, spirit of the chicken:

Today they celebrate,[12]

30   his recovery,

because he is alright now,

Because made so by grandfather Tenangan,

because made so by grandmother Bungan,

because made so by grandfather Jalong Pesalong,[13]

because of spirits of grandparents$_1$ spirits of grandparents$_2$

spirits of sacred plants, of house stones,[14]

spirits of community, of farms, of fight magic,[15]

spirits of prayer stations, dragons, water monsters,[16]

because of spirit guides, spirits of the mountains,[17]

40   because of spirits of the lake,

because of spirit of the moon, spirit of the sun,[18]

to whom they prayed[19] long ago.

Tell them this, spirit of the chicken:

This is the sacrificial$_1$ chicken, the sacrificial$_2$ chicken,

for you, grandfather Penyalong (with this pig,

wherever that pig is just now),

verse continues uninterrupted

- tu díek la díek líwa[20]
- no uko Jalong Penyalong[21] ngan bíkuí tu
- tu díek la díek líwa
- no uko Tenangan   50
- lo nangan lakíp nangan uríp tuo Ukat tu
- mulong jìn mulong genín cì' ya
- mulong tanyít mulong la'ít cì' ya

◆ píléo telang dèíng telang nèíng
◆   telang jo telang sío
◆   telang sa'an telang kenumaan
◆ sema díek
◆ masak lum naa lum usaa
◆ tupo Ukat na'a

Pause

■ tu borèk ícung ngan kaam   60

• ngan kau uko Penyalong
◆   kau uko Jalong Pesalong
◆ ngan kau uko Bungan Malan
■   kau uko Tenangan

■ tu borèk ícung ngan kaam tu

◆ kaam bílì' dacíen bílì' aman
◆   bílì' vì' bílì' sadì'
◆ kaam bílì' luppéé

verse continues uninterrupted

this is the sacrificial$_1$ chicken, the sacrificial$_2$ chicken,

    for you, grandmother Bungan,

this is the sacrificial$_1$ chicken, the sacrificial$_2$ chicken,

50   for you, grandfather Tenangan,

        who give life$_1$ give life$_2$ to little Ukat,

        a good life, a cool life for him,[22]

        a healthy$_1$ life, a healthy$_2$ life for him.

Charge with power to augment$_1$ power to augment$_2$

    power to satisfy, power to give life,

    power to convey, power to feed,[23]

        the blood of the chicken;

        let it enter the body$_1$ enter the body$_2$

        of little Ukat afterwards.[24]

Pause

60   This is the rice wine we give to you:

To you grandfather Penyalong,

    you grandfather Jalong Pesalong,

to you grandmother Bungan Malan,

    you grandfather Tenangan.

This is the rice wine we give to you:

You spirits of water creatures, spirits of omen creatures,

    spirits of grandparents$_1$ spirits of grandparents$_2$

you spirits of dreams,

verse continues uninterrupted

◆ kaam bílì' luvak

◆ kaam bílì' dita' bílì' tanaa 70

◆ kaam bílì' sau bílì' dacíen

◆ kaam bílì' agang bílì' síkíp

◆ kaam bílì' ca bílì' lasaan

▪ kaam bílì' tapo'

■ tu borèk ní ícung ngan kaam

• urok jíu mulong nyí

◆ urok jíu mo tupo Ukat selamat

◆ kícung acì' sítong borèk

• ní jíu rè malam

■ tu borèk jajjì' ícung ngan kaam 80

Pause

■ tu tíku

▪ pat tíku

▪ tu pakaan

▪ tu borèk

◆ tu kaju unong lenga unong tíga

◆   unong seken unong maren

▪ tupo' Ukat tu mulong

▪ nak putéé ulo'

▪ ngalawèk sílo'

verse continues uninterrupted

you spirits of the lake,

70   you spirits of the plain, spirits of the land,

you spirits of water monsters, spirits of water creatures,

you spirits of valor, spirits of fight magic,

you spirits of the longhouse, spirits of the farms,

you spirits of the prayer station.[25]

This is the rice wine we give to you:

Because we said if he lived,

because we said if little Ukat were safe,

we would give one large jar of rice wine,

that's what we said that night.[26]

80   This is the rice wine we promised to give to you.

Pause

These are the eggs,

four eggs.

This is the tray of offerings.[27]

This is the rice wine.

This is the tree of $good_1$ life, $good_2$ life,[28]

$noble_1$ life, $noble_2$ life.[29]

May little Ukat live,

until his head is white,

his nails curly with age,

verse continues uninterrupted

- urok kaam rèng na'a   90
- rèng tubo rèng batu
- sarong usau sarong lakau
- sarong lasat sarong penalat nyí
- unong lenga unong tíga
- unong seken unong maren nyí

90   because you protect him afterwards,

protect his body$_1$ protect his body$_2$[30]

wherever he settles, wherever he goes[31]

wherever he travels$_1$ wherever he travels$_2$[32]

a good$_1$ life, a good$_2$ life,

a noble$_1$ life, a noble$_2$ life.[33]

5.

Pataí—A Prayer at a Funeral

Solitary prayer, Weber tells us, is not a social act (1968:4). This is a test that Berawan prayer is in no danger of failing. **Píat** requires an audience, and there is no way to tell where appeal to spirits ends and appeal to the crowd begins. Nevertheless, there is a serious religious purpose in each of the prayers that we have looked at so far. To understand it, we examined the ritual in which it occurred. But the prayer in this chapter has more to do with the biography of the speaker than the occasion of the prayer. In the terms of chapter two, it is deeply hypocritical. It provides a nice example of the bending of ritual language to political ends.

Addressing a Corpse

Addresses made over and to corpses are a feature of Berawan death rites. For example, when a relative of the deceased arrives back at the longhouse

154

after having been summoned by messengers or after having heard the boom of the great gong (**padung**) that announces a death, he or she will go directly to the corpse. If the death occurred more than an hour ago but less than thirty-six, the body will probably be displayed on a special throne, dressed in all kinds of finery and surrounded by valuables. Later, the corpse is likely to be stored within a coffin or large jar. Whichever it is, the relative talks directly to the dead individual. The tone is chiding: Why have you left those that love you? Why couldn't you wait?

Such one-sided conversations go on throughout the funeral, and for months afterwards in small mourning rites. In addition, there may be a whole second phase of public ritual—a kind of second funeral—a year or more later. As we shall see in the next chapter, the remains of the deceased are even then being flattered and cajoled. To explain why it is that Berawan find it natural to talk to corpses in this manner requires an account of Berawan notions of death. Since I have set this out in detail elsewhere (1982a), I will not repeat the account here. The key point for present purposes is that Berawan think of death as a slow transmutation of the mortal soul (**telanak**) into the immaculate stuff of ancestors (**bílî'**). Until this process is completed, the temper of the deceased is unreliable, to say the least, and there is every reason to flatter and to cajole in order to avert further death.

Uking Engages in Propaganda, June 1973

In view of these beliefs and practices, it is not surprising to find Uking standing over the coffin of his uncle Tama Avit, and making an impassioned prayer. He was not the first to do so since Tama Avit had passed on a few days before. Dirges had been made, and **píat** spoken by senior male relatives. Uking was also not the last person to honor Tama Avit; on the final night of the ten-day funeral (**íccem mugé**) visiting dignitaries made formal speeches honoring the dead man. There was even a speech that had been prepared by Tama Avit himself, which was full of unimpeachable sentiments concerning the need for cooperation and brotherly feeling among the living. This speech, which supposedly had been composed by Tama Avit on his deathbed, was read out by a grandson, in suspiciously schoolboyish Malay.

As an element in this dialogue, there are various themes that we might expect to find in Uking's prayer, most that turn on the benefits that the ancestors, together with their new recruit, should bring to the community.

It would be tactless to mention the risks that the recently dead pose to the living; instead much is made of them as envoys to the benign ancestors. Yet Uking touches on these themes only cursorily. His main theme turns out to be the leadership of the Long Teru community, and its inability to handle the problem of encroachment on Berawan land. While nominally addressing the spirits, he is in fact pontificating to the crowd assembled before the coffin of Tama Avit. He uses—or abuses—the form of **píat** to make pointed remarks that in any other context would have been shouted down or ignored. In this context, the people that he attacks cannot even answer.

The unpopularity of Uking's views, not to mention the man himself, has to do with intercommunity relations, which are convoluted because Berawan villages are more labile social units than is immediately apparent. The massive structure of the longhouse, raised on great piles and floored with heavy hardwood planks, seems to guarantee the stability of the community it houses. Nevertheless, the historical record is one of movement; villages migrate, or disaffected factions decamp elsewhere, or wholesale fragmentation occurs. This is the stuff of Berawan politics, so that Berawan seem constantly to be arguing about something that happened in the last century. It is not easy to explain a contemporary rivalry without being trapped into a rambling history of the entire Berawan people, but some account of Uking's affiliations is necessary in order to understand his sallies in this prayer.

In chapter four, I pointed out that Tama Avit had spent most of his life at Long Jegan upriver from Long Teru. His grandfather was the leader of a major faction of the Long Jegan folk that had at the turn of the century temporarily split off and built a separate longhouse. Tama Avit's own political career took him into government service. In the 1950s he was a leader of the conservative party at Long Jegan, favoring retention of the traditional religion over the adoption of Christianity or the revivalist Bungan cult. (For details of the last, see chapter eight.) At this time, he became the mentor of his sister's son, Uking, who was of the same mind. This faction lost the debate, and the entire community converted to the Bungan cult, led by a descendant of those who had won at the turn of the century. Tama Avit's reaction was to move to Long Teru, a community that retained the old religion. There he married the widow of the late Penghulu (government appointed chief) Lawai.

Uking's reaction was to attempt to split the longhouse, just as his ancestors had done almost a century before. He led a small group, mostly close relatives, to an area of fertile land at Long Teran, downriver from the main village. These people had made their farms in this area for many years anyway, so that what was basically involved was the construction of a house more grand than the usual temporary farm houses. Uking went further. He invited a party of Kayan to join him there, themselves a disaffected faction from some parenting community. The Kayan built a longhouse across the river from Uking's people. Many at Long Jegan considered it scandalous to give away Berawan land to ancient enemies in this way, and they tried to restrain Uking. Meanwhile, Uking constantly schemed to detach more people from Long Jegan. Whenever there was a major ritual there, Uking would show up. He pushed his way into pleasant social occasions, and made loud disruptive speeches in an attempt to embarrass his rivals. He was shameless, and extremely difficult to silence. He was loathed by many people at Long Jegan who considered him boorish in the extreme.

Nevertheless, Uking had his own charisma. Early on in life he had gained a reputation as a shaman, and he had the classic unstable personality often associated with that role. His moods would change with lightning speed: I once saw him fulminate violently against a crowd of workers at a tomb site, and then go and sit up to his neck in the river, where he cried pitifully. Though occasionally ridiculous, he could at times be impressive, a small wiry man, electric with energy. Even his detractors were unwilling to discount his supernatural powers. Moreover, Uking's arguments were not without merit. He said, over and over again to anyone that would listen, that the great threat to Berawan lands came not from traditional upriver rivals like the Kayan, but from the far more numerous Iban. The Iban are not closely related in ethnological terms to the Berawan and other folk of central northern Borneo. They come from a homeland far to the south, but they have for centuries expanded northward absorbing by weight of numbers the small ethnic groups that lay in their path. Uking argued that his twin community at Long Teran would act as a dam, blocking the spread of Iban further upriver. The proof of Uking's arguments, from his point of view, was the fate of Long Teru, surrounded by Iban interlopers.

No one was surprised that Uking came to Tama Avit's funeral at Long Teru. The two men were close, and it was right that he be there. No one objected to him participating in making decisions about how things should be done. But people very soon began to object to his high-handed manner and his noisy interference. Avit, the dead man's son by his first wife at

Long Jegan, was driven to distraction by constant demands for money. This poor young man was a school teacher in a village far upriver. He had a cash income and some savings, which, Uking decided, would conveniently finance construction of a grand tomb. This tomb soon became controversial. Tama Avit had said before he died that he wished to be buried across the river from the Long Teru house, and his widow, the influential Kasi, concurred with this plan. Yet, Uking wanted to take Tama Avit back to Long Teran, where he promised a massive concrete tomb that Tama Avit's sister, and Kasi too, could share in due course. Only the firmest language could deter Uking from his plans. When Uking lost that battle, he threw himself into the construction work at Long Teru. Since this was already well advanced, his interference was less and less appreciated. Kajan, the young headman of Long Teru, told Uking several times, in effect, to mind his own business. Yet Kajan rapidly discovered what the elders of Long Jegan had discovered before him—that Uking was difficult to silence. Uking saw that Kajan was insecure, suffering from doubts about his own ability to handle the difficult tasks before him, and he bored in remorselessly.

Such was the situation when Uking made the prayer recorded in this chapter. It was late one afternoon, on about the fifth day of the funeral, and there had been heavy rain. Unable to work outside, people had returned to the longhouse, and there was a considerable crowd seated around the coffin of Tama Avit when Uking jumped up to make his **píat**. Many of those present were women or younger men—an appropriate audience for his propaganda. The senior men who might perhaps have made a counter **píat** were busy elsewhere trying to keep a complex event running on schedule. Kasi, who was obliged to stay beside the coffin at all times because she was the widow, could say nothing because grieving widows must remain silent in public. Uking's first argument was that Long Teru is in deep trouble. It is surrounded by Iban settlements, particularly in the Teru river. These settlers move onto Berawan land, and despite all the agreements and the legal battles, invite their kin to join them, and refuse to pay their rent. His second argument was that only the firmest leadership— no doubt following his own example—can stem this flow. Kajan, however, is not such a leader.

By way of epilogue, we may note that Uking was right in his main thesis. In the last decade, more and more Berawan land has been lost. At Long Teru, the situation threatens the vitality of the community, and even Long Jegan has not been immune. But Uking is no longer making speeches about it. He died only a few months after Tama Avit in strange circumstances; many believe that he was poisoned. Whether in the end his breakaway community defended the Long Jegan folk, as he claimed it would, or weakened them by internal division, it is not possible to say.

Prayer Four

Speaker: Uking

Time: 3 minutes and 20 seconds

Summary: The opening lines of the prayer are missing because it took me a moment to realize what Uking was doing and to start the tape recorder, which had been brought to the veranda to record music. However, the topics were probably similar to those in the first twenty-three lines below, namely the important leaders of Long Teru in past generations, the benevolence that they should provide, and the imminent arrival of his uncle Tama Avit (Alang).

Lines 24–38 are aimed at Kajan, the young headman at Long Teru. Uking asks that Kajan be granted the disposition to act justly toward his own people and the firmness necessary to deal with the "people that bother us"—implying, of course, that Kajan currently has neither of those attributes.

In lines 39–45 he develops the apparently erroneous proposition that the lake near Long Teru is named after a famous leader of the turn of the century. People at Long Teru say that this is a false etymology (see note 19 of this chapter). He follows with a piece of mythology that he changes around to suit his own purposes by substituting Iban settlers for a race of ogres (see note 23 of this chapter). This myth is told differently at both Long Jegan and Long Teru, and Uking uses the name of the hero employed at the former (Tot Manyem) rather than the latter (Anak Tau). He may have intended to confuse his audience by implying that his emendations were received dogma at Long Jegan.

Next the sacrificial chicken is presented (lines 59–66), and Uking addresses the spirit of the chicken, charging it with more responsibilities than is normal (see note 25 of this chapter).

Uking is soon back to his favorite themes. In lines 67–73 he hands out advice to his audience not to mistrust their headman, Kajan. He does not say who suggested that they did. In lines 74–81 Uking is wringing his hands over the fate of Long Teru: it is the most downriver of Berawan or Kenyah communities; it has been forced to "make peace," or more explicitly, to tolerate its Iban neighbors; it deserves "pity." In lines 82–86 we find the list of great men of Long Teru once again, with Kajan's name ingenuously tagged on at the bottom, as if to say: and now *him*. Lines 87–89 add further barbs, but lines 90–96 are more of a battle cry.

Finally, he closes with some phrases about the effectiveness of sacrifice. Compared to the full figures, as they appear for instance in prayer one (lines 32–48), these are truncated and hard to follow, as if to emphasize that they are not the point of his prayer.

Style: Despite noise from the crowd on the tape, I could still hear Uking clearly most of the time. His voice is high-pitched, almost shrill, and it

---

- unyín maséé
- ke[1] sadì' Orang Kaya Luwak

◆ kaa mé kaa supé
- tanyat melígat
- anak Melawan
- tanyat melígat
- anak Bíto' Kala
- tanyat melígat
- anak Lelak

■ ní jíu ko ke sadì' Orang Kaya Luwak   10
-    ke sadì' Tama Julan Tínggang
-    ke sadì' Lawaí

cuts through the chatter effectively. Almost the whole prayer is spoken loudly and with the words pronounced crisply. Occasionally, Uking is definitely shouting, and it is clear that he means to be heard. All of this makes transcription of Uking's prayer much easier than for other prayers, such as those spoken by Tama Aweng and Tama Jok, who both vary speed and loudness for artistic effect. In fact, there is very little artistry at all in Uking's **píat**. His use of parallelism is perfunctory. What primarily makes this recognizable as **píat** is the staccato mode of delivery. Each line comes out separately with clear pauses between. The effect is like a burst from a machine gun—not subtle, but powerful.

Note: For an explanation of the conventions of notation, see chapter one. A synopsis of these conventions is provided on the last printed page of the book.

Have pity on us,

    grandfather Orang Kaya Luwak.[2]

Don't fail$_1$ don't fail$_2$[3]

    to make active$_1$ to make active$_2$[4]

the Berawan children,[5]

    to make active$_1$ to make active$_2$

the Batu Belah children,[6]

    to make active$_1$ to make active$_2$

the Lelak children.[7]

10   That's what I say, grandfather Orang Kaya Luwak,

        grandfather Tama Julan Tinggang,[8]

        grandfather Lawai.[9]

- tu tama Alang mang leta'
- kíku kelo'
- muléí ngan kelo'
- tutok pì' kelo'
- lo tína lo tama
- kaam lo sadì'

- tu anyam tu anak kelo' lo la'a
- tubor lamèng Long Teru   20
- kaam bílì' sadì'
- píon lía tu
- tubor lía tu

- tu Kajan
- lo tua kampong Long Teru

- tu atan kelo'
- mano' unyín Kajan tu uccíu
- kuva kelo' mano' unyín Kajan tu jìn
- kuva kelo' mano' unyín Kajan tu merèng
- píon lía lo ka nacau   30
- tubor lía tu

- ra Kajan tu cì' nusíng dé
- ra nyí mupé
- ra nyí tepo'
- ano' lo lía kíng lía kraí
- atan lía Long Teru

Our father Alang is dead now,[10]

    he follows you,

    he returns to you,

    he is together with all of you,

        his mothers, his fathers,

        you his grandparents.

    These are your grandchildren, your children, left behind,

20   to look after the longhouse of Long Teru,

    you spirits of the grandparents,

        defend this community,[11]

        guard this community.

    This is Kajan,

    headman of Long Teru.[12]

It is for you,

    to make Kajan's disposition just,

    to try to make Kajan's disposition goodhearted,[13]

    to try to make Kajan's disposition firm,

30   to challenge people that bother us[14]

        to look after this community.

Don't let Kajan be cheated by them,[15]

don't let him fail,

don't let him be soft,

    in dealing with people upriver and down,

    for the community of Long Teru.[16]

- ke sadì' Orang Kaya Luwak
- ♦ ní jíu ko ngan no

- íno pa[17] bang
- ■ luvak ano' dé luvak   40
- ♦ yo rè kíku ngaran no
- ▪ Orang Kaya Luwak
- ♦ urok luvak ní ano' dé
- ♦ ngaran no luvak

- ▪ ní a'an[20] ko jíu ní

    ooo . . .

- ▪ tupaan kaam
- ▪ bílì' puwíeng bílì' ngaputíeng
- ▪ kaam bílì' Tot Manyem
- ▪ lo ngasan kamé lamulong   50

- ▪ spak atong luvak
- ▪ kura Ivan
- ▪ kín kakíng kín kan
- ▪ lo a'an Tot Manyem bawa uní
- ▪ a'an payau kílong
- ▪ ní sabeb Ivan ní aroo
- · bawa Manyem
- · ngayan payau kílong ngan apo

- ■ kaam bílì' díek
- ■ katé bílì' jat   60

verse continues uninterrupted

Grandfather Orang Kaya Luwak,

    that's what I say to you.

So great a reputation,[18]

40   that they made the lake,

    named after you,

    Orang Kaya Luwak,

    because they made the name of the lake,

    your name.[19]

That's why I'm saying this.

Calling noise[21]

All of you,

    spirit that holds, spirit that creates,

    you spirit of Tot Manyem,

50   who are the origin of we human beings.[22]

In the tributaries around this lake,

    how many Iban are there,

    to left and to right,

    that Tot Manyem fought long ago;

    at the place where the deer bailed,

    that's why those Iban are so many,

    that Manyem fought,

    at the place where the deer bailed the rivers.[23]

You spirit of the chicken,

60   cast away bad spirits,

verse continues uninterrupted

- tuman co^{24} lunaa co usaa
- tupaan Melawan Long Teru
- díccu anak laké lo lía tu

■ bílì' puwíeng
◆ no pekena no pelíka
◆ kamé Melawan tu

■ tupaan díccu laké
■ kaa kaam muvíu jíu Kajan
■ kaa kaam muvíu jíu komítí
- lo wakíl Kajan   70
- co lía tu

- atan no nelíka pekena
- bílì' díek

◆ íno pa maséé ulong
◆ íno pa maséé lía kíng
■ urok Long Teru tu pang buno
- tilo' tu lo kíng bangsa Kenyah
- bangsa Melawan

◆ ní a'an ko jíu ní
■ bílì' díek   80
· no cì' nelíka no cì' pekena tu

■ tama Alang tero leta'
■ kaman Lawaí tero leta'
- lo dukep bítang lamèng tu
- Oyang Ajang pun tero leta'
- Kajan lo gaté

from the bodies[1] the bodies[2]

of all the Berawan of Long Teru,

the women, the children, the men of this community. [25]

Spirit that holds, [26]

you set things right[1] set things right[2] [27]

for us Berawan.

All you women and men, [28]

don't you mistrust what Kajan says,

don't you mistrust what the committee says,

70   that is deputy to Kajan,

in this community. [29]

It is for you to set things right[3] set things right[1]

spirit of the chicken. [30]

Have pity on their lives,

have pity on this downriver community,

because Long Teru has made peace, [31]

being the most downriver of the Kenyah people,

the Berawan people. [32]

That's why I say to you,

80   spirit of the chicken:

you go and set things right[3] go and set things right[1]

Father Alang is dead now,

uncle Lawai is dead now, [33]

that ruled this house, [34]

Oyang Ajang is dead now, [35]

it is Kajan that replaces them. [36]

◆ kuva kelo' nelíka pekena

◆ unyín tílo' lo umí

◆ díccu laké co lía tu

▪ íno pun mulong ka Melawan   90

■ cì' mé cì supé

■ mano' lía lo sakí ní'è sakí diccì

■ mano' dé lo sakí malam

■ mano' dé lo buwau mang

▪ íno pa maséé tubor Melawan

▪ bílì' díek

◆ kuva no bílì' puwong bílì' ngaputong

◆ no Bungan Malan tílé tílo'

▪ ra urok kamé umok

▪ kumaan pa'a kumaan líèk kuman kulèk   100

▪ no bílì' díek

◆ co kamé papì' mekí tupaan lía tu

▪ kíjì' butí selí sema díek

◆ masak da masak uma

◆ masak lunaa masak usaa

◆ masak líèk masak pa'èk

◆ dé bílì' unyín dukep katè

◆ unyín jat unyín purok

■ mupok tupaan

■ no bílì' díek tu   110

Try to restore$_3$ to restore$_1$

    their morale, the small ones,[37]

    the women, the men of this community.

90   What life for the Berawan,

    if defeated$_1$ if defeated$_2$

    by people who arrived just now, arrived recently,

    by those who arrived last night,

    by those immigrants?[38]

Pity and care for the Berawan,

    spirit of the chicken.

    Try, you spirit that holds, spirit that creates,

    you Bungan Malan, to look out for them.

It's not because we want

100   to eat your thighs, eat your wings, eat your skin,[39]

    you spirit of the chicken,

    but to make prayers and sacrifice for all of us in this community.

Though as small as a grain of grass, let the blood of this chicken,

    enter your house$_1$ enter your house$_2$

    enter your bodies$_1$ enter your bodies$_2$

    enter your arms$_1$ enter your arms$_2$[40]

Those spirits that rule emotions, throw away

    bad feelings, rotten feelings,

    cast them all out,

110   you spirit of the chicken.[41]

6.

Nulang—A Prayer at the Graveyard

Like the preceding prayer, the one in this chapter is made over the mortal remains of an important man, but there the resemblance ends. **Nulang** is performed with the remains of someone dead for months rather than days. More significantly, the motivation of the speaker is not hypocritical. When making this prayer the spirits are his genuine concern—indeed his anxiety—for no one enters a graveyard without foreboding.

Tama Suleng's Posthumous Wanderings

The remains in question belonged to Tama Suleng, a man whose social standing depended more on who he was related to than anything he achieved himself. His father-in-law was Oyang Ajang, who for two decades

170

was the headman and controlling influence at Long Teru. In early 1972 it was plain that Tama Suleng was ill, probably with tuberculosis. He tried every treatment available to him, without avail. In April 1972, in a last desperate attempt, he sought out a shaman that he had not tried before at the Berawan village of Long Terawan near the Tutoh river. But it was of no avail, and there he died.

His companions were now in a quandary. Should they bury him at Long Terawan? If they did so, there would be no kinsmen around to perform a proper funeral. Should they rush the decaying corpse all the way back to Long Teru? Even there, it would be absolutely proscribed to bring him into the longhouse. In the end, they came up with a neat solution. They brought the body as far as Batu Belah, a Berawan village on the Lower Tutoh. He was then rapidly put into a large jar and deposited in the graveyard of the village, housed in a crude temporary **salong** (raised tomb). The beauty of this solution was that Batu Belah was Tama Suleng's native village. Consequently, he was decently stowed among the bones of his ancestors. At the same time, he had lived most of his adult life at Long Teru, and his family would want him there. This could be achieved through the ritual of **nulang**, "fetching the bones." In technical language, **nulang** is a rite of secondary treatment of the dead reserved for those of high status. In practical terms, it is a great festival in which an entire longhouse community pools its resources to put on an eight- or ten-day party with food and drink for the assembled crowds, and often also to build an impressive mausoleum. Costly though it is, a **nulang** may be beneficial for its sponsors. Cosmologically, it allows a life-renewing contact with the entire company of the ancestors. Socially, it secures the standing of the leading family whose kinsman is honored by the ritual, and memorialized in the grand mausoleum. In this case there was a special benefit: it would enable the two villages of Long Teru and Batu Belah to renew by mutual cooperation a long-standing alliance.

The complex details of the **nulang** ritual need not detain us here, and I have described them elsewhere (1982a:155–231). Suffice it to say that the opening move is a small rite at the graveyard called **neken**. It involves the playing of two innocuous-seeming games that nevertheless are absolutely taboo at any other time than the season of **nulang**. After that, the coffin or jar may be removed from its place of temporary storage, opened if it is necessary or desirable to clean the bones, and transported back to the longhouse. The first necessity, however, is to make a prayer announcing what is intended.

In May 1973, a couple of dozen people went from Long Teru to collect the bones of Tama Suleng, and they returned with a contingent from his native village. (As a note to chapter five, Uking also appeared at Batu Belah, though he had little to do with the affair.) About a dozen people went to the graveyard to carry Tama Suleng's coffin to the barge that would carry it to Long Teru. The jungle had been cleared from around the temporary mausoleum the day before, so as to alleviate the gloom and make room to play the special games. As the party struggled up from the river, close female relatives of the deceased rushed forward to the tomb, and threw themselves down in front of it. With their hair thrown forward over their faces, they wailed just as they had done over the newly deceased corpse. Somewhat hesitantly, a middle-aged man named Lian began to make **píat**. He had been drafted to perform this task because he was the senior man going to the graveyard. He was related affinally to the dead man, being married to the sister of Tama Suleng's famous father-in-law. This degree of distance was appropriate; it would be unseemly for immediate relatives to make the prayer. Lian was not prominent in community affairs, and he is not skilled at **píat**. Nevertheless, he knew well enough what he needed to say. It is this prayer that is recorded.

Lian Prays at the Graveyard

Lian's prayer neatly expresses the combination of awe and hope that surrounds the dead. They have the power to help and also to harm, to give life, and to kill. Their blessing is constantly solicited, but too close contact, particularly with their relics, makes everyone extremely nervous. Lian has three main themes. First, he announces to Tama Suleng that his **nulang** is about to commence. This should be a welcome message, and indeed there are stories about lax relatives being confronted by unhappy ghosts demanding to know when was the appointed day (see note 28 of this chapter). Nevertheless, there is a distinct undertow of fear: maybe the ghost of Tama Suleng will be startled and lash out unpredictably. Maybe the disturbed ancestors will be expecting a new recruit, or perhaps some evil spirit has gained control of the corpse—or what is left of it—and is laying in wait inside the temporary mausoleum. Second, and partly to offset at least the first of these hazards, Lian wants to assure Tama Suleng that disturbing his bones in this fashion is not just his idea. He is careful to point out that Tama Suleng's close family are all there: his widow Bilo Meneng (**bílo'** means "widow"); his wife's mother Bilo Unut, also called Sadi Suleng (**sadì'** means "grandparent"), the widow of Oyang Ajang; his daughter Suleng, from whom he takes his own teknonym (**tama** means "father"); and his son-in-law Yo. Not only that, but the whole community of Long Teru has concurred in carrying out the **nulang**. His third theme is to explain that there will be certain changes in the way the ritual is done this time, that these changes were also a collective decision, and that Tama Suleng should not let any of this cause problems.

The innovation Lian refers to is the rehabilitation of the death songs (**gu**). These songs are in many ways the ritual core of the **nulang**, recounting the journey of the soul to the land of the dead. They are very sacred, and they possess in full measure the ambiguity of the ancestors. Shortly before Tama Suleng died it had been decided to stop singing them because there were few people left who were fully competent to do so and mistakes are risky. But enthusiasm for this **nulang** caused public opinion to reverse itself and favor their reintroduction. The danger now feared was the displeasure of the ancestors at all this indecision and change.

These were the circumstances surrounding Lian's prayer. It should be noted that in the full account of Tama Suleng's **nulang** (Metcalf 1982a:155–70), he is referred to by his personal name, Lanau. Both names were in frequent use at Long Teru, and I use the former here because it is used by Lian in the prayer. Lian used no teknonym, but he was often referred to by a patronym as well: Lian Yang.

Prayer Five

Speaker: Lian Yang

Time: 4 minutes and 45 seconds

Summary: The **píat** begins during a lull in the wailing. In contrast to Uking standing over the coffin of Tama Avit, Lian immediately addresses Tama Suleng. He does not prefix the word **bílì'** (spirit) onto his name, although Tama Suleng is by now presumably a spirit. He also does not attach the respect terms often employed before the names of prestigious ancestors (**ke sadì'**, see chapter three, prayer one, notes 3 and 4). Lian does not call on any other spirits, either at the outset or later in his **píat**: he has no need to summon the ancestors to that place, and he wishes only to communicate as directly as possible with the ghost of Tama Suleng. The tone is respectfully conversational.

The first message (lines 2–6) is "let no other disturb you." The unnamed others are those nightmarish demons that prowl graveyards and try to reanimate corpses.

This anxiety expressed, Lian briefs Tama Suleng on what is in progress (lines 7–23). The implication of including the names of Lawai and Tama Julan Tinggang (see chapter three, prayer one, notes 5 and 6) is that the initiative to move Tama Suleng actually comes more from the ancestors (who need not fear his wrath) than from humans.

Lines 24–33 point out that a chicken is to be sacrificed to "awaken" Tama Suleng auspiciously so that he will not "disturb" the Long Teru or the Belah communities; rather he should help them obtain fish and game, which is after all to be used for his **nulang**.

A recapitulation of these points in lines 34–49 mentions Tama Suleng's father-in-law, called Tange here, and emphasizes the group decision. Tama Suleng is urged to be affectionate as in life to his kin, not vengeful as are the newly dead. Lines 50–65 cover the selfsame agenda, including lists of living kin and prestigious forebears.

There is then a short pause while Lian pours generous quantities of rice wine onto the posts of the temporary mausoleum. He makes a metaphor out of the wine: let it be sweet, he says, not sour. In other words, let the festival go well (lines 66–74).

- a Tama Sulèng

- rè lo an^2 co^3 kedíín ko tílo

◆ ngan no Tama Sulèng

- kaa karoo dé

- lo acì'

- ngelabang ngekalang Tama Sulèng

- tu lo an ko

- pattéé ngan no

verse continues uninterrupted

Finally, Lian deals with the reintroduction of the **gu** (lines 75–87). He appeals to Tama Suleng not only to accept this himself, but also to use his skills to persuade the other "ghosts" (**uted**) to accept it also.

Style: Lian's style bears comparison with Uking's, despite the great temperamental difference between the two men. Lian's voice can be heard clearly over the sound of the women's keening. He speaks at almost the same level throughout, which is just loud enough to be heard. If he were to be too loud, he would summon all the spirits that might be nearby. His pace is measured; there is only the occasional phrase spoken at high speed, often one on a potentially embarrassing topic. There are few parallel structures, and many verses are brief and to the point. As with Uking, the feature of style that makes his speech most easily recognizable as **píat** is the staccato effect of phrases shot out machine-gun fashion. Unlike Uking, there is no shrillness or histrionics. Lian's whole manner of making **píat** is workmanlike but artless, just what one would expect of a head of a household who is not usually forward in ritual matters.

Note: For an explanation of the conventions of notation, see chapter one. A synopsis of these conventions is provided on the last printed page of the book.

Where are you, Tama Suleng,[1]

   it is I here to tell,

   you, Tama Suleng:

Let no,

   other,

      disturb$_1$ you, disturb$_2$ you, Tama Suleng.[4]

This is why I'm,

   talking to you,

verse continues uninterrupted

- urok lo ka[5] ngíso no tu
- urok lo ka mala no tu   10
- muléí co ukuk no síndírí
- ◆   co lamèng no síndírí
- mala no tutok ngan Lawaí
- mala no tutok ngan Tama Julan Tínggang
- ◆ co luvak

- ■ tu'o ma[10] ngaran no
- ■ tuman Bíto' Kala
- an no tupo'

- urok kedung no wong ukuk
-                 no wong selakík Tama Sulèng   20
- ní an metelo' no muléí
- mala no tutok ngan Lawaí
- mala no tutok ngan Tama Julan Tínggang

- tu díek Tama Sulèng
- díek lo co nyíkí no tu

- ◆ bí'é no ngelabang bí'é no ngekalang
- lamèng Long Teru
- lamèng Bíto' Kala

- ■ lukí tílo'
- mala bíkuí   30
- mala síju
- lo co tubor no
- lo co pínyít no

because you are going to be moved,

10   because you are going to be brought,

back to your own apartment,[6]

to your own longhouse,

to bring you together with Lawai,[7]

to bring you together with Tama Julan Tinggang,[8]

at the lake.[9]

It's true that your name,

is from Batu Belah,[11]

where you were born.

Just because you have a home$_1$

20   you have a home$_2$, Tama Suleng,[12]

that's why we want to return you,

to bring you together with Lawai,

to bring you together with Tama Julan Tinggang.

This is the chicken, Tama Suleng,

the chicken we use to awaken you.

Lest you disturb$_1$ lest you disturb$_2$

the longhouse of Long Teru,

the longhouse of Batu Belah.[13]

Let them have good luck,

30   in getting pig,

in getting fish,

to be used in taking care of you,

to be used in attending to you.[14]

- tutok ngan Lawaí
- ◆ co Ikíung Peté
- tutok ngan díken no
- Tangé
- ní lo an ngíso no tuman ato'

- ◆ bukan tu rè lamèng no lamèng tu ma
- tetap kedíín unyín lía Long Teru   40
- ngan no
- ní an mala no tu muléí Tama Sulèng

- utan no
- lukí dé mala
- cìn tubor no tu
- lukí dé mala síju dé mala bíkuí
- Tama Sulèng

- ◆ a pa kedíín unyín no to mulong
- ní atan no

- ní an nyíkí no tu Tama Sulèng   50
- ní an tílo ko ngan no

- tu la[19] bun ício pínyít no tu
- Sulèng Yo
- Bílo' Meneng
- Bílo' Unut
- lo mala no muléí

Together with Lawai,

at Ikiung Pete,[15]

together with your father-in-law,

Tange,

that's why we move you from here.

Not that that house is your house,[16]

40   but this is how the people of Long Teru felt,

about you:

that's the place to bring you to, Tama Suleng.[17]

Give,

them luck in obtaining,

money to take care of you,

luck in obtaining fish, luck in obtaining pig,

Tama Suleng.

As if you were still alive let your feelings,

be for them.[18]

50   That's why we wake you up, Tama Suleng,

that's why I'm telling you this:

This is the first day they attend to you,[20]

Suleng and Yo,

Bilo Meneng,

Bilo Unut,

it is they that bring you back.[21]

- tupaan lamèng Long Teru mala no muléí
- mala no maccì' co lía
- co an ke sadì' Lawaí leta'
- co an ke sadì' Lawaí param   60
- co an ke sadì' Suraí param

■ ní jíu pattéé ko ngan no Tama Sulèng

- kaa no ngelabang ngekalang Bíto' Kala
- kaa no ngelabang ngekalang Long Teru
- ní lo tubor no

Pause

- tu borèk ícung Yo
- tu borèk ícung Sulèng
- nyíkí no tu Tama Sulèng
- bí'é no ra kanaí
- kaa no mano' rè maccam   70
- kaa no mano' rè jat lèng
■ bawaa ngaran ba[24]

- maséé lamulong tubor no
■ tu Tama Sulèng

- yo jíu bun mekì naté gu
- tu no mala
- Sulèng ra umok
◆ no ra kena gu
- Yo ra umok

verse continues uninterrupted

The whole house of Long Teru brings you back,

transports you back to their community,[22]

to the place of dead grandfather Lawai,

60   to the place of the late grandfather Lawai,

to the place of the late grandfather Surai.[23]

That's what I say to you, Tama Suleng:

Don't disturb$_1$ disturb$_2$ Batu Belah,

don't disturb$_1$ disturb$_2$ Long Teru,

those that care for you.

Pause

This is the rice wine given by Yo,

this is the rice wine given by Suleng,

to wake you up, Tama Suleng,

lest you not know,

70   don't make it sour,

don't make it taste bad,

let people say it is sweet.[25]

Pity the people that care for you,[26]

Tama Suleng.

Although we said at first we would abolish the death songs,[27]

you will have them,

Suleng did not want,

you not to have them,

Yo did not want,

verse continues uninterrupted

◆ no ra kena gu

▪ místi no kena gu

▪ no manaí tílo ngan uted

▪ urok ní barang malam tero naté

▪ kaa rè wong alé

▪ kaa rè wong kedíín

▪ ngan matelo'

▪ co ubín tu na'a

80   you not to have them,

you must have the death songs.

Be skillful in explaining to the ghosts, [28]

why these things were previously abolished, [29]

don't let it be harmful,

don't let it do anything,

to us,

your descendants.

7.
Ngelaké—A Prayer to Call the Major Omen Bird

The Berawan have a great variety of modes of divination, ranging from the trivial to the serious. The most striking is a system of augury employing omen animals (**aman**); comprising about eighteen species of birds, two species of deer, and two species of snakes. The weightiest of all forms of divination is the seeking of signs from the eagle **plaké** (*Ictinaetus malayensis*). The prayers that are part of this process are distinctive in content and form: they are addressed predominantly to one spirit agency that is asked to manifest itself physically, and they exhibit many of the stylistic attributes of **píat** in extreme form.

Calling **Plaké**

The distinction between **plaké** and the other omen creatures is most clear in the way that omens are obtained. Sometimes a chance sighting of **plaké**

184

will be taken as an omen, but primarily **plaké** is summoned to a location previously prepared for the purpose. The augur's prayers entreat the bird to appear and to give council to men. The lesser omen animals give promise of success or warning of danger through—from our point of view—chance encounters in the jungle, on the farm, or by the river. **Plaké** is called, the other **aman** never are.

The calling of **plaké** is a serious matter not to be undertaken lightly. Of the half dozen occasions that I saw **plaké** called, one was to ask about the chances of a good rice harvest, two concerned the chances of recovery of critically ill persons, two inquired about the likelihood of further deaths in the community after the completion of mortuary rites, and one, the least serious matter, was to reverse a man's bad luck at hunting. This last caused public censure: to call **plaké** on too small a context might anger the spirit and endanger the whole community. In earlier times, **plaké** was consulted before all major decisions in warfare and headhunting. Indeed, there is a general symbolic association between **plaké** and warfare, so that Hose describes him as a god of war (Hose and McDougall 1912, 2:15). That this bird is seen as powerful is illustrated by the nature of shamans who are possessed by his spirit. They are expected to be violent and unpredictable, but of great use to the community. But **plaké** is not associated with death as, for instance, the crow is in Western mythology. Rather he is seen as life-giving: he is said to be "hot" and "red."

The procedures for calling **plaké** (**ngelaké**) are well defined and not greatly subject to idiosyncratic variation. A start is made early in the morning since the process may be a long one. It may continue, if necessary, for four to six hours on one day, and resume on the next day, up to a limit of three days. After a few days of rest, the augur may try again if he has the stamina. The day should be fine, and the threat of rain will cause cancellation because it is tactless to ask **plaké** to appear in inclement weather. The spot chosen needs a good view over the surrounding jungle, such as a knoll in the middle of a rice field, preferably with a shade tree. If the augury is taken at the longhouse, a spot on the riverbank, with a view across the river, is invariably chosen.

The standard procedure is first to set up two sticks (**telejang**), which are decorated with ruffs of raised shavings. These sticks frame a segment of the sky for the augur who sits behind them, and **plaké** must appear within this restricted field of vision. The augur is also equipped with a small tray of offerings for the bird, consisting of some rice wrapped in little bundles (**kelupé**), some sliced hard-boiled eggs, cigarettes, and maybe some candy, often contained in a small upturned gong. He also needs two bottles half filled with water (**pí plaké**), each with a crudely carved stick figure (**lèngaí plaké**) inserted in the neck, and a chicken, which is often a tiny chick. Some adepts keep "luck hooks" (**angèk**), small forked pieces of twig, in the bottle necks as well, as another way of securing the blessing of **plaké**. The adept lights a small fire of twigs, which he will keep burning throughout the performance, and settles himself comfortably behind his sticks. He begins his prayer to **plaké** with a high-pitched humming noise, which he maintains as long as possible. During the prayer he mentions the chicken that will be sacrificed on a successful augury while pulling out a feather, which he singes in the fire so that it releases a pungent smell. He then sits back and waits, chatting to any observers or passersby. At intervals of half an hour or so he repeats his prayer. If a **plaké** should appear, he immediately addresses it. People nearby, hearing the urgent note in the prayer, rush up to watch.

The instructions that the augur gives to **plaké** and the subsequent interpretation of the bird's behavior are straightforward enough once we realize that the process has two stages. I was initially confused by conflicting reports about whether the bird is supposed to fly to the right or to the left, as others had been before me (Hose and McDougall 1912, 2:52–53; Furness 1902:161–62). The resolution is simple: the bird must do both.

Having entered the augur's field of vision, preferably near the middle, the bird should circle. This is a holding pattern, which indicates the bird's willingness to begin. Sometimes the pattern of flight is called **ngelaco,** "to dance." The augur vigorously urges the bird to fly to the left (**ngabèng**), and if it eventually does so, a shout of triumph goes up since this is a good omen. The augur will grab up one of the bottles and, waving it after the disappearing **plaké**, bless the water, which is thereby imbued with the power to ward off harm (**pí plaké ngabèng**). If, however, the bird sails off to the right, then neither a good nor a bad omen is deduced. People say that the bird is "playing," or that it is an inexperienced bird, or even that it does not hear well! They then settle down to persevere in their attempt to have one fly to the left. Should the **plaké** fly directly toward the onlookers and over their heads (**mupok**), then a gasp of dismay emerges from the crowd, for this is clearly a bad omen. In this case, the augury is over, and everyone drifts off disconsolately. If the bird should suddenly disappear from sight (**lacèk**), or if it should suddenly dive (**tukong**), or fly in a violently ungraceful manner, then a similar reaction will be provoked, and a similar meaning construed. Should the bird fly directly away from the onlookers, or

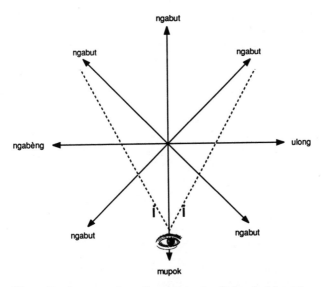

Figure 7. Interpretation of omens in the flight of **plaké**. The dotted lines indicate the field of vision of the augur, who is limited to the space between his two sticks.

diagonally to the right or to the left (**ngabut**), then the omen is mixed, partly good and partly bad (see figure 7).

If a good or a mixed omen is received during the first stage, the augur proceeds to the second stage—summoning **plaké** to fly to the right this time. Ideally it should be a different bird that answers the call, and it is convenient in this respect that eagles move in pairs. Sometimes the augur will even mention that he calls the eagle's wife now, aware that the birds are a pair. It is sufficient, however, if the first bird flies out of vision and then reappears. If another bird is not sighted, the augur may continue on the following day, up to the maximum of three days. This time the bird must fly off to the right in order to provide a favorable outcome, and the augur can dedicate the other bottle of water (**pí plaké ulong, ulong** means "life"), which is even more potent to cure illness than the first bottle. Flying left, conversely, will be described as playing, and the other omens are as before.

A range of outcomes is thus possible. A bad omen in either part of the performance is final. A good omen in both parts is the happiest possible outcome, or it may be diluted with a mixed omen in one part or the other.

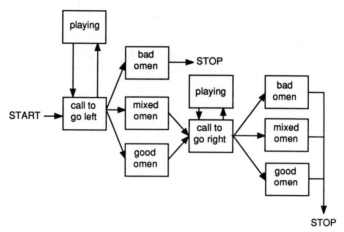

Figure 8. Summary of procedures for calling **plaké.**

A mixed omen in both parts does not inspire much confidence. If omens were being taken before a war party set out, for instance, such a result might cause the party to abandon or delay the entire project. (See figure 8 for a summary of procedures.)

In contrast to the cut-and-dried procedures for reading **plaké,** the interpretation of portents from the lesser omen creatures is idiosyncratic—a mixture of imaginative symbolism, personal preference, and previous experience. Most adult men have some knowledge of the lesser **aman,** and are particularly watchful at the time of making farms. But the interpretations of one man can vary radically from or even directly conflict with another.

Tama Aweng Seeks Advice, June 1973

The great majority of instances in which **plaké** is called employ a basic procedure. What is required is an answer of yes or no: Will there be more deaths in the community? Will the rice crop fail? Will so-and-so recover? Occasionally, however, some other kind of answer is required, and then it is possible to modify, within limits, the routine. The next prayer recorded was such an occasion.

It arose because of the chronic illness of a small boy named Balleng, the grandson of Tama Aweng. As we noted in chapter four, infant mortality is high, and the health of children is a subject of constant concern. But this case had some specially disturbing features. The infant would seem normal for long periods of time, but then would without warning go into a muscular paroxysm. His small body became stiff, his breathing irregular, and he lost consciousness. It was evidently some kind of epileptic fit. What shocked his family was the sudden resemblance to a corpse, suggesting the most sinister of supernatural attacks. Even after the child recovered his normal appearance, his parents remained alarmed. Tama Aweng, as head of the household and a ritual specialist, cast about for the right response. In his role as shaman, he might make a seance and call on his familiars for help. Or he could prepare a prayer station, and ask the Creator Spirit to intervene. In the end he did both these things and more. Yet his first thought was to consult **plaké**. **Plaké** could reveal the root cause of the illness. With the etiology of the illness known, the appropriate cure would be easier to find.

Tama Aweng chose a spot on the riverbank in front of the longhouse; it was a shady spot where he could sit all day if necessary, and where the trees framed an expansive view across the river and the jungle. This spot had been chosen for the same purpose before, for the reason noted in the summary. The usual offerings were set out, but instead of two **telejang** sticks, Tama Aweng set up three—one directly in front of him, and one on each flank, all three pointing slightly forward. Since this arrangement was novel, his prayer needed to explain what they meant. Each stick signified a different cause of the child's illness: the one on the left means attack by an evil spirit (**kenacau bílì'**), which has waylaid the child's soul. The middle one signifies retribution for some error on the part of the parents (**palé ano' kellèjjé tína tama**), or accidental exposure to some enervating influence (**tekena**). The former occurs because of a breach of one of the innumerable taboos on a pregnant woman and her husband (see note 34 of this chapter). The latter involves forces of the natural world. What these etiologies have in common is an unmediated or automatic action (see notes 31 and 32 of the chapter). Finally, the right-hand stick means that the cause of the child's sickness is none of the above but something else (**íno íno ka**). Tama Aweng does not say what that might be. It could include, for instance, physical injury.

There are two things about this passage that make it particularly interesting. The first is the semiotic sophistication that Tama Aweng displays. The usual view that Westerners have is that divination and augury try to read what is random by an overextension of determinist causality, a branch of the science of the concrete. In this view, signs inhere in nature, put there perhaps by gods or the fates, and it is up to men to figure out what they say.

Astrology is the example that most influences our concept of divination; the stars are there, and we look up at them wonderingly. Tama Aweng's approach is by contrast, thoroughly communicative. He makes up the code, and it is spirits—suitably briefed in prayer—that must talk the language of men. The same approach governs the interpretation of signs from the lesser omen creatures. As noted above, men often give radically different, even contradictory, interpretations of the same behavior. They are not abashed when this is pointed out. The bird has become accustomed to them personally over the years, they say, and each speaks the other's language.

The second thing to note about this passage is that it offers us a classification of the etiologies of illness. If one were to ask a Berawan directly what kinds of diseases there are, I suspect that it would take a great deal of probing to obtain any kind of ethnotaxonomy. This one is produced spontaneously, and moreover it provides a guide to treatment, which is why Tama Aweng set about calling **plaké** in the first place. If the root cause of the child's illness is soul loss, then it is the skills of the shaman, the psychopomp, that are required. If the child is sick because of the breach of a taboo, then only an appeal to the Creator Spirit can have any effect, only he can restore the *status quo ante*. If neither of these is indicated, the only recourse in traditional medicine is the herbal healer, who deals with conditions that are considered to have purely physical causes. Formerly there was a great body of magical and herbal lore, but it has largely disappeared because of the increased availability of Western medicine. Herbal medicines were used on wounds and injuries, and it is possible that the child's condition was the result of brain damage in childbirth. Berawan midwives press down upon the abdomen of a mother in labor in order to speed delivery, and the baby sometimes emerges so rapidly that it is injured in the process. (For more details on concepts of the etiology of illness see Metcalf 1982b.)

Tama Aweng's modification of the procedures for calling **plaké** also necessitates new ways of interpreting the behavior of the bird when it appears. In the prayer, we hear him ask the bird to appear and to fly to the left, just as in the standard procedure. But significance is now also placed on the segment of the sky in which **plaké** appears. Wherever it is, flying off to the left will provide a diagnosis. The ominous and noncommittal omens are the same as in the standard routine. Next, the bird should show up in the same quarter and fly off to the right, thus confirming the diagnosis and predicting a successful cure. How Tama Aweng planned to evaluate a bird that showed up in a different quarter and flew off to the right, I do not know. Such are the hazards of innovation. Perhaps he would have concluded that the affliction of the child had multiples causes. In the event, he obtained the result that he wanted on his second day of trying, and the child in due course stopped having the fits.

Tama Aweng as Augur

Tama Aweng's willingness to tinker with ritual forms is entirely in character. When we met him in chapter three he was playing a leading role in the community-wide festival of **papì' lamèng**, and experimenting with poetic expression in his **pìat**. We saw that he is a man without resources of prestige in the community, who yet wants to play a prominent part and win acknowledgement. Tama Aweng is also an active shaman, following the style of Long Teru's great **daíyung**, Tama Ukat Sageng.

His efforts as an augur are less showy, but more exceptional. There is only one other person at Long Teru who calls **plaké** with any frequency, an old man, who is not a shaman. No one else at Long Teru attempted it while I was there, and certainly no woman would try. There is no ritual by which a man qualifies to call **plaké**. Tama Aweng made much of the need for dream inspiration, but it is mainly the skills in **pìat** that need to be acquired. Beyond this basic prerequisite the neophyte needs only the daring to try, and I suspect that it is the risk of public ridicule that is the major inhibition, rather than any supernatural sanction. Tama Aweng is well respected in this role. His shamanistic powers were often denigrated, and people sometimes sneered at his attempts to be forward in ritual matters, but he had earned a solid reputation as **manaí ngelaké** (skilled at calling **plaké**). In more warlike times, the man who **dukep aman** (held the omen creatures) or **dukep plaké**—if the job was divided up—was an important figure, effectively charged with making all kinds of decisions. Even today the role has its importance, and Tama Aweng is asked to officiate when the need arises. After a funeral, for instance, the kin of the deceased are obligated to discover whether more deaths are to be expected. On one such occasion Tama Aweng managed to obtain an entirely positive omen—two birds appearing and flying just as bidden—within minutes of beginning his **ngelaké**. His audience was stunned, and he was very pleased with himself.

The Identity of **Plaké**

Tama Aweng's prayer appeals again and again to **bílì' plaké**, or in the Kenyah form he often prefers, **balí plakí**. But if one asks who or what **bílì' plaké** is, one asks in vain. What can be known about Berawan conceptions of the identity of **plaké** must be deduced from references in ritual and in prayer, notably in the prayers of **ngelaké**.

The first issue, and the easiest, concerns the species of birds that provide omens. All of the hawks, kites, and eagles in the submontane habitat are referred to by the Berawan as **plaké**, but only some species are used for augury. The most common **plaké** is the brahminy kite *Haliastur indus intermedius*, which is often seen circling low over the riverbank. For this reason, previous writers about the peoples of the Baram river have identified it as the principal omen bird of the Kayan and Kenyah (Hose and McDougall 1912, 2:51; Haddon 1901:384). If one asks to be shown a **plaké**, the one pointed out will most likely be a brahminy kite, which the Berawan call **plaké ulo' putéé**, the "white headed **plaké**." However, this bird is never used for augury because it is so common that its appearances lose all significance. Also, its flight patterns are inappropriate. I strongly suspect that the same was true for the Kayan and the Kenyah augury, although it is hard to prove my case since these people have now abandoned the practice.

Adepts are perfectly capable of describing the appearance and the habits of the preferred augural species. Moreover, I was at an advantage over earlier observers because I could show my informants the colored illustrations in B. E. Smythies' *The Birds of Borneo*, which was published in 1960. The species that they selected as best for augury were the eagle-hawk *Spizaetus alboniger* and, particularly, the Malaysian black eagle *Ictinaetus malayensis*, which they call **plaké tudok ulo'**, the "**plaké** with the crest on its head." According to Smythies, this bird is found throughout Borneo from the coasts to the mountains but is not common anywhere. This is consistent with the hypothesis that all the Kayan and the Kenyah, whether in the hilly interior or the coastal plain, relied upon the same species, and with the assumption by the Berawan themselves that sightings of the augural **plaké** will not be frequent. Moreover, Smythies says that black eagles move in pairs, are "usually seen sailing in small circles over a forested hillside," and have a "slow deliberate round winged flight" (1960:154), all features that lend themselves to Berawan interpretation of omens.

This identification does not, however, solve the problem of the identity of **plaké**. Although it is an eagle—a bird—that is called, it is evidently not this creature that Tama Aweng is constantly addressing as **balí plakí**. This is made clear in several striking passages in the prayer. In lines 148–64, for instance, Tama Aweng asks **balí plakí** not to send a bird that is lax or careless, but to send instead one with "old wings," that is, an experienced bird. Clearly, **balí plakí** is not identical to the bird that appears before Tama Aweng's eyes. The spirit remains veiled, mysterious.

As we saw in chapter one, Berawan pronouns do not indicate gender. So we cannot even be sure whether **balí plakí** is thought of as male, female, or neuter. I speak of **bílì' plaké** as "him" because of a structural equivalence with him and **bílì' ngaputong**, the Creator Spirit. The eagle is unique among the omen creatures in the same manner that the Creator is unique among the spirit agencies that rule Berawan cosmology. This is clearly expressed when Berawan talk as if **bílì' plaké** were the special representative of **bílì' ngaputong**. Such representatives have powers of their own, powers to intercede for one person rather than another, to give priority to some cases over others. That is why, in the case of **plaké**, Berawan frequently stretch to the breaking point the principle that omen animals only give counsel about what is going to occur, and that they themselves cannot influence those events. In lines 42–45 of the prayer, **balí plakí** is told that only he knows how to cure the sick child. In lines 112–20, he is instructed to "fly in order to heal," as if the flying did the healing. In line 180 he is told that it is up to him to "care for" poor human beings, in a phrase that echoes those used about the ancestral spirits in prayers one and two.

The Berawan hold **balí plakí** in awe because of his special relationship with the Creator Spirit. Yet there is also an intimacy about **balí plakí**, because he responds directly and palpably to the appeals of men. Not all eagles are manifestations of **balí plakí**, that is clear. Most are just birds going about their business like any other. But there is something special about an augural **plaké**. Is it just that **balí plakí**—the spirit—beckons some passing eagle and instructs it to run an errand, as the passage noted above might imply? Or does **balí plakí** somehow inspire the birds that appear to the augur in the manner that spirit familiars inspire a shaman, so that **balí plakí** is manifested in a deeper sense? Does **balí plakí** take on the shape of an eagle, so that some eagles are not eagles at all but gods in disguise? What does **balí plakí** look like when he is not answering some augur's plea? Does he resemble an eagle or a man or neither? These are precisely the sort of questions that have no answers, or alternatively, as many answers as your imagination can provide. To wonder about them is to enter into the poetry of **ngelaké**, and the compelling drama of bird augury.

Prayer Six

Speaker: Tama Aweng

Time: 4 minutes and 50 seconds

Summary: Contrary to what might be expected, the opening lines (1–17) do not focus on **plaké**, but instead focus on the spirits of prayer sites (**tapo'**), sacred plants (**daren**), and house stones (**bíto' tíloí**). This is because the spot that Tama Aweng chose for taking omens is adjacent to a sort of sacred grove, a shady place in front of the longhouse where many **tapo'** had been made in the past, and where ritual paraphernalia of various kinds has accumulated. Had Tama Aweng been calling **plaké** at some other place— his farm, for instance—it is less likely that he would have begun in this way. In line 14, Tama Aweng calls on one of the minor omen birds. This is because he sees the bird across the river just as he begins speaking, and so weaves a reference to it into his prayer just as Tama Jok did in line 107 of prayer one. It is not an exception to the hard and fast rule that only **plaké** is called.

Finally, Tama Aweng summons **plaké**, and immediately explains his business (lines 18–41). It is a serious matter. It concerns an illness that has peculiar symptoms, which are described in some detail. Note that the sick child is called Ukat in line 27, as one might expect of a child that has frequently been sick (see chapter four). The child's personal name is also mentioned, with emphasis on its inspired origin. Tama Aweng may be ensuring that **bílì' plaké** knows exactly which "Ukat" is being discussed, and he may also be boasting, since he himself was the shaman who supposedly discovered the child's identity.

Lines 42–49 make several exhortations, employing formulae that are repeated. The spirit of the eagle is bluntly instructed not to dawdle. Irreverent language is not uncommon in prayers addressed to **bílì' plaké**, who may be told to leave his rice untasted, or his mate alone. The next section (lines 50–75) specifies the code by which the eagle is to signal what is wrong with the child, and whether a cure will be effective.

Exhortations similar to those in lines 42–49 are repeated in lines 78–91, with the addition of a special calling noise reserved for **plaké**. This sound is characteristic; to hear it is to know that this most serious form of augury is in progress. The noise often made at the beginnings of prayers to get the attention of spirits is loud but brief. This noise is pitched higher, has a slight vibrato, and is maintained as long as possible.

The next sixty lines employ poetic imagery, with the repeated request to the bird to fly first to the left so as to secure a good omen (lines 89–91, 112–15). Tama Aweng's vantage point was chosen so as to frame his view of the open sky, and he likens this view to a window, to which **plaké** should come though it be "no bigger than a winnowing tray or a cutting board" (lines 92–108). Once within the augur's view, **plaké** should fly "as gracefully as a Kayan dancing," an image that neatly relates cultural, natural, and supernatural beauty (lines 109–111; see note 45 of this chapter). Meanwhile, Tama Aweng's voice should rise up to **bílì' plaké** sounding as sweet as the music of **keluné** and **sapé** (lines 138–44; see note 50 of this chapter). The musical imagery is appropriate since Tama Aweng makes a great attempt to create a melodious prayer. The rising up of Tama Aweng's voice is described in a passage reminiscent of those used about sacrifice in prayer two (see note 68 of this chapter).

The qualifications of the eagle that is to answer his call are Tama Aweng's next topic (lines 150–64). It should not be a careless or inexperienced bird, and it should be one that nests near the deity.

In the closing section (lines 165–200), the exhortations "show your feathers," "fly like a Kayan dancing," and do not dawdle are repeated. In addition, the offerings in front of Tama Aweng are pointed out, and the seriousness of the procedure is emphasized by alluding to the taking of omens in war (lines 176–80).

Style: Of all the prayers, this one is perhaps the most polished, and the most pleasant to listen to. The reason for this is that the augur has many opportunities to practice his prayer during the hours or even days that it takes to complete a reading. There is no other event that allows a prayer to be repeated over and over in this fashion. Tama Aweng's style of **píat**, which we have already observed in prayer two, is clearly molded by his practice of **ngelaké**: the striving after long runs of parallel phrases, the modulated voice level varying in a studied way between loud and soft, and similarly the variation of speed, with some phrases lingered over lovingly and others shot through with dazzling speed. This prayer demonstrates more of these characteristics than does prayer two, but the effort to use them is present in both.

Tama Aweng begins in an almost conversational style. His audience is small and relaxed, unlike the noisy crowds that often surround prayer sites at large festivals. Consequently he has no need to raise his voice. The red-leafed **daren** plants are all around him, and the house stones are nearby. He addresses the spirits without histrionics, effectively conveying a sense of easy familiarity between the ritual habitué and the supernatural resources of the community.

Soon the tension increases, but he does not accomplish this by raising his voice. Throughout the prayer, Tama Aweng continues to speak in normal tones, in contrast to the exhortative style of prayers one and two. The feeling conveyed is correspondingly different: at the festival of Prayers of the House, the ancestors are summoned to a prearranged ritual. Here, a lone supplicant is coaxing a soaring bird to a rendezvous.

This increase in tension is caused by rhythmic devices. First, there is the constant repetition of the phrase **balí plakí**. This is a Kenyah pronunciation of **bílì' plaké** (see note 10 of this chapter), which alone makes it sound strange to Berawan ears. Also the long vowels of the Kenyah words, in contrast to the crisp Berawan ones, enable Tama Aweng to linger over them. The phrase is used anacrustically, as is indicated by the deep indentation. Often, it is said rapidly in the same breath as the last line, then

---

ooo . . .

- a kaam
- bílì' daren bílì' tapo'
- tu ko ngajoí ngaluroí
-     ngelíok ngeluwok tekelo'
- kaam bílì' ca

- tu díek la díek líwa telo'
- ngan kelo'

verse continues uninterrupted

there is a slight check, and a new line is said. At other times, it is said separately and slowly with a falling cadence. The hard vowels in the phrase make it conspicuous in either case.

Second, the passages that lie between the repetitions of **balí plakí** grow longer, are said more rapidly, and display formulaic parallelism as the prayer goes on. Though dispersed among slower, descriptive segments, the rapid, repetitive passages provide much of the rhythmic character. They are hard to hear on the tape, and in such passages lines are frequently run together breathlessly. By the same token, parallelism is occasionally flawed, that is, terms appear in a list without a pair word. In the avalanche of words, the flaws are not conspicuous. It is only the overall effect that matters.

The tension is relieved twice by the high-pitched, drawn-out calling noise described in the previous section. In each case the pace picks up again immediately afterwards, since the necessary descriptive passages are completed and only repetition remains.

Note: For an explanation of the conventions of notation, see chapter one. A synopsis of these conventions is provided on the last printed page of the book.

Calling noise

Where are you,

    spirits of sacred plants, spirits of the prayer station,[1]

    this is what I'm calling$_1$ calling$_2$

        shouting$_1$ shouting$_2$ to you,[2]

            you spirits of the community.[3]

This is our sacrificial$_1$ chicken, sacrificial$_2$ chicken,[4]

    for all of you,

verse continues uninterrupted

◆ kappì ngan no

◆ bílì' plaké apíu ní   10

▪ tupaan kaam

▪ bílì' tapo'

▪ kaam bílì' aman

▪ no kèta'u sekotèk tu'o

▪ kaam bílì' daren bílì' tapo'

▪ kaam bílì' bíto' tíloí

▪ kaam bílì' ca bílì' lía

◆ ra pu'ong ko mígín melín

▪   balí plakí

◆ ra pu'ong ko metun mugun   20

▪   balí plakí

▪ ícío tu

◆ urok kamé bulu mulong tu

▪ kíjì' penusaa kamé

· tílé sakèk bulu mulong ní

▪ sakèk lo gaya ní

◆ sakèk bukan sakèk kedíín

▪ urok tupo' Ukat

▪ anak Dau

▪ ano' ngaran Ballèng   30

▪ ano' bílì' daíyung ma[14] ní

◆ ano' bílì' buwan bílì' tekena'

◆ lo mano' nyí ngaran ní

◆ lo mano' nyí nanong ní

to ask for you,

10   spirit of the eagle up there.[5]

All of you,

spirits of the prayer station,

you spirits of the omen creatures,[6]

you noble, true tailorbird,[7]

you spirits of sacred plants, spirits of the prayer station,

you spirits of the house stones,[8]

you spirits of the community$_1$ spirits of the community$_2$[9]

I'm not lying when I call$_3$ I call$_4$

spirit of eagle,[10]

20   I'm not lying when I call$_5$ I call$_6$[11]

spirit of eagle,

today.

Because we human beings[12]

have a big problem;

look at this human illness,

an illness that appears,

sick-and-not-sick.

Because my grandson Ukat,

the child of Dau,

30   given the name Balleng,[13]

by the spirits of the shaman,[15]

by the spirits of songs, the spirits of stories,[16]

that gave him that name$_1$

that gave him that name$_2$[17]

- urok nyí lo sakèk
- mattacèk matta
- teleman kedíín lo mapan
- teleman mattacèk
- usaa nyí ugeng
- gejen gejen kedíín   40
- matta lapíu jiwé nyí

- ní a'an[20] kamé bulu mulong tu
- ra kanaí lo co[21] kamé tubor
- acì' no bílì' plaké ma lo kanaí kedíín ní

- ní an mínya an míka an metun an mugun
- balí plakí

- kaa no uram selawan
- kaa no metok semílok
- balí plakí

- tu raan telejang tu   50
- balí plakí

- telejang kín kakíng tu
- balí plakí
- bí nyí kelabé uted kenacau bílì'
- lo wong kabé nyí
- ané a'an no mada lécu
- mada bulu no
- balí plakí

Because he that is sick,

    rolls up his eyes,

    as if suddenly startled,

    suddenly rolling,

    his body stiff,[18]

40   and sort of shivering,

    his eyes going up into his head.[19]

That is why we humans,

    do not know how to care for him;

    you alone, spirit of eagle, know how.

That's why I call$_7$ why I call$_8$ why I call$_5$ why I call$_6$[22]

    spirit of eagle.

Don't waste time, dawdle,

don't hide$_1$ hide$_2$[23]

    spirit of eagle.

50   Here is what the augury sticks look like,[24]

    spirit of eagle:

The augury stick at the left here,

    spirit of eagle,

if he is bothered by a ghost, disturbed by a spirit,

that's what bothers him,[25]

there is where you should show your feathers$_1$

    show your feathers$_2$[26]

    spirit of eagle.

- tu telejang co jumé ko tu
-      balí plakí   60
- bí nyí tekena
- bí nyí palé
- ano' kellèjjé tína tama nyí díséí[29]
- ◆ jaka díséí nyílèng uní
- ní a'an no lívaí
-      balí plakí

- bí nyí tekena
- · íno íno ka nelían melínan ngan díséí
- · lo ngalacau ngan nyí
- ◆   balí plakí   70
- dekat tu telejang kín ketu'o
- ◆ ní a'an no lupo'
- ◆   balí plakí
- ◆ ní a'an no mada lécu mada bulu
- ◆   balí plakí

- ◆ kaa no meluwan seluwan
- ◆   balí plakí
- ◆ kaa no sengetok sengílok
- ◆   balí plakí

        ííí . . .   80

-      balí plakí
- · kuva no mapau matok sarok
- ◆   balí plakí

verse continues uninterrupted

This augury stick in front of me,

60   spirit of eagle,

      if he is bespelled,[27]

      if he is tabooed,[28]

because of something his mother or father did,

during the pregnancy,[30]

that's where you come,

             spirit of eagle.

If he is bespelled,

by whatever else might trouble$_1$ trouble$_2$ those two,

or disturb him,[31]

70   spirit of eagle,

near the right hand augury stick,

is where you should appear,

             spirit of eagle,

that is where you show your feathers$_1$ show your feathers$_2$

             spirit of eagle.

Don't dawdle$_3$ dawdle$_2$[32]

             spirit of eagle,

don't hide$_3$ hide$_4$[33]

             spirit of eagle.

80   *High pitched calling noise*[34]

          Spirit of eagle,

just answer for a moment$_1$ a moment$_2$[35]

          spirit of eagle,

verse continues uninterrupted

- íno kellèjjé
- íno kedíín kaam apíu
-         balí plakí
◆ kuva acì' usaa kelo' mapau jíu ko
-         balí plakí

- bíra ko ngabong ngabèng
◆   ngabong nyírèng   90
-         balí plakí

◆ nak umí pun[39] mílèk líma
◆ mílèk putéé co jumé ko
-         balí plakí
- ané a'an no mada lécu mada bulu
-         no balí plakí

◆ nak kíjì' tapaan kíjì' sagín
◆ langít manèng langít marèng
◆ langít buwéé langít putéé
◆ co jumé ko tu   100
-         balí plakí

◆ ní a'an no
◆ mada lécu mada bulu
◆ mada dètor mada èkor
◆ mada kepík mada pawèk
◆ mada peca mada tíma
◆ mada tegen mada aren
-         no balí plakí

whatever you're doing,

whatever you're up to up there,[36]

    spirit of eagle,

  just one of you, answer my call,[37]

    spirit of eagle.

I ask you to fly to the left$_1$ fly to the left$_2$

90   fly to the left$_1$ fly to the left$_3$[38]

    spirit of eagle.

However small the window of sky,[40]

of bright sky in front of me,

    spirit of eagle,

there is where you show your feathers$_1$ show your feathers$_2$

    you spirit of eagle.

Even if no bigger than a winnowing tray, a cutting board,[41]

  the blue$_1$ sky, the blue$_2$ sky,

  the bright$_1$ sky, the bright$_2$ sky,[42]

100   in front of me,

    spirit of eagle.

That is where you,

  show your feathers$_1$ show your feathers$_2$

  show your tail$_1$ show your tail$_2$

  show your wings$_1$ show your wings$_2$

  show your coverts$_1$ show your coverts$_2$

  show your pinions$_1$ show your pinions$_2$[43]

    you spirit of eagle.

◆ íko mejong tau la⁴⁴ ní ngan mejong saga Kayan

◆ co jumé ko tu   110

■   balí plakí

◆ bíra ko ngabong ngabèng

◆ ngabong nyírèng

■   balí plakí

◆ co ko ngabo co ko maso

◆ co ko masat co ko ngabat

◆ co ko katé co ko pela

◆ co ko nga co ko konga

■   balí plakí

◆ sakèk tuman co lunaa tuman co usaa tupo' Ukat   120

■   balí plakí

· atan kaam bílì' kaam pì' bílì'

■   balí plakí

■ kaam bílì' plaké ma

· nyí rapulé nyí ramulé

■   no balí plakí

■ ngabong ngabèng

◆ kaam lo manaí katé manaí ngelabé

◆   manaí ngíso

◆   manaí lígat manaí masat   130

◆   manaí katé manaí pulé

■   balí plakí

◆ ní a'an ko mínya ko míka

◆   ko metun ko mugun

verse continues uninterrupted

Fly now as gracefully as a Kayan dancing,[45]

110   in front of me,

spirit of eagle,

I ask you to fly to the left$_1$ fly to the left$_2$

fly to the left$_1$ fly to the left$_3$

spirit of eagle.

In order to expel$_1$ in order to expel$_2$

in order to heal$_1$ in order to heal$_2$

in order to throw away, in order to sweep away,

in order to eject$_1$ in order to eject$_2$[46]

spirit of eagle,

120   sickness from the body$_1$ from the body$_2$ of grandson Ukat,[47]

spirit of eagle.

It's for you spirits, all you spirits,

spirit of eagle,

you spirits of eagles,

to cure$_1$ him, to cure$_2$ him,

you spirit of eagle.[48]

Fly to the left$_1$ fly to the left$_2$

you that are skilled at throwing out$_1$ skilled at throwing out$_2$

skilled at removing,

130   skilled at healing$_3$ skilled at healing$_1$

skilled at throwing out$_1$ skilled at throwing out$_3$[49]

spirit of eagle.

That's why I'm calling$_7$ I'm calling$_8$

I'm calling$_5$ I'm calling$_6$

verse continues uninterrupted

◆   ko melín ko mígín

▪   no balí plakí

◆ díku keluné díku sapé

◆ díku kurèng díku pagíng

◆ attéé ko tu

◆ sakí co da sakí co uma   140

▪ sakí co dong sakí co padong

▪ sakí co lamín co lírín

▪ sakí co jalan

▪   no balí plakí apíu ní

◆ kaa kaam meluwan seluwan

◆ kaa kaam sengetok sengílok

▪   balí plakí

◆ kaa bíra plaké lo nyíbu lo muju

◆ kaa bíra plaké lo keléjéo lo seluréo

▪ a plaké lo laan lo kelabaan   150

▪ plakè lo mukong lièk mukong pawèk

▪ akí sema díek

▪   sema bíkuí

▪ uvì'sadì'

◆ ukun dupun ko uní

◆ ní lo mapau jíu ko mínya

◆   jíu ko míka

▪ a plaké lo sara urau sara padong

▪ Bungan Penyalong

verse continues uninterrupted

I'm calling$_4$ I'm calling$_3$

you spirit of eagle.

Like the tune of the pipes, the tune of the strings,

the tune of the mouth harp, the tune of the harp,

let my voice be,[50]

140 arriving at the house$_1$ arriving at the house$_2$

arriving at the fastness$_1$ arriving at the fastness$_2$

arriving at the house$_3$ arriving at the house$_4$

arriving at the paths,

of you spirit of eagle up there.[51]

Don't dawdle$_3$ dawdle$_2$

don't hide$_3$ hide$_4$

spirit of eagle,

don't send an eagle that is careless$_1$ that is careless$_2$

don't send an eagle that is offhand$_1$ that is offhand$_2$[52]

150 Where is the eagle that is proper$_1$ that is proper$_2$[53]

the eagle with old wings$_1$ old wings$_2$[54]

because of the blood of the chicken,

the blood of the pig,

of my grandparents$_1$ of my grandparents$_2$

of my grandparents$_3$ of my grandparents$_4$ long ago;[55]

that's the one to answer my call$_7$

my call$_8$

Where is the eagle that is near the seat, near the fastness,

of Bungan Penyalong,[56]

verse continues uninterrupted

- nyí lo mapau lívaí   160
- nyí ko mínya nyí ko míka
- nyí ko metun nyí ko mugun
- nyí ko melín nyí ko mígín
-         balí plakí

- tu díek la díek líwa
-     díek turíp díek takíp
-         no balí plakí

- tu laam tu supa' tu pakaan
- tu agung tu sanang
- síngau sapau   170
-         no balí plakí

- kaa no lacík
-         balí plakí
- kaa no meluwan seluwan
-         balí plakí
- sadeng pun bawa gíku bawa gíto'
-         balí plakí
- wong dé metun no
-         balí plakí
- atan no tubor bulu mulong   180
-         balí plakí
- co díta' co tanaa tu
-         balí plakí
- kuva kuva pa no mapau jíu ko
-         balí plakí

160   he is the one to answer, to come,

                 he I call$_7$ he I call$_8$

                 he I call$_5$ he I call$_6$

                 he I call$_4$ he I call$_3$

                         spirit of eagle.

This is the chicken of sacrifice$_1$, the chicken of sacrifice$_2$[57]

       the chicken of life$_1$ the chicken of life$_2$[58]

              you spirit of eagle.

This is the tobacco, this is the betel, these are the offerings,[59]

       in this gong$_1$ in this gong$_2$[60]

170   to feed$_1$ to feed$_2$[61]

              you spirit of eagle.

Don't be frightened,

              spirit of eagle,

      don't dawdle$_3$ don't dawdle$_2$

              spirit of eagle,

although it was a war of hundreds$_1$ a war of hundreds$_2$[62]

              spirit of eagle,

still they called you,[63]

              spirit of eagle,

180   it is for you to care for the human beings,

              spirit of eagle,

in this plain, in this land,

              spirit of eagle,

try to answer what I say,

              spirit of eagle.

ííí . . .

▪   balí plakí

◆ mada lécu mada bulu

◆ mada dètor mada èkor

◆ mada kepík mada pawèk   190

◆ mada tegen mada aren

▪   balí plakí

◆ anyí co lírín pakaan

▪   balí plakí

· ngelínga atong anak metun

▪   balí plakí

◆ íko mejong ma tau mejong saga Kayan

▪   balí plakí

◆ kuva pa no sagem lupo'

▪   balí plakí   200

High pitched calling noise

Spirit of eagle,

show your feathers$_1$ show your feathers$_2$

show your tail$_1$ show your tail$_2$

190   show your wings$_1$ show your wings$_2$

show your pinions$_1$ show your pinions$_2$

spirit of eagle.

receive the offerings in your house,

spirit of eagle,

hear our call,[64]

spirit of eagle,

as gracefully as a Kayan dancing in front of me,

spirit of eagle,

appear now quickly,

200   spirit of eagle.

8.

Adèd Bungan—A Prayer for the Festival of Bungan

The last prayer is the longest, as long as the first two put together. It resembles them also in that it is intended to secure the welfare of the entire community for the coming year. Like them, it is spoken at an annual longhouse festival, but this festival is not the **papì' lamèng** of the traditional religion. Instead the festival belongs to a new indigenous faith, a revivalist cult of sorts, named after its principal deity, Bungan.

The Spread of the Bungan Cult

Hard data about the origins of the Bungan cult, as it has come to be called, is difficult to come by. Only a couple of brief descriptive articles are in

214

print, written by people who were not close to the events. These accounts agree that the cult was initiated by a man called Jok Apoi in the late 1940s in Indonesian Borneo, on the far side of the mountain range that bisects northern Borneo. They disagree about whether Jok Apoi was a Kayan or a Kenyah (although the latter seems likely since Bungan is a Kenyah deity), and whether he was following the traditional religion or christianity prior to his revelation. The latter confusion is significant since the Bungan cult constitutes a rejection of both and an attempt to integrate their perceived advantages.

In the most frequently told version, Jok Apoi was a poor man who year after year failed to produce enough rice to feed his family. Then, he had a dream in which he was confronted by Bungan, a gentle female deity often portrayed as the wife of the supreme deity, Bali Penyalong. She told Jok Apoi that his crops failed because he observed all the traditional taboos, rather than tending to his farm. This is the same pragmatic message that missionaries were urging on interior folk at the time, as an inducement to become Christian. Bungan instructed Jok Apoi to disregard the bad omens that previously kept him at home, and to disregard also the expensive or inconvenient taboos, such as those surrounding trophies of the headhunt. Jok Apoi did as he was told, and his farm prospered. Despite the ridicule of the noble elite, others increasingly followed his example.

In the 1950s, the Bungan cult spread over the mountains into Sarawak, but the details of that expansion need not concern us here. The point is that it provided a third alternative in the bitter competition then in progress between the old religions, slightly different in each community but everywhere offering a rich ritual life, and the powerful but alien Christianity. To many, the cult seemed to offer the best of both religions. It abolished those usages that seemed to stand in the way of progress, but it drew upon indigenous sources. In 1956, a party of Bungan missionaries traveled down the Baram, preaching as they went. They converted many among both the old religionists and those who had recently gone Christian. Yet they were more successful with the former than the latter, and in the next decade that was to prove fatal. At its zenith of influence in the late 1950s and early 1960s, Bungan could probably claim as many adherents in the Baram river watershed as Christianity. The traditional religions had meanwhile all but disappeared. Since then, there has been a steady, piecemeal erosion of Bungan adherents, and no one goes back to the old religions, which cannot operate without full communal support. With the wisdom of hindsight, it becomes clear that Bungan only prepared the way for Christianity by undermining the shared certainties of the old religions.

A *Berawan Prophet*

For many years the Berawan were insulated from these disruptive currents. Several features served to keep them apart: first, the designs of the Christian missionaries, who set their sights on the large ethnic groups of the interior and passed by the less numerous and more worldly Berawan. Second, the relative social isolation of the Berawan. The Kayan and Kenyah (see the introduction) in the Baram river area are connected by a network of noble marriages, so that influences flow readily from one community to another. But the Berawan, earlier immigrants to the region, kept themselves apart. Third, Berawan cosmology is unreceptive to the Bungan cult in one major respect. The Kayan supreme deity Laki Tenangan has a consort, Doh Tenangan, just as the Kenyah Bali Penyalong has Bungan. The Berawan Creator Spirit has none.

Ultimately, these features only served to delay innovation. As for the Bungan, it made no progress against Berawan indifference until a prophet emerged from among their own ranks.

Sadi Pejong comes from a noble family at Long Jegan, and his elder brother was headman in the immediate postwar period. However, Sadi Pejong was slow to emerge as a leader himself. He was an introspective young man, and he formed idiosyncratic opinions about matters of ritual. As a teenager, he helped reopen a large and already well-stocked mausoleum so that a new corpse could be inserted. He was disgusted by the experience, and he decided that the long decline that the Berawan had suffered in population and power, according to their legends, was the result of the practice of secondary treatment of the dead (see chapter six). No doubt, he also heard about the new Bungan cult among the Kayan and the Kenyah. In the mid-1950s he began to experience strange dreams, a composite of Berawan cosmology and things that he had seen during the Second World War. In one dream, a mystical airplane landed on the river outside the longhouse and took him on a heavenly tour. After a particularly intense vision in which he received instruction from Bungan herself, he made his inspiration public and announced a new order. Initially he was followed by the residents of only three rooms in the longhouse, but even this small minority was sufficient to force intense discussion. Most people wanted to avoid a religious split in the community: either everyone should hang on to the old religion or adopt Christianity, or follow Sadi Pejong's version of Bungan. This desirable consensus was already doomed, however, and the old religion consequently weakened.

There were three mutually incompatible opinions. Some wanted to preserve the old way come hell or high water. In this party were Tama Avit and his nephew Uking, whom we met in chapters four and five respectively. Some were prepared to accept some change, but distrusted the foreign missionaries. Yet others were contemptuous of Sadi Pejong. They were prepared to stay with the old way, or go Christian en masse, but not to follow Bungan. No clear resolution was possible, and dissension continues to this day. The result was similar to that in the Baram river generally. At first, Bungan appeared to triumph. By 1960, the majority of families at Long Jegan had agreed to follow it, and religious unity was almost recovered. Under Sadi Pejong's leadership, all the taboos of the old religion were abolished and ritual life was drastically simplified. In particular, the long, complex, and expensive death rites were abridged, and secondary treatment of the dead terminated. Sadi Pejong looks back wistfully on those years when the annual festival of Bungan animated almost the entire community. But there were from the start those who remained recalcitrant. Some moved away, either to Long Teru where the old religion was determinedly maintained, or to found a daughter community. Others stayed put but showed their disapproval by converting to Christianity. The ranks of this minority were swelled by political rivals when Sadi Pejong became headman after his brother's death. Missionaries maintained a steady pressure, seeing to it that any non-Christian who married a Christian converted first. Every defection weakened Sadi Pejong's authority. By 1973 the community was split about evenly between the two, just the circumstances that most people had wanted to avoid.

February 3, 1973

Sadi Pejong's revised ritual year climaxed in a festival oddly synchronized by reference to a calendar irrelevant to Berawan life. The date he chose was Chinese New Year, a major event in the towns and cities of the coast, but virtually unknown upriver. In 1973 harvesting was not yet completed at that time, which made for some inconvenience. However, it was already clear that the harvest would not be good, a fact repeatedly mentioned in Sadi Pejong's prayer.

The days prior to the festival were busy with preparations, principally to ensure that there would be enough food and rice wine. Early on the appointed day, women were busy setting up tables at two places on the longhouse veranda, both decorated with cloths, artificial flowers, and valuable brassware. The resemblance to an altar was obvious. On the tables were those offerings that Sadi Pejong enumerates at the beginning of his prayer—special delicacies, rice wine, tobacco. By nine o'clock about fifty people were seated around the table outside Sadi Pejong's room, much less than the total Bungan congregation but including the heads of most households. Other adherents joined in later in the day. The proceedings began with a prayer by Sadi Pejong, the prayer that is recorded in this chapter. It was the longest that I ever heard, and dealt exhaustively with all aspects of longhouse welfare. It was received attentively, in contrast to the irreverent chatter that often accompanies prayers at Long Teru. The atmosphere was indeed similar to a prayer meeting of the Christians, but that was to change as the day wore on.

One distinctly non-Christian element was the sacrificial chicken, which Sadi Pejong waved about by its feet during his prayer, charging it with messages for both the Creator Spirit and Bungan together. This combination distinguishes Sadi Pejong's version of Bungan from that of neighboring Kayan and Kenyah adherents. The latter have retired their male supreme deities, who are regarded as having little interest in the affairs of men anymore, and address their prayers instead to the friendly figure of "grandmother Bungan." If Sadi Pejong had done the same, he would have been left with a goddess lacking a counterpart in Berawan cosmology. His compromise was to retain the properly Berawan Creator Spirit in addition to Bungan, and indeed to give him priority over her. Lesser spirit agencies, usually talked about in terms of the harm that they might do, were not addressed directly. Instead, the Creator and Bungan were asked to intervene to control them. The ancestral spirits, so prominent in the prayers of papì' lamèng at Long Teru, were inconspicuous in Sadi Pejong's prayer.

Once he had completed the prayer and sacrificed the chicken, Sadi Pejong beckoned other leading men in the community to join him. This they did with gusto, raising their voices to a crescendo of prayer, and finally merging them in a loud humming noise. This is the sound that the crowd at a party makes to encourage some individual who is currently the center of attention to down his glass of rice wine in one go. The procedure was repeated five times, causing everyone to became more animated. Bottles of rice wine circulated freely among the crowds until it was time to move over to the other table of offerings. This table was set up outside the room of Sadi Pejong's most important backer, Sadi Ulau, a man of impeccable pedigree who nevertheless preferred to let others take the lead in day-to-day affairs. There the prayers were repeated, first by Sadi Pejong alone (but briefly this time), and then by the senior men together, who were joined by a couple of latecomers. Everyone drank more rice wine before the party moved off to a third location, inside the apartment of a staunchly Bungan family. The party traveled from there to a fourth location, and then to a fifth, always saying prayers—though successively less formal at each stop—and always drinking plenty of rice wine.

By early afternoon an easy sociality was well established, with knots of people wandering from room to room to sample the food prepared for the occasion, to drink, and to chat. The early starters, Sadi Pejong included, retired to take a nap before the evening's events, but not before a pig had been sacrificed with due ceremony before the **kaju uran** (**kaju** means "wood," **uran** is untranslatable). This mysterious structure, mentioned several times by Sadi Pejong in his prayer, consisted of a carved post set up outside the longhouse in front of the apartment of Sadi Ulau. The original **kaju uran** was built by a prestigious ancestor of Sadi Ulau, who had received the inspiration for it in a dream. The structure has been renewed every decade or so, in effect proclaiming the superior social status of its owners.

That evening, and far into the night, kerosene lanterns burned brightly along the veranda. An elaborate party had been organized with all manner of games to amuse young and old. Despite the disapproving presence of a Christian missionary, almost everyone was successfully drawn into the festivities. Over a filled glass, convert and conservative alike agreed that the only important value was neighborliness. The festivities continued the next day. Though the festival of Bungan was completed, it was followed by a wedding, and then a **kumaan selamat** (see chapter four), initiating an informal ritual season.

Prayer Seven

Speaker: Sadi Pejong

Time: The entire prayer runs 22 minutes and 10 seconds, over four times as long as the average of the other six prayers (4 minutes and 40 seconds), and nearly three times as long as the next longest, Tama Aweng's prayer in chapter three (8 minutes). At the time, I thought that the length of Sadi Pejong's prayer, as well as some of its themes, might have been provoked by my presence. But on reflection, I doubt that this is true. This prayer is a set piece; there would be no similar occasion for a whole year. Because **tapo'** (prayer stations) are not prepared by adherents of Bungan, there are few opportunities during the year for formal prayer. Other prayers at this festival were made by many speakers simultaneously, or in particular rooms in the longhouse. It is appropriate that this opening prayer, made by the prophet himself, should be weighty.

Two short passages have been elided in order to make the text that much briefer and more readable. They had little to offer in understanding either form or content. Substantively, they rehash in summary topics already covered. Stylistically, they reveal nothing that is not already more than adequately displayed in the bulk of the prayer. What does appear is about eighty percent of the whole, and the locations of the cuts are indicated.

Summary: It is interesting to compare Sadi Pejong's prayer with those in chapter three. There are many similar themes, each dealing with the general welfare of the community and the role of sacrifice. There are even figures that recur, for instance when Sadi Pejong asks for "a good life, a cool life, a happy life," (lines 224–26), or speaks of the spiritual power (**ketí balí**) of sacrifice (line 107), in phrases similar to those used by both Tama Jok and Tama Aweng.

But such similarities of language are few, and Sadi Pejong's prayer is different in at least three major respects. First, it is more self-conscious. While Tama Aweng and Tama Jok begin with the theme of invocation, launching directly into their appeals, Sadi Pejong starts out with an explanation, a lengthy statement of what is happening and why. Second, when Sadi Pejong does come to invocation, it is handled in a different way. Only the Creator and Bungan are invoked directly, and the formula linking their titles is indeed the single most conspicuous metrical device in the prayer. Other spirit agencies are acknowledged but dealt with only through the Creator and Bungan. Those two are asked to summon benign spirits to share the offerings, and to intermediate with dangerous or malign ones. The ancestors, so prominent in the prayers of Tama Jok and Tama Aweng, are inconspicuous here. It is easy to see the influence of Christian teaching in all this. Third, Sadi Pejong's prayer contains more references to modern circumstances, such as travel and schooling. However, it would not do to overstate this difference: his principal concerns are the familiar ones of health and wealth, and Tama Jok and Tama Aweng do not avoid mentioning anxieties novel to the last two decades.

At times, Sadi Pejong sounds like a company director making his annual report to the shareholders, those adherents sitting at his feet. Despite a superficial appearance of moving erratically from topic to topic, an appearance mainly produced by the repetition of passages *sotto voce*, he in fact deals methodically with a handful of general themes. Evidently, he thought out in advance what he was going to say. The main topics are as follows:

1) an opening apologia;
2) the instructions to the sacrificial chicken;
3) the message to be delivered;
4) his concerns about the prevalence of sickness;
5) people away from the community;
6) a supplication for help with topographical spirits;
7) and, lastly, a desire to "wall off" the community against malign outside influences.

Sadi Pejong begins soberly with a description of the religious division in the community, and the origins of his version of the Bungan, which emerged only a little over a decade before the prayer was made. There are two things to note about the translation: first, the context requires that the word **adèd** be glossed in two ways, as "festival" and as "religion," since the concept is wider than either (see the introduction). Second, the entity **bílíe ngaputíeng** is rendered as "Creator Spirit." The same title in every preceding prayer is translated "spirit that creates." The difference here is that Sadi Pejong does not employ the dual formula that is characteristic of prayer in the traditional religion (see chapter two). Instead the Creator Spirit is balanced, time after time, against the personally named Bungan. In lines 11–20, he lists the offerings that are set on the table before him, presumably for the benefit of the Creator Spirit and Bungan, although he gives the impression that he is checking everything over for himself. In lines 21–36 he introduces the notables of the community, casting his eyes around the crowd as he does so. This list makes a nice contrast with the one that Tama Jok gives at the outset of his prayer at **papì' lamèng.** Tama Jok's great men are the leaders of past generations, the ancestral spirits. Once the introductions are completed, Sadi Pejong fussily lists the offerings again (lines 37–47) before describing the purpose of the festival, which is to allow the spirits and humans "together to sit in this very place" (lines 48–79). A mention of rice and "fullness" leads to the first of several plaintive interjections about the poor rice crop (lines 80–89). Lines 90–102 repeat the message of lines 48–79.

For so important an occasion, one might expect a pig to be sacrificed. Yet the animal repeatedly addressed from line 103 onward is only a chicken. Sadi Pejong expresses the hope that it will have great spiritual power anyway (lines 103–108), and then charges it to carry all the offerings to the Creator and Bungan (109–118). The correct path to take is described in detail (lines 119–38), as is what is to be expected when the chicken arrives at the house of the Creator, with its golden stairs (lines 139–49).

There the burdened chicken is to serve all the offerings, again listed (lines 150–59), before delivering its message from "all the Berawan" (lines 160–68). This begins with reverent salutations, but rapidly turns into a complaint about the poor rice crop (lines 169–81). This complaint is rubbed in by pointing out that they are again spending good money on offerings for the festival of the new year. Lines 182–88 contain an image of worship, involving giving "greetings from their feet to the crowns of their heads." Before moving to the next theme, there is a reprise of the purpose of the festival of the new year, this time with an emphasis on the participation of the ancestors (lines 189–202).

In a long section (lines 203–242), Sadi Pejong talks about the illness and hardship that afflict the community. First, the epidemics of flu that occur during the season when certain jungle flowers bloom (lines 203–207). Next, Sadi Pejong complains that there is too much hunger and death in the community, despite the faith of the people and their pleas for a good life (lines 208–260). It is up to the Creator and Bungan to expel "devils" that cause "frailty," and death. The note of complaint is briefly reversed in lines which ask for "forgiveness." Since Berawan lacks a word for this concept, Sadi Pejong adapts the Malay term **ampun**. The following lines (261–99) are concerned with errant souls, and contain two interesting images of the Creator as bookkeeper, reckoning the days of peoples' lives. In the first, the Creator keeps a string (**tebukau**) with a knot for each day. Sadi Pejong urges the Creator to subvert the system by tying new knots so that everyone will live a hundred years. The second envisages the Creator keeping track of "signs" (**sa'ín**), so that they should not become "enough" (see note 89 of this chapter).

Sadi Pejong's is next concerned with people absent from the community (lines 300–316). Some are away seeking modern medical attention, others are at school, and others are working for logging companies. Sadi Pejong insists that their absence does not mean a loss of faith. He seems to be intuitively aware, however, that the indigenous religion cannot operate outside the environment of a cohesive longhouse community.

The next theme displays a more traditional concern with spirits of the place, showing that the simplification brought about by Bungan did not extend to elimination of minor spiritual agencies (lines 317–43). The Creator and Bungan are asked to intercede with the spirits of the land and the river to prevent them from harming humans. Sadi Pejong is particularly worried that the noise of children playing on the soccer field by the elementary school will disturb the spirits of the nearby mountain.

Finally, Sadi Pejong speaks movingly of the need to insulate his community against all manner of disruptive influences, both human and spiritual (lines 344–87). He talks of a mystical barrier (**rèng**), much like the ones shamans used in the past to keep out the epidemics that swept periodically through the Baram watershed. He wants to exclude not only malign spirit forces, but also humans who sow dissension within, and slander without, the community. Most of all, he is concerned about Iban and Kayan moving onto village land when Berawan are already hard pressed to find good soil for farms. This theme is one we have heard before—in chapter five—and Sadi Pejong is no doubt thinking of the trouble-making Uking throughout this passage. Sadi Pejong's prayer closes with a last reference to the food offered to the Creator and to Bungan.

Style: Stylistically, Sadi Pejong's prayer contrasts with those spoken by Tama Jok and Tama Aweng in chapter three. Just as the Bungan cult brought a simplification in ideology and particularly in ritual, so the mode of **píat** becomes less internally structured, almost bland.

Sadi Pejong begins his prayer slowly. The phrases are clearly separated and easy to understand, almost conversational. After the first fifty lines or so he begins to speed up, gathering momentum throughout his long performance. But even after he gathers speed, Sadi Pejong's prayer continues to resemble normal speech more closely than the **píat** of either Tama Jok or Tama Aweng. The verses into which the translation is assembled are sometimes mere paragraphs, lacking internal organization. A simple syntactical parallelism is most evident, with whole lines repeated verbatim. Sadi Pejong does not employ the staccato mode of delivery that marked the **píat** of Uking and Lian Yang (in prayers four and five, respectively); quite the contrary, he allows lines to run on until he runs out of breath.

Sadi Pejong's main device is a variation between two voice levels. Typically, he opens a segment with an appeal to the Creator and Bungan. Next follows the main message of the segment, produced in phrases that are sometimes run together and spoken rapidly. Phonologically, these constitute lines that are, however, too long to be accommodated on one line of transcription. Consequently, they are broken up into two or more lines of the transcription and the translation. Such run-on lines are indicated by devices both in the transcription and the translation. Three ellipsis points at the end of a line of Berawan text indicate that there is no real pause in voice production, or change in intonation, before the next line. In the translation these part-lines have no ending punctuation.

At the close of a succession of long phrases, Sadi Pejong typically drops his voice to a whisper, producing a series of lines that are highly repetitive, often garbled. In the transcription, all four intonations are indicated, but the principal contrast is simply between these two modes of delivery. In the former, Sadi Pejong talks just loud enough to be audible to most of his audience, which is for the most part quiet and attentive. If there is shuffling, Sadi Pejong raises his voice a little more but not much. Apart from the occasionally rapid delivery, there is little difficulty in making out what is said. Even a casual listener could follow the general drift of the prayer. In the latter mode, Sadi Pejong evidently does not intend to be heard. Even though the microphone was positioned closer to him than was most of his audience, it did not pick up his words clearly. It is as if he were talking quietly to his spirits, forgetting for the moment his human audience.

Two minor idiosyncracies of Sadi Pejong's **píat** are also worth pointing out. First, he tends to muddle personal pronouns. Often when he means "we" (**kaméí**), meaning his congregation, he says "they" (**déí**). This is because, after line 159, all Sadi Pejong's statements are words that the sacrificial chicken is instructed to repeat to the Creator and Bungan. To remind himself and us of this, he occasionally inserts the phrase **jíu no díek** (you say, chicken). For the second person singular he uses indiscriminately the forms **kau** and **no,** and sometimes one of these forms when he clearly should employ the plural form (**kaam**). Second, he employs many words that are borrowed or adapted from Malay. This feature is consistent with the nontraditional nature of the Bungan cult and is particularly significant when Sadi Pejong is discussing abstract concepts for which there is no counterpart in traditional Berawan religious ideas.

Note: For an explanation of the conventions of notation, see chapter one. A synopsis of these conventions is provided on the last printed page of the book.

Figure 9. Sadi Pejong says a prayer at the annual festival of the Bungan cult described in chapter eight. A table set with offerings is before him and in his hand is a whip made of **caang** leaves. In earlier times, these leaves were used to decorate the trophies of headhunting raids.

- tu adèd bílíe ngaputíeng
- co[1] uko Bungan

- tu'o pa[3] adèd kaméí ma rè duvéí
- adèd sebayang sebarèng
- adèd bílíe ngaputíeng uko Bungan sebarèng
- tapí rè adèd uko Bungan . . .
- ngan bílíe ngaputíeng lo co mukéí . . .
- pang lum lía lum lamèng kuvít
- tuman bun staat
- kaméí píléo adèd   10

- a kau díek kau tíku . . .
- kau caang kaam dínu kelupéí
- supa' sígup kaam borèk
- wíong píe cukup
- wíong kopí wíong lotí
- wíong arak
- wíong píe nyíkínan

- barang lo tenítèng
- kaméí wíong píe
- wíong píe sedía atau   20

- tu píe tupaan lo kíjíe
- tu'o pa ma rè jat
- kedíín

verse continues uninterrupted

This is the festival of the Creator Spirit,

and grandmother Bungan.[2]

It's true that our religions here are two,

part Christian,[4]

part Bungan,[5]

but this is the festival of grandmother Bungan

and the Creator Spirit that we have used to open

gatherings in the community, in the longhouse,

from the start,[6]

10   when we changed our religion.[7]

Where are you chicken, you eggs

you palm leaves, you cooked food, savory rice,[8]

betel nut, tobacco, you rice wine,[9]

there is enough of everything,

there is coffee, there is bread,[10]

there is liquor,[11]

there are all kinds of food.

The things that needed arranging,

we have completed,

20   everything is ready here.

These are all the leaders,[12]

truly not without merit,

like:

verse continues uninterrupted

- Sadíe ulau kedíín
- Sadíe Payau tílau
- Tama Píno tílau
- Tama Lanyíng ngan tupaan dínak wíong píe atau
-                tupaan anak umí wíong píe atau
- Sadie Ujan déi
- Melawan Long Jegín tu   30
- lakéí díccu
- anak umí kíjíe
- wíong píe turau pupang atau
- ngabenar ngabesar
- adèd bílíe ngaputíeng adéd uko Bungan
- lo an[20] kaméí suva an lava

- ní a'an puku an bíra . . .
- akí díek
- kau kíku kau cang
- kílaan dínu kílaan kelupéí . . .   40
- supa kílaan sígup
- kílaan borèk
- kílaan rotí kílaan nyíkínaan dítíu
- kílaan kopí
- co ngusaí co ngelamaí
- co makan co nguman
- adèd bílíe ngaputíeng ngan uko Bungan

- arap ngan no bílíe ngaputíeng . . .
- arap ngan no uko Bungan
- nyípang tupaan bílíe sadíe kaméí   50

verse continues uninterrupted

Sadi Ulau,[13]

Sadi Puyan and his people,[14]

Tama Pino and his people,

Tama Lanying and all the young people are here,[15]

all the small children are here,

Sadi Ujan and his folks,[16]

30   the Berawan of Long Jegan,[17]

the men and women,

children large and small,

are all sitting here,[18]

    to celebrate$_1$ to celebrate$_2$[19]

    the festival of the Creator, the festival of Bungan,

    in which we take pride$_1$ take pride$_2$[21]

That's why we may ask$_1$ why we may ask$_2$[22]

    because of the chicken,

    you eggs, you palm leaves,

40   bringing cooked food, bringing savory rice

    betel, bringing tobacco,

    bringing rice wine,

    bringing bread, bringing the food here,

    bringing coffee,

        to make festive$_1$ to make festive$_2$

        to provision$_1$ to provision$_2$[23]

    the festival of the Creator Spirit and grandmother Bungan.

We hope that you Creator Spirit,

we hope that you grandmother Bungan,

50   will gather all the spirits of our grandparents,

verse continues uninterrupted

- lo tuman tero tuman penga
- sadíe kaméí lo ngasan kaméí atong Meletíng tu
- Melawan lo bun mulong atong Meletíng tu

- a bílíe sadíe kaméí
- lo tubor kaméí . . .
- co lía co pang . . .
- lo tuman tero tuman penga
- bílíe kaju uran mang

- arap no bílíe ngaputíeng tawa tutok . . .
- turau co an co sedang   60
- bílíe daíyung mang
- bílíe luppéí
- kaméí Melawan Long Jegín co laméng kuvít tu ní

- arap no bílíe ngaputíeng
- tawa lívaí tutok seluyok
- turau acíe an acíe sedang

- mala déí jíen ngelínga jíu
- tupaan lakéí tupaan dínak
- tupaan anak umí tupaan díccu

- menamba menabí   70
- bílíe ngaputíeng
- menamba menabí
- bílíe sadíe kaméí
- bílíe paraí kaméí mang
- bílíe pecco kaméí mang

from the past, from old times,[24]

our ancestors that are our origin along the Meleting,[25]

the Berawan that first lived along the Meleting.

Where are our ancestors,

who looked after us

in our community, in our gatherings

from the past, from old times,[26]

also spirits of the uran post.[27]

We hope that you Creator Spirit will call them all

60   together to come to this place,[28]

also spirits of shamans,

spirits of dreams,[29]

of us Berawan of Long Jegan in this longhouse.

We hope that you Creator Spirit,

will call them to come together$_1$ together$_2$

to sit in this very place$_1$ very place$_2$[30]

Make them listen well to what is said,

all the men, all the young people,

all the small children, all the women.

70   We greet you, salute you,[31]

Creator Spirit,

we greet you, salute you,

spirit of the grandparents,

and again, our spirits of rice,

and again, our spirits of fullness.[32]

- arap ngan no bílíe ngaputíeng vaí turau . . .
- nutok nyululok tílau . . .
- turau kaséí uko Bungan
- mala dítíu déí lo kumaan lo kanaan

■ arap kaméí Melawan tu selalu cukup   80
■ arap kaméí Melawan tu selalu semup
- mala jíen paraí

- aroo ní lo nacau lírèk kaméí tau tu
- kenacau ulan kenacau cen
- ní a'an puku paraí kaméí ra berapa mulong

- arap bílíe ngaputíeng tawa
- bílíe paraí kaméí
- tawa bílíe sadíe kaméí
- vaí turau acíe an acíe legan

■ urok kaméí ícío tu   90
■ tu ícío bulíin
■ tau lo lupau mang
- kaméí selalu naku nyíkínaan
■ co ngusaí ngalamaí
- bílíe ngaputíeng
- ngusaí ngalamaí
- uko Bungan
- ngusaí ngalamaí
- bílíe luppéí kaméí
- bílíe bítau kaméí   100

verse continues uninterrupted

We hope that you Creator Spirit will come and sit

together$_1$ together$_3$ with them[33]

sit with grandmother Bungan, you two,[34]

to partake of these comestibles, this food.[35]

80   We hope we Berawan will always have enough$_1$

we hope we Berawan will always have enough$_2$[36]

getting good rice.

There are many things that damage our farms this year,

damaged by worms, damaged by animals,

that's the reason our rice is not much to live on.[37]

We hope the Creator Spirit will call,

the spirits of our rice,

call the spirits of our grandparents,

to come and sit in this very place$_1$ very place$_3$[38]

90   Because we, this day,

this day of the month,

each new year,

we always serve food,

to celebrate$_3$ to celebrate$_4$[39]

the Creator Spirit,

to celebrate$_3$ to celebrate$_4$

grandmother Bungan,

to celebrate$_3$ to celebrate$_4$

the spirits of our dreams,

100   the spirits of our stones,[40]

verse continues uninterrupted

- bílíe lo tubor kaméí lo jaga kaméí
- kaméí Melawan tu

- arap ngan no díek
- tu'o peno kíjíe ka sekotèk
- ra kíjíe ka temenggang
- ♦ ra kíjíe ka tepíon
- tapí kíjíe ketí balí
- ngan luvat ngan balat

- kau kabí mekí
- kau kílaan tupaan   110
- dínu kelupéí supa sígup
- kílaan nyíkínaan
- borèk dítíu
- barang dítíu
- ♦ nuvang a'an nuvang sebang . . .
- ♦ nuvang lenaa nuvang usaa . . .
- ♦ bílíe ngaputíeng ngan uko Bungan
- ♦ bílíe víe bílíe sadíe

- kau bílíe díek cíe ngusau cíe lakau
-             cíe dítaí cíe selaí   120
- kíku ngapulu nun . . .
- lo abang lo mawang . . .
- lo líma lo mengada
- ní a'an ngusau an lakau bílíe díek
- kaa kau pabéí kaa kau peréí

the spirits that look after, that guard us,

us Berawan.

We hope in you, chicken,

although no bigger than a tailorbird,[41]

not as big as a black hornbill,

not as big as a rhinoceros hornbill,[42]

yet big as charm, as spirit,[43]

with $strength_1$ with $strength_2$[44]

You carry these offerings,

110   you carry all,

the cooked food, savory rice, betel, tobacco,

carry the food,

this rice wine,

these things,

to meet at the $place_1$ to meet at the $place_2$

to meet the $persons_1$ to meet the $persons_2$[45]

of the Creator Spirit and grandmother Bungan,

the spirits of $grandparents_1$ of $grandparents_2$.

You spirit of chicken, $travel_1$ $travel_2$[46]

120   across the $plain_1$ across the $plain_2$[47]

$follow_1$ $follow_2$ the path

that is $clear_1$ that is $clear_2$

that is $bright_1$ that is $bright_2$[48]

that's where you $walk_1$ where you $walk_2$

don't get $lost_1$ don't get $lost_2$[49]

- macau lakau bílíe díek

- apabíla wíong nun lo semèk lo sapat . . .
- lo jat lo pelaya bíkín kakíng
- atan no tíléí atan no ngelatéí
- nun lo bílíe leta ní   130
- kaa nun ní

- a nun
- lo abang mawang . . .
- lo líma lo mengada tu'o
- ní nun macau lakau
- kau bílíe díek

- macau lakau bílíe díek
- kíku ngapulu nun lo líma lo mengada

- bíla metau numau acíe lamèng mang
- lamèng líma lamèng mengada   140
- ní lamèng temaga ní lamèng bílíe ngaputíeng . . .
- ní a'an lakau ní a'an kílaan nyíkínaan dítíu

- sakí co acín bílíe ngaputíeng . . .
- acín mat bílíe ngaputíeng
- 　　　　bílíe díek
- síka co acín mat bílíe ngaputíeng
- síka co lamèng bílíe ngaputíeng
- síka co sebang bílíe ngaputíeng
- 　　　　bílíe díek

Walk$_3$ walk$_1$ spirit of chicken.[50]

Whenever there is a path that is wet, that is overgrown

that is bad, that is made all to the left,

watch out$_1$ watch out$_2$[51]

130   that is the path of the dead,[52]

don't take that path.

> Where is the path
>> that is clear$_1$ that is clear$_2$
>> that is bright$_1$ that is bright$_2$ truly,
>>> that's the path to walk$_3$ walk$_1$
>>> spirit of chicken.

Walk$_3$ walk$_1$ spirit of the chicken,

follow$_1$ follow$_1$ the path that is bright$_1$ that is bright$_2$

When you next espy$_1$ espy$_2$ a house,[53]

140   a bright$_1$ house, a bright$_2$ house,

that house of brass, that is the house of the Creator[54]

that's where you go, where you carry this food.

> Arriving at the stairs of the Creator Spirit,
> the golden stairs of the Creator Spirit,[55]
>> spirit of the chicken,
>> stop at the golden stairs of the Creator Spirit,
>> stop at the house of the Creator Spirit,
>> stop at your destination, the Creator Spirit,
>>> spirit of chicken.

- ní an selu naku   150
- dínu kelupéí supa sígup
- selu naku borèk
- selu naku lotí
- selu naku kopí
- co juméí bílíe ngaputíeng
- selu naku barang
- co juméí uko Bungan
-                         bílíe díek

· tu kau pattéí mang bílíe díek

- tu nyíkínaan   160
- tu kelèjjéí
- tuman tupaan Melawan tu
- tuman lakéí muléí ngan
- dínak muléí ngan
- anak umí ngan díccu tu
◆ co menabí co menamba bílíe ngaputíeng
◆ co menabí co menamba uko Bungan
· ní jíu no díek

- tu déí kícung ngan no bílíe ngaputíeng
◆ urok tau lo tero tau lo penga réí malam   170
- déí melí déí kappíe ngan no bílíe ngaputíeng
- déí melí déí kappíe ngan no uko Bungan
◆ melí déí kappíe ulong jíen ulong genín
◆ meli déí kappíe belurí . . .
◆ paraí míran paraí kapan
· ní jíu no díek

150   That's where you serve$_1$ serve$_2$

the cooked food, the savory rice, the betel, the tobacco,

serve$_1$ serve$_2$ the rice wine,

serve$_1$ serve$_2$ the bread,

serve$_1$ serve$_2$ the coffee,

in front of the Creator Spirit,

serve$_2$ serve$_2$ all the things,

in front of grandmother Bungan,

spirit of chicken.

This is what you say then, spirit of chicken:

160   This food,

these products,[56]

are from all the Berawan,

from the adult men and,

the young people and,

the small children, and these women,

to greet, to salute the Creator Spirit,

to greet, to salute grandmother Bungan,

that's what you say, spirit of chicken.

This they give to you, Creator Spirit,

170   because last year, the year that just ended,

they sought, they asked of you, Creator Spirit,[57]

they sought, they asked of you, grandmother Bungan,

they sought to ask for a good life, a cool life,

they sought to ask to receive

plenty$_1$ of rice, plenty$_2$ of rice,[58]

that's what you say, chicken.

- tau tu ra déí berapa mala
- bílíe ngaputíeng ngan uko Bungan
- tu'o pun paraí déí ra berapa ra berapa aroo

- tu déí ngabayan budíe ngabayan gajjíe   180
- ngan no bílíe ngaputíeng

- ◆ tu acíe icío acíe bulíín tau lo lupau mang
- ◆ tu icío déí ícung ngan no bílíe ngaputíeng
- ◆   ícung ngan no uko Bungan
- tabí tuman co gímad sakí co bukeng ulau . . .
- no bílíe ngaputíeng
- tabí tuman co gímad sakí co bukeng ulau . . .
- no uko Bungan

- arap ngan no bílíe ngaputíeng
- arap ngan no uko Bungan   190
- tawa bílíe sadíe . . .
- tuman tero tuman penga
- ◆ Melawan lo atong Meletíng tu uní
- ◆ lo bun mulong atong Meletíng tu
- urok sadíe déí aroo lo jíen lo lakín
- lo tuman tero tuman penga

- a mang bílíe ngaputíeng
- mang uko Bungan
- ◆ bílíe paraí rè mang
- ◆ tawa bílíe pecco rè mang   200
- vaí tutok seluyok ngan no . . .
- turau acíe an acíe sebang

This year they didn't get much rice,

    Creator Spirit and grandmother Bungan,

    it's true their rice was not much, not very much.

180   Here they are paying for gifts, paying our their wages,

    for you, Creator Spirit.[59]

This is the first day of the first month of the new year,[60]

    this day they give to you, Creator Spirit,

        give to you, grandmother Bungan,

    greetings from their feet to the crowns of their heads[61]

        you Creator Spirit,

    greetings from their feet to the crowns of their heads

        you grandmother Bungan.

    We hope that you, Creator Spirit,

190   we hope that you, grandmother Bungan,

        will summon the spirits of the grandparents

        from the past, from old times,

        the Berawan that were in the Meleting long ago,

        that first lived along the Meleting,

        because many of those ancestors were good and brave,[62]

        in the past, in old times.

    Where are you again, Creator Spirit,

    again, grandmother Bungan,

        those spirits of rice again,

200   summon those spirits of fullness again,

        to come $together_1$ $together_2$ with you

        to sit in this very $place_1$ very $place._4$

- urok wíong acíe bacau bílíe
- bílíe busèk
- busèk kaju íno íno pa rè . . .
- apabíla wíong jaka busèk . . .
- memang wíong lamulong lo sakèk akí senga

- íno tajun íno puwíeng . . .
- Melawan tu pegéí semín
- íno tajun íno puwíeng . . .   210
- Melawan tu pegéí leta pegéí susaa

- tu tau lo tero lo penga
- aroo déí leta
- bílíe ngaputíeng ngan uko Bungan

- ra wíong déí napíu
- ngan no bílíe ngaputíeng
- ngan no uko Bungan
- ra wíong déí ngalíngo kaséí

- mengkalí ní nasíb . . .
- mengkalí ní sa'ín nyí cukup   220
- jíu bílíe ngaputíeng
- jíu uko Bungan

- sukau mawa
- mulong jíen mulong genín
- mulong tína mulong tava
- mulong tanyít mulong la'ít

Because there is one type of spirit,

    the spirit of flowers,

    flowers of various trees

    whenever it is the season of those flowers

    always there are people sick with 'flu.[63]

    What's the cause, what's the reason[64]

        we Berawan are too often hungry?

210   What's the cause, what's the reason

        we Berawan suffer too much death, too much hardship?

    This last year, the year that's ended,

        many of them have died,

        Creator Spirit and grandmother Bungan.

    They are not rude,

        to you, Creator Spirit,

        to you, grandmother Bungan,

        they haven't abandoned you two.[65]

    Perhaps it's luck

220   perhaps it's that they have enough signs,

        says the Creator Spirit,

        says grandmother Bungan.[66]

As long as we have anyway,

    a good life, a cool life,

    a happy life, a laughing life,

    a healthy$_1$ life, a healthy$_2$ life.

◆ menamba déí lo to no bílíe ngaputíeng

◆ déí lo kara lo la'a atan no bílíe ngaputíeng

• selamat píe déí atan no uko Bungan

■ a mang bílíe ngaputíeng . . .   230

■   mang uko Bungan

•   jíu no díek

■ jau wíong ríbelí jau wíong shaítan

■ lo to co lamèng

■ lo to co ukuk ní

■ a'an déí pegéí lasoo . . .

■ a'an déí pegéí pa jat kedíín . . .

■ a'an déí pegéí sakèk . . .

■ a'an déí pegéí leta

• kau bílíe ngaputíeng tíléí ngelatéí   240

• kílaan déí muléí

• kílaan déí kísau

◆ tu nyíkínaan co déí kappíe apun kappíe tabí

• ra déí bíra mawa

■ arap ngan no bílíe ngaputíeng

■ ngetu ngattéí

■ tupaan Melawan

■ tupaan lakéí tupaan díccu tupaan anak umí

• sakí déí co an no bílíe ngaputíeng

Those that are still here greet you, Creator Spirit,[67]

    those that remain behind because of you, Creator Spirit,

    they are all safe because of you, grandmother Bungan.

230   Where are you again, Creator Spirit

again, grandmother Bungan,

        (you say, chicken)

    if there are demons, if there are devils,[68]

    that are still in the longhouse,

    that are still in the apartments,

        where they cause too much frailty

        where they cause too much evil

        where they cause too much sickness

        where they cause too much death,

240   you see$_1$ you see$_2$ Creator Spirit,

        carry them away,

        chase them away.

This food they use to ask forgiveness, to ask greeting,[69]

    they don't ask just anyhow.

They hope that you, Creator Spirit,

    will listen to what they say,[70]

    all the Berawan,

    all the men, all the women, all the little children,

    let them arrive at your place, Creator Spirit.[71]

- déí kappíe apun kappíe tabí   250
-    kappíe tunok kappíe ngeluok
- déí mara sakèk unyín ngan tu bílíe
- ra patut kedíín déí leta lo jat . . .
- leta lo sakèk leta lo neku . . .
- kedíín tau lo tero tau lo penga

- kaméí pecaya adèd no bílíe ngaputíeng
-        adèd no uko Bungan

- tu ícío ngusaí ngalamaí
- a mang bílíe ngaputíeng
- a mang uko Bungan   260

- jau wíong jat telanak
- jau wíong telenak lo ka pabéí
- arap ngan no uko Bungan . . .
-    ngan no bílíe ngaputíeng
- ◆ katau petalau
- ◆ tawa kara
- ◆ co lenaa co usaa
- ◆ tam lenaa tam usaa
- ◆ a'an no tubor
- ◆ a'an no pekena   270
- telenak déí
- pekena pelíka
- tupaan déí lo Melawan

- a mang bílíe ngaputíeng
- a mang uko Bungan

verse continues uninterrupted

250   They ask forgiveness, they ask greeting,

ask for your patience$_1$ ask for your patience$_2$[72]

they are angry, upset with those spirits,[73]

it's not fair how they cause bad death

death from illness, sudden death

like last year, the year that's over.

We believe in the ritual of you, Creator Spirit,[74]

the ritual of you, grandmother Bungan.

This is the day of the festival$_1$ of the festival$_2$[75]

where are you again, Creator Spirit,

260   where are you again, grandmother Bungan.

If there are bad souls,[76]

if there are souls that are inclined to go astray,[77]

we trust in you, grandmother Bungan

in you, Creator Spirit,

to call$_1$ them, to call$_2$ them,[78]

to keep them,

close to yourself$_1$ close to yourself$_2$[79]

each one$_1$ each one$_2$[80]

where you can care for,

270   where you can set right,

their souls,[81]

set right$_1$ set right$_2$[82]

all the Berawan.

Where are you again, Creator Spirit,

where are you again, grandmother Bungan,

verse continues uninterrupted

- ní jíu no díek
- arap ngan no bílíe ngaputíeng
- tíléí ngelatéí
- temau tebukau ulong nyí

- jau wíong temau tebukau déí . . .   280
- ka mukéí ka kuréí . . .
- kau bílíe ngaputíeng . . .
- pekena peneka
- ◆ ka míkat ka mera déí mang
- ◆ cukup gítau cukup tangau
- ◆ tam lenaa tam usaa

Passage omitted

- ra Sadíe Pejong manaí
- metun ngaran tam lenaa tam usaa Melawan
- anak anyam nyí
- sadíe nyí   290
- cukup co an co lía pupang

- arap ngan no bílíe ngaputíeng
- urok sa'ín déí wíong tutok sebutok
- ◆ ngaran tam lenaa tam usaa
- ◆ no bílíe ngaputíeng tíléí ngelatéí
- tam lenaa tam usaa
- déí lo anau adèd urok déí
- arap ngan no bílíe ngaputíeng
- arap ngan no uko Bungan

(that's what you say, chicken)

we trust in you, Creator Spirit,

to look out for$_1$ to look out for$_2$

the tally lines$_1$ the tally lines$_2$ of their lives.[83]

280 If there is a tally line$_1$ a tally line$_2$

   that is open$_1$ is open$_2$[84]

   you, Creator Spirit

   set it right$_1$ set it right$_3$[85]

   tie it up$_1$ tie it up$_2$ again[86]

  enough for a hundred years$_1$ enough for a hundred years$_2$[87]

  for everybody$_1$ for everybody$_2$

Passage omitted

Sadi Pejong isn't skilled,[88]

  at calling the names of everybody$_1$ everybody$_2$ that's Berawan,

  his children and grandchildren,

290 his grandparents,

  enough they are here, in this community, at this gathering.

We trust in you, Creator Spirit,

  because their signs are together$_1$ together$_3$

  the names of everybody$_1$ everybody$_2$

  for you Creator Spirit to look out for$_1$ to look out for$_2$[89]

  everybody$_1$ everybody$_2$

  who participates in the ritual because they,

   trust in you, Creator Spirit,

   trust in you, grandmother Bungan.

- a mang bílíe ngaputíeng   300

- mang uko Bungan

· jíu no díek

- urok déí co tam lakanak co tam luking ukuk

- wíong déí lo cíe pubèd kíng

- wíong déí lo cíe pubèd kraí

- kau bílíe ngaputíeng tíléí ngelatéí

♦ a kara tína tama déí

♦ a kara sadíe déí

♦ lo to ngenung co ukuk

- tu ko metun attéí tupaan déí   310

- lo cíe kíng cíe líkang . . .

- ngan déí lo ra wíong lum lamèng jaka tu

♦ ra ma urok déí muvíu ngan no bílíe ngaputíeng

♦ ra urok déí muvíu ngan no uko Bungan

· déí pecaya ngan no bílíe ngaputíeng

· déí pecaya ngan no uko Bungan

Passage omitted

- a mang bílíe ngaputíeng . . .

- mang uko Bungan

· ní jíu no díek

- jau bílíe díta bílíe tanaa . . .   320

- co kelupa lamèng dítíu

♦ arap ngan no bílíe ngaputíeng

♦ arap ngan no uko Bungan

♦ kappíe apun kappíe tabí ngan déí

♦ tílo jíu Melawan tu

300 Where are you again, Creator Spirit,

again, grandmother Bungan,

(you say, chicken)

because from each family, from each room,[90]

there are those going downriver for medical attention,

there are those going upriver for medical attention,[91]

you Creator Spirit look out for$_1$ look out for$_2$ them,

and their mothers and their fathers,

and their grandparents,

who stay at home.[92]

310 I am speaking for all those,[93]

who have gone downriver on business

and for those who aren't in the house at this season,[94]

it's not because they doubt you, Creator Spirit,

it's not because they doubt you, grandmother Bungan,

they believe in you, Creator Spirit,

they believe in you, grandmother Bungan.[95]

Passage omitted

Where are you again, Creator Spirit,

again, grandmother Bungan,

(This is what you say, chicken)

320 if there are spirits of the plain, spirits of the land

underneath our house,

we trust in you, Creator Spirit,

we trust in you, grandmother Bungan,

to ask their forgiveness, ask their greeting,[96]

to tell them what we Berawan say.

- tu nyíkínaan co menamba menabí déí . . .
- bíyaí déí ka manau jat ka peleta kaméí
- ní kedíín ngan bílíe líkau mang
- arap ngan no bílíe ngaputíeng
- arap ngan no uko Bungan   330
- tílo déí tunok tílo déí ngeluok

- bílíe tukung mang . . .
- urok déí tunéí tukung kíjíe
- bíyaí bílíe tukung ngelínga . . .
- benau anak anyam déí sekolaa . . .
- kara ícío kara íccem
- benau déí ngeluwok benau déí tugéí
- co an déí sekolaa
- bíyaí bílíe ka mara ka meka
- arap ngan no bílíe ngaputíeng   340
- arap ngan no uko Bungan
- tílau unyín tílau ba'ín
- tílau attéí tílau pattéí

- pecaya ngan no bílíe ngaputíeng
- pecaya ngan no uko Bungan
- acíe kau bílíe ngaputíeng ngan kau uko Bungan
- lo a'an dukep mulíín melaín . . .
- merèng ngadèng déí
- tam lenaa tam usaa
- merèng ngadèng kampong   350

verse continues uninterrupted

With this food we salute, greet them

we don't want them to do harm, to kill us,[97]

the same with the river spirits again,

    we trust in you, Creator Spirit,

330   we trust in you, grandmother Bungan,

        to tell them to have patience$_1$ have patience$_2$

Spirits of the mountains again

    because they are near big mountains,

    we don't want the mountain spirits to hear

    the screams of their children at the school

    morning and evening,[98]

    the screams, the shouting of them at play,

    on the school playing field,

    we don't want the spirits to get angry$_1$ get angry$_2$[99]

340   we trust in you, Creator Spirit,

    we trust in you, grandmother Bungan,

        to tell them our feelings$_1$ our feelings$_2$

        to tell them what we say$_1$ we say$_2$[100]

We believe in you, Creator Spirit,

we believe in you, grandmother Bungan,

    in you alone, Creator Spirit and grandmother Bungan,

    because you are trusted to wall off$_1$ to wall off$_2$[101]

    to fence them off$_1$ to fence them off$_2$[102]

    every one$_1$ every one$_2$ of them,

350   fence off$_1$ fence off$_2$ the village,

verse continues uninterrupted

- merèng ngadèng lía déí
- ní jíu no díek

- bíyaí wíong bílíe lo ka musíng
- kaméí Melawan
- wíong déí lo ka manau unyín jat
- kaam bílíe píon déí
- kaam bílíe ngalarak déí
- urok selalu déí ngeluppéí . . .
- lamulong vaí bawa Long Jegín

- arap ngan no bílíe ngaputíeng   360
- arap ngan no uko Bungan
- jau wíong bílíe lo ka musíng . . .
- jau wíong bílíe lo ka manau pesana pupok
- Melawan tutok Melawan
- ra wíong kedíín ní
- arap ngan no bílíe ngaputíeng
- arap ngan no uko Bungan
- pupok tílau kedíín mawa
- tu nyíkínan co kaméí menamba
-          co kaméí menabí   370

- a mang bílíe ngaputíeng
- ngan no uko Bungan
-          jíu no díek
- íno tajun íno puwíeng
- Melawan tu pegéí daréí paraí

verse continues uninterrupted

fence off[1] fence off[2] their community,[103]

(that's what you say, chicken).

We don't want spirits that are devious[104]

we Berawan,

there are those who make bad feelings,[105]

you spirits challenge them,

you spirits oppose them,

because always someone is dreaming[106]

that people are coming to attack Long Jegin.

360 We trust in you, Creator Spirit,

we trust in you, grandmother Bungan,

if there are any spirits that are devious

if there are any spirits that make slander, or attack,

the Berawan, all the Berawan,[107]

don't let it happen,

we trust in you, Creator Spirit,

we trust in you, grandmother Bungan,

to strike them instead,

this food we use to salute you,

370 we use to greet you.

Where are you again, Creator Spirit,

are you, grandmother Bungan,

(you say, chicken)

what's the cause, what's the reason

these Berawan are too often without rice?

verse continues uninterrupted

- tu'o pun tanaa jat tanaa pepat . . .
-       tanaa urau tanaa bítau

- kau bílíe ngaputíeng . . .
- kau uko Bungan . . .
- a'an déí melí kappíe paraí   380
- kícung jo kícung sí'o . . .
- kícung sa'an kícung kenumaan

- urok lía lo aroo buwau . . .
- sakí co tunéí lamèng Melawan tu . . .
- masak lum tanaa Melawan masak lum sepadan Melawan tu
- bíyaí wíong Ivan wíong Kayan . . .
- ka petatau ka pelalau tanaa kaméí

- arap ngan no bílíe ngaputíeng
- arap ngan no uko Bungan
- tu píe nyíkínaan . . .   390
- co awa Sadíe Pejong . . .
- co awa a'an pupang kaméí
- co ícung attéí
- nuvang ngan no bílíe ngaputíeng
- nuvang ngan no uko Bungan

It's true that the land is bad, the land is hilly

the land is grassy, the land is stony.[108]

It's you, Creator Spirit

it's you, grandmother Bungan

380   from whom they seek, ask rice,[109]

to give satisfaction, to give life

to give sustenance, to give nourishment.[110]

Because there are races of whom many migrate

arriving near this Berawan house

moving onto Berawan land, moving into Berawan areas,

we don't want there to be Iban or Kayan

taking away$_1$ taking away$_2$ our land.[111]

We trust in you, Creator Spirit,

we trust in you, grandmother Bungan,

390   all this food

on Sadi Pejong's veranda[112]

the veranda where we gather,

is to give our speech,

meeting with you, Creator Spirit,

meeting with you, grandmother Bungan.

Conclusion

Writing under the heading "Prayer (Introductory and Primitive)" in the *Encyclopedia of Religion and Ethics*, E. N. Fallaize offers this account:

> In its simplest and most primitive form prayer is the expression of a desire, cast in the form of a request, to influence some force or power conceived as supernatural . . . though the ostensible influence in determining the form is largely colored by a desire to compel or command. Genetically, prayer is related to the spell or charm; and it is frequently a matter of difficulty to determine whether a particular formula should be assigned to one category or the other. (Fallaize 1919:154)

His use of the adverb "genetically" hints at the argument which lies behind this bald assertion. Just as James Frazer argues that magic precedes and evolves into religion, so Fallaize assumes that spells underlie prayer (Frazer [1890] 1963:56–68).

How difficult it may be to distinguish prayer and spell remains to be seen. In the introduction, a working definition of prayer was employed that seemed adequate to disallow some forms of ritual speech, and to include others, though of a diverse nature. Certainly the Berawan case presents no ambiguities. However "primitive" Fallaize might have found Berawan prayer to be, yet he would have had no difficulty in telling it from spells. In common with many of the peoples of central northern Borneo, the Berawan have remarkably little interest in magic or witchcraft. When they want their crops to grow, or their enterprises to prosper, or their enemies to be frustrated, they do not mumble formulae learned rote and in secret from some adept.[1] Instead, they seek the occasion to offer prayers, publicly and loudly. All of their approaches to the spiritual are, in W. H. R. Rivers's term, "vocative" (1906:272).

An instructive limiting case that I happened to witness concerns an act of cursing. One morning Tama Jok returned to the longhouse in a towering rage. He had gone to look at his fishing platform in the Bunok river, but the raft had disappeared, drifted away on the current. (See prayer two, note 16, for a description of these rafts and their uses.) He was certain that this was sabotage. He showed the ends of the lines that had secured the raft, clearly cut through rather than frayed. What made it worse was that it could only be someone within the community, a jealous neighbor. Tama Jok had his suspicions, but no evidence on which to base an accusation. So he set up a prayer station in front of his house, using only two tapo' sticks instead of the regulation four. He found a chicken and a bottle of rice wine, and went to make his prayer in front of the tapo'. No one would accompany him because they did not want to be associated with the antisocial message that they knew the prayer would contain. Their apprehensions were correct; instead of the usual appeals for health and wealth, Tama Jok called throatily on the ancestors to send misfortune and disease to the miscreant and coward who had attacked him. Once he had finished his diatribe, Tama Jok took a long pull from the bottle of rice wine, poured some onto the tapo', and looked around for someone to seal the act by drinking with him. The area in front of the longhouse was apparently abandoned, though there were eyes watching from concealment. The only person in view, timidly and uncomprehendingly watching from thirty yards away, was the hapless ethnographer. Tama Jok beckoned, and I walked stiffly over to take the proffered drink. Then, wordlessly, he cut the head off the chicken, and smeared its blood on the tapo', but not on himself or on me. He walked over to the river bank, and threw the carcass into the river, as one disposes of rubbish.

Table 2. Metrical devices by prayer and verse.

Verse	One	Two	Three	Four	Five	Six
			Prayers			
1	R1 F1	L(7)	F9	—	—	L F8
2	L F1	F8 1	F9	L 2	1	R2
3	L	R1 L 1	F2	L	F11 2	L(6) R3
4	L	F8 R3 L	1	2	—	P(2)
5	F2	L(7) 2	2	2	F11 1	—
6	F3 F4 1	F7	1	—	—	L 1
7	F5 2	4	—	L(4)	2	—
8	F6	F3	L(17)	L 1	2	—
9	F5 F7	P(5)	R2 L F2	—	F11	2
10	1	R2, 4 F6 L	F6, 5	—	—	2
11	L	F8	L(4)	R4	1	—
12	P(4)	—	L(14)	1	—	3
13	2	F2	—	2	—	1
14	P(2) 1	F3 1	—	1	L	2
15	F5 R1 2	R3, 4 L	—	1	F11	2
16	1	F1	—	1	2	1
17	F2	L	F10	1	P(2)	F12
18	F3 F4	R2, 5	F10 4	1	—	1
19	L 2	P(3) R4		L	1	P(2) 1
20	P(6)	P(6)		2	1	F13
21	F5	P(2)		3		R7 F12
22	F6	F3, 4 1		—		P(5)
23	F7	L R6		R4		1
24	R2 1	P(3)		3		P(3) 1
25	3	L(5) R1		F5		F8
26	2	R1 3		1		P(5)
27	F5	3				P(4)
28	F6	2				P(2) R1 1
29	P(2)	F7				F8 2
30		F9 R1				R2,5
31		P(2) R4				L 2
32		2				3
33		R2 F2 4				F13 R7

Key

R = formula, numbered according to the sequence set out below. Formulae may occur alone or within lists.

F = figure, numbered according to the sequence set out below. Figures must occur, by definition, at least twice in the corpus.

L = list. If the list includes more than three items, the number of them is shown in brackets, thus: L(n).
P = novel parallel structure. The number of dyadic sets used in the structure is shown in brackets, thus: P(n).
A number without a preceding letter indicates how many dyadic sets appear in the verse, exclusive of those found in formulae, figures, lists, and novel parallel structures, indicated separately.
— = a verse lacking parallel structures or dyadic sets.

In the following numbered formulae, the English translation may vary slightly in different contexts, but the Berawan is invariant. They are given in the order in which they occur:

R1 = Spirits of grandparents$_1$ spirits of grandparents$_2$
spirits of grandparents$_3$ spirits of grandparents$_4$
R2 = The sacrificial$_1$ chicken, the sacrificial$_2$ chicken.
R3 = Spirits of the community$_1$ spirits of the community$_2$
R4 = Spirit that holds, spirit that creates.
R5 = The chicken of life$_1$ the chicken of life$_2$
R6 = Spirits along the Bunok, spirits around the lake.
R7 = Fly as gracefully as a Kayan dancing.

The numbered figures listed below are not invariant (see chapter one), and the wording given here identifies their most characteristic phrase or phrases. Three periods at the end of a phrase (. . .) indicate that it may be repeated one or more times with different dyadic sets. To be counted in the table as a use of such figures, there must be at least *two* lines. A single line counts as a dyadic set not incorporated in a figure. In order of occurrence:

F1   = Who rule over this lake, rule over this Bunok.
F2   = A good life, a cool life . . .
F3   = Let us have money, let us have rice . . .
F4   = luck$_1$ luck$_2$ . . .
F5   = Let the blood of my chicken enter, into the house$_1$
into the house$_2$ . . .
F6   = Charge it with power to convey, power to nourish . . .
F7   = Take it to be charm, to be spirit . . .
F8   = We are calling$_1$ thus, we are calling$_2$ thus . . .
F9   = Go, spirit of the pig, go to . . .
F10 = A good$_1$ life, a good$_2$ life, a noble$_1$ life, a noble$_2$ life.
F11 = To bring you together with X, together with Y.
F12 = I ask you to fly to the left$_1$ fly to the left$_2$
F13 = Show your feathers$_1$ show your feathers$_2$

It is curious that even a curse takes the form of a disqualified prayer. The ancestors do not normally appear in a judgmental capacity, and they do not mete out retribution. The antilife sentiments, the incomplete **tapo'**, the rejection of the blood and meat of the sacrificial animal, all present a parody of normal prayer. Yet even this prayer required some minimal congregation. Had I not been there, I was told later, Tama Jok would have marched into the longhouse and taken hold of some boy to come and share his rice wine.

The social intensity of **píat** exceeds anything with which we are familiar in the prayer in Judeo-Christian tradition. There is no concept of private prayer; prayer is always public. Moreover, the function of praying is delegated to senior men, who speak on behalf of the group. Whole classes of persons are excluded: women, children, and young men. Even among older men, some are forward, and some are not. Competence in **píat** is indicative of a wider social performance.

Variation in Competence

Now that the prayers have been set out in full, the descriptions provided in chapters one and two can be substantiated, and even to some extent quantified. Though it might well be argued that the genius of a poetic genre cannot ultimately be captured by statistics, they nevertheless do have the advantage of compactness.

I begin with the issue of the considerable variation in competence between speakers, which is itself a major characteristic of **píat**. Presumably, such variation is less marked in the ritual languages of Eastern Indonesia, the performance of which is a specialized role, requiring considerable skill even in a lesser exponent. By contrast, competence in Berawan prayer varies across the spectrum of the social hierarchy. Table 2 provides a verse-by-verse breakdown of the use of metrical devices for each of the prayers, excluding for a moment Sadi Pejong's marathon statement in the new Bungan style. This table's extensive key provides a summarized guide to all the figures and formulae used in the corpus. Lists are too variable in content to be usefully summarized in this way; it is quicker simply to look them up. In addition, dyadic sets occurring outside these structures are also enumerated, as are original parallel structures, that is, those that do not recur int he corpus and so do not qualify as figures.

A general impression of the competence of speakers can be gained at a

Table 3. Numbers of different metrical devices by prayer.

	Prayers					
	One	Two	Three	Four	Five	Six
Formulae	3	13	1	2	0	6
Figures	18	12	7	1	4	6
Lists	5	13	4	5	1	4
Totals	26	38	12	8	5	16
Novel structures	4	7	0	0	1	7
Lone dyadic sets	16	19	8	22	13	26
Verses with two devices	10	16	3	0	2	9
Verses lacking any devices	0	1	5	5	6	4

glance. The prayers of Tama Jok (prayer one) and Tama Aweng (prayers two and six) are longer than those of Tama Avit (prayer three), Uking (prayer four), and Lian Yang (prayer five). They are also more densely packed with metrical devices, which is revealed by a further tabulation. Table 3 shows the number of different kinds of metrical devices in each prayer. Inevitably, there is some loss of data when aggregating in this manner. It suppresses, for instance, the variety of figures or formulae employed. All four figures in prayer five are the same, and unique to that prayer, whereas prayer two employs seven different figures. Again, the baroque lists in prayer three are counted as equivalent to some much less impressive examples elsewhere, so the special quality that they lend to Tama Avit's style is discounted.

Nevertheless, the fourth line of table 3 convincingly demonstrates the poverty of prayers four and five as compared to prayers one and two. The fifth line, enumerating novel parallel structures, confirms the impression, and especially shows how much originality is displayed by Tama Aweng (prayers two and six) in comparison with all other speakers. However, the sixth line has some surprises. Uking's poor showing so far is somewhat offset by his use of single dyadic sets sprinkled around his **píat** without articulation into structures. He has a trick of using only one line of a figure, as if in too much of a hurry to bother with the whole thing.

The last two lines of table 3 present an interesting inversion of one another. The former shows how many verses in a given prayer simultaneously employ two or more items of metrical device, providing a simple measure of complexity in the building of verses. Again, Tama Aweng and

Tama Jok are clear leaders. The latter shows how many verses lacked any kind of device. There is still an obvious difference between speakers, but a better contrast is between the first two prayers and the rest. Most prayers have to explain themselves, and so are led willy-nilly into less readily structured passages. What is special about prayers one and two is their social context; spoken at the annual festival of **papì' lamèng,** they deal with only the most general, time-honored themes of Berawan prayer. This observation draws our attention to the fact that there is variation in metrical structure, not only from one speaker to another, but also from one theme to another.

Variation in Themes

Table 4 shows the themes of successive verses in prayers one through six. Table 5 shows the number of verses on different themes in each prayer, and in the whole corpus. In view of Fallaize's characterization of prayer, it comes as no surprise that the most common theme overall is supplication. However, we might not suspect in advance that the second most common would be sacrifice, and this juxtaposition of themes highlights the inequality of the sacrificial bargain, of which, Valeri says "the sacrifier gives little in exchange for much." In other words:

> For a god, giving much is giving little; for a man, giving little is giving much. Hence man's small gift to the god is as valuable as god's big gift to man, but at the same time, this equivalence of the gifts signifies and establishes the nonequivalence of the givers, of god and man. It is in this way that reciprocity can coexist with hierarchy and that the sacrificial exchange can represent the god's superiority over men. (Valeri 1985:66)

By contrast, the theme of offering occurs in only a third as many verses, confirming the conclusion drawn in chapter two that the communicative aspects of sacrifice outweigh the digestive suggestions of offerings.

Only slightly less frequent than supplication and sacrifice are the themes of invocation and explanation. The former is inescapable since prayer invariably begins with invocation. It would in fact be better represented but for the accident that in two cases (prayers three and four) the tape recorder was switched on too late to catch the first couple of verses. The latter is almost as frequent, but does not occur in all the prayers, as is the case with all the remaining, less prominent themes.

Indeed, the totals for different themes give little hint about their representation in particular prayers, which vary widely in this regard. Even

Table 4. Themes of verses by prayer.

Verse	Prayers					
	One	Two	Three	Four	Five	Six
1	I	I	S	P	I	I
2	I	I	S	P	E	S
3	I	T	P	I	E	I
4	O	I	S	E	E	D
5	P	S	E	T	E	E
6	P	S	E	T	S	E
7	S	P	E	P	P	E
8	S	P	I	P	P	E
9	S	P	S	I	E	D
10	T	S	S	Z	E	D
11	P	I	I	I	P	E
12	P	T	I	Z	P	E
13	S	P	E	P	E	E
14	O	P	O	P	E	E
15	O	I	O	X	E	D
16	T	I	O	P	P	D
17	P	O	O	P	O	D
18	P	S	P	P	P	D
19	P	S		E	E	D
20	P	S		P	P	D
21	S	S		Z		D
22	S	P		P		P
23	S	I		P		P
24	S	Z		S		D
25	S	I		S		D
26	I	I		P		D
27	S	Z				D
28	S	Z				D
29	S	S				D
30		I				S
31		I				O
32		I				D
33		S				D

Key

I	= invocation	T	= identity
P	= supplication	E	= explanation
O	= offering	D	= divination
S	= sacrifice	Z	= unclassified

X = anomalous verse in prayer four, addressed to the audience.

Table 5. Numbers of verses by theme and prayer.

	Prayers						
	One	Two	Three	Four	Five	Six	Total
Invocation	4	12	3	3	1	2	25
Supplication	8	6	2	13	7	2	38
Offering	3	1	4	0	1	1	10
Sacrifice	12	9	5	2	1	2	31
Identity	2	2	0	2	0	0	6
Explanation	0	0	4	2	10	8	24
Divination	0	0	0	0	0	18	18
Unclassified	0	3	0	3	0	0	6

prayers one and two—made on the same occasion—show differences that can only reflect the temperaments of the speakers. Tama Jok puts heavy emphasis on the theme of sacrifice, whereas Tama Aweng, while not slighting sacrifice, is far more insistent in his acts of invocation. The distributions of themes in the remaining prayers are clearly slanted toward particular ritual contexts. Tama Avit, in prayer three, touches evenly on the main themes, but requires almost a quarter of his verses to explain the special circumstances of the illness of his grandchild. For Lian Yang, the theme of explanation is an even greater concern. He devotes half of his verses to trying to ensure that the recently dead man whom he addresses knows exactly what is happening and why. Prayer six is equally specialized. The theme of divination is predominant in it, and restricted to it. In prayer four, Uking chooses to disguise his calumnies largely as supplication.

Metrical Devices and Themes

Let us return to the issue of variation in metrical structure from one theme to another; table 6 shows how may verses there are on each theme that utilize the various devices of **píat**. This table can be difficult to read because the total numbers of verses on different themes varies so much, so table 7 displays the same data with the frequencies of verses of various kinds shown as percentages of all the verses on that theme in the entire corpus. Table 7 shows that themes do indeed vary in the characteristic manner in which they are expressed, as was suggested in chapter two. This is especially true of the four most common themes. If we begin with sacrifice, we see

Table 6. Numbers of verses incorporating different kinds of metrical devices, by theme.

	P	S	I	E	D	O	T	Z
Complex verses	6	10	10	0	4	2	1	0
Verses containing:								
a figure	10	17	8	4	6	2	0	0
a formula	1	8	9	0	3	1	1	0
a list	5	3	13	3	0	3	1	0
an original parallel structure	4	4	1	0	5	1	1	1
Verses containing only odd dyads	14	4	3	7	6	0	3	4
Verses lacking any metrical device	4	1	2	9	0	3	2	1
Number of verses	38	31	25	24	18	10	6	6

Key: P = supplication, S = sacrifice, I = invocation,
     E = explanation, D = divination, O = offering,
     T = identity, Z = unclassified.

NB: 1. A *complex verse* is one containing two or more specimens from the inventory of formulae, figures, and lists, *or* one such, and at least two separate dyadic sets.
    2. The columns in table 6 do not add up to the totals shown on the bottom because a verse is counted for each kind of metrical device it incorporates. For the same reason, the columns of table 7 do not add up to 100 percent.
    3. A verse containing *two* formulae, or *two* figures, or *two* lists is counted as only one instance of a verse with one of these structures. It is, however, a complex verse.

that over half its verses contain a figure, significantly more than in any other theme. By contrast, invocation is largely expressed by means of lists, which are relatively rare in other themes. Supplication is not obviously associated with any one device, and its largest bloc of verses are those containing only a couple of unconnected dyadic sets, reflecting the variety of boons that may, in different situations, be requested of the spirits. This situational particularity is even more marked in the theme of explanation, where the most numerous type of verse is that containing no metrical devices of any kind.

These contrasts between major themes are confirmed by a further manipulation of the data contained in table 2. If we count up the occasions when different figures are used, we are able to show that three of the most common are those concerned with the blood of sacrificial animals (F5, F6, and F7, the first being the most common figure of all). Together, they make up a third of all the figures used in all six prayers. Another third is provided by three figures often used in verses containing supplication (F2,

Table 7. Verses incorporating different metrical devices, expressed as a percentage of all the verses on that theme in the entire corpus.

	P	S	I	E	D	O	T	Z
Complex verses	16	32	40	0	22	20	17	0
Verses containing:								
a figure	26	55	32	17	33	20	0	0
a formula	3	26	36	0	17	10	17	0
a list	13	10	52	12	0	30	17	0
an original parallel structure	11	13	4	0	28	10	17	17
Verses containing only odd dyads	38	13	12	29	33	0	50	66
Verses lacking any metrical device	11	3	8	38	0	30	34	17

Key: P = supplication, S = sacrifice, I = invocation,
    E = explanation, D = divination, O = offering,
    T = identity, Z = unclassified.

NB: 1. A *complex verse* is one containing two or more specimens from the inventory of formulae, figures, and lists, *or* one such, and at least two separate dyadic sets.
    2. The columns in table 6 do not add up to the totals shown on the bottom because a verse is counted for each kind of metrical device it incorporates. For the same reason, the columns of table 7 do not add up to 100 percent.
    3. A verse containing *two* formulae, or *two* figures, or *two* lists is counted as only one instance of a verse with one of these structures. It is, however, a complex verse.

F3, and F4). Figures are not inherently restricted to verses of one particular theme. Nevertheless, it so happens that these six almost invariably are found with the themes indicated, so that sacrifice and supplication between them account for more than 70 percent of all uses of figures. Invocation however makes little use of figures.

This situation is reversed for formulae. The two most common formulae are the titles of the Creator (R4) and the ancestors (R1). They often occur, though not invariably, in verses concerned with invocation. So do two others (R3 and R6), and the four together make up 66 percent of the total used. A further 28 percent comprise two formulae (R2 and R5) that are mostly employed in verses concerned with sacrifice.

Other findings of table 7 are worth notice. Invocation and sacrifice both employ a high percentage of complex verses, as defined in the key. Yet original parallel structures are rare in invocation, compared to supplication and sacrifice, and absent from explanation. The theme with the most original structures, even in absolute numbers, is divination. This state of affairs may be partly a result of the restriction of the theme of divination to prayer six, thus limiting the opportunities for these structures to recur, but the creativity of Tama Aweng is clearly the major factor in it. Not surprisingly, lists are the most conspicuous metrical device involved in the theme of offering. For the remaining two themes, the numbers of verses are so small that it skews the percentage figures, but it is clear that they seldom employ much more than the odd dyadic set.

The Bungan Style

Finally, a brief review of the statistics concerning Sadi Pejong's prayer seven will supplement the account of his style offered in the last chapter. Table 8 shows how each verse is composed in terms of theme and metrical devices. One new formula and one new figure are introduced, as shown in the key. Some skewing of the data is possible as a result of text abbreviation (by approximately 20 percent, or 100 lines), but I doubt that this is large enough to distort the overall picture.

The most suitable comparisons can be made with prayers one and two, which were spoken in a similar ritual context at an annual festival. In terms of the prevalence of different themes, the same three are predominant, but in the reverse order. Sadi Pejong uses fully a third of his verses for supplication, trying to avert a range of misfortunes, both spiritual and material, that he spells out in detail. Invocation is covered in 19 percent of his verses, and sacrifice in a mere 14 percent, all coming in a single section near the beginning. By contrast, Tama Jok and Tama Aweng return again and again to the theme of sacrifice, allotting it the largest number of verses (34 percent). Invocation is next most prominent (26 percent), with supplication third (22 percent).

More prominent than sacrifice in Sadi Pejong's prayer are the unclassified verses. Several of these take on a mournful or carping note so that I am tempted to label a new theme for Sadi Pejong's benefit, the theme of complaint. One or two provide a kind of credo, classifiable neither as invocation nor supplication. For instance in the brief verse beginning at line 256:

We trust in the ritual of you, Creator Spirit,
    in the ritual of you, grandmother Bungan.

Table 8. The themes and metrical structures of the verses of prayer seven.

Verse	Theme	Structure	Verse	Theme	Structure
1	E	R8	33	I	R8 L 1
2	E	R8 1	34	Z	—
3	O	L	35	Z	2
4	O	—	36	Z	—
5	Z	L R8 2	37	Z	R8
6	O	L 3	38	Z	R8
7	I	R8 3	39	P	F2
8	I	2	40	I	R8 1
9	I	L	41	I	R8
10	I	2	42	O	1
11	P	L	43	P	L
12	I	L 2	44	P	2
13	I	1	45	Z	R8
14	P	1	46	E	R8
15	Z	1	47	P	R8 5
16	I	1	48	P	R8 2
17	E	L 3	49	P	6
18	S	F7 2	50	T	L 1
19	S	R8 L 3	51	P	R8 4
20	S	F14 3	52	P	R8 4
21	S	1	53	P	R8 1
22	S	3	54	P	R8 2
23	S	F14 1	55	P	R8 2
24	S	2	56	P	R8 3
25	S	L	57	P	R8 5
26	S	L 1	58	P	1
27	O	R8 L 1	59	P	R8 1
28	P	R8 2	60	Z	R8 L 1
29	Z	R8	61	P	R8 2
30	Z	—	62	P	2
31	I	R8 2	63	I	R8
32	I	R8 L 2			

Key

P = supplication, S = sacrifice, I = invocation, E = explanation, O = offering, T = identity, Z = unclassified, L = list, — = verse lacking dyadic sets.

A number without a preceding letter indicates how many dyadic sets occur outside other structures.

R8 = Grandmother Bungan, Creator Spirit, F2 = A good life, a cool life,
F7 = Take it to be charm, to be spirit, F14 = Follow the path that is clear$_1$ is clear$_2$

Structurally, these lines might be regarded as a figure, with variable introductory phrases, "we trust in you," or "we believe in you." But I prefer the
alternative analysis, which is to identify a formula in them that recurs in
other contexts. This formula (R8) is a Bungan equivalent of the dyadic
reference to the Creator in traditional **píat** (R4). It has the peculiarity that it
may appear split between two lines, as above. Toward the end of the
prayer, it is used in this form to open verses on the theme of supplication.

This formula is the most obvious metrical device of Sadi Pejong's
prayer. A full 45 percent of all his verses contain it and he uses no other.
His use of figures is minimal, and they are found in only 8 percent of his
verse. Lists are more common, occurring in 25 percent of the verses. A
comparison with the figures for prayer two tells its own story. Tama Aweng
uses formulae slightly less frequently—40 percent of his verses—but he
uses a diversity of them. He employs figures in 36 percent of verses, and
lists in 40 percent. It seems clear that Sadi Pejong's prayer is less polished
than Tama Aweng's.

There are, however, a couple of statistics that seem to argue against this
conclusion. The first concerns complex verses, which are only slightly less
common in Sadi Pejong's prayer (31 percent) than Tama Aweng's (36
percent). But a closer inspection shows that this effect is largely an artifact
of the long verses that Sadi Pejong often employs, verses that display little
internal structuring yet manage to pile up sufficient dyadic sets to qualify as
complex. Second, Sadi Pejong has a high percentage of verses (24 percent)
containing one or more dyadic sets, but no parallel structures; this is in
direct opposition to Tama Aweng's prayer, which has only 12 percent of
the verses containing dyadic sets. Is this simply another way of expressing
the proposition that Sadi Pejong is unsophisticated in the use of figures and
formulae? Or is there an alternative style that prefers the metrical effect of
isolated dyadic sets to the routine of predictable parallel structures? Perhaps
Sadi Pejong resembles Uking in this respect. As a simple test, a count was
made of all the lines in both prayers that contain one or both elements of a
dyadic set, regardless of the presence or absence of other metrical devices.
In Sadi Pejong's prayer 29 percent of lines exhibited this kind of parallelism; in Tama Aweng's 61 percent did. The impression of relative simplicity
in Sadi Pejong's prayer consequently persists.

Nevertheless, we must concede that there is a power and an artistry in
Sadi Pejong's verse, even if they are not derived from those stylistic features
of traditional **píat** that the statistics are designed to capture. Instead, by
loosening the constraints of parallelism, Sadi Pejong manages to display
more emotion than is characteristic of Berawan prayer. **Píat** generally, by

making a virtue out of deadpan delivery, seems to speak of a world that is predictable, and governed by the customs of the ancestors. Sadi Pejong, innovator and preserver, busy putting new wine into old bottles, does not speak about that world. In his verses, there is a poignant sense of looking backwards and forwards, of balancing irresistible new forces and old norms. When Sadi Pejong demands of his gods, the one old, the other new:

> What's the cause, what's the reason,
>   we Berawan are too often hungry?
> What's the cause, what's the reason,
>   we Berawan suffer too much death, too much hardship?

His perception of a problematic future overrides the declamatory conventions of prayer.

The Resources of Prayer

The idiosyncracies of Sadi Pejong's style, the protraction of lines and verses (not to mention the prayer itself), the expository manner of dealing with themes, the simple alternation of loud and soft passages, the wistful feeling that is conveyed, all extend the parameters of **píat**, of what is recognizable as prayer. What makes this extension possible is an inherent pliability. The style of Uking, noisy propagandist for the old way, is hardly less quirky. Tama Avit is more sober in his presentation, as befits a respected elder. Nevertheless, his peculiar use of anacrustic lines challenges the procedures for identifying verses. Both Tama Jok and Tama Aweng, who provide models of competence in **píat**, have a definite, individual style.

The nature of **píat** as a genre is that it provides resources from which individual speakers fashion their own productions. They select from among a range of devices of parallelism, of theme, and of intonation, few of which are indispensable. Little is governed by rule or rote, and no one is coached or contradicted. The conventions of prayer not only allow for variety, they produce it. In this way, they display a nice fit with social realities. Prayer is not restricted to specialists but it is not practiced with equal frequency by all men. Where some are forward, and seek to make an impression, others hang back. Yet others have a workmanlike attitude. There are as many ways to pray as there are roles in a society that leaves a great deal of room for choice, spontaneity, and drama. **Píat** is as individualistic as the Berawan themselves.

Notes

Chapter One

1. **Píat** is a nominal; there is also the verbal form **níat.** It is confusing to use inflected forms in a little-known language so I say that so-and-so "makes píat."
2. It would be foolish to suggest that in all the literature on the area there is no discussion of forms of ritual language, but I know of no work that offers any extended metrical analysis. One source—W. Kern's (1956) study—that was pointed out to me also uses material from Borneo, but not from interior folk. Instead it employs the court annals of the Sultanate of Kutai on the Mahakam River and is, like much similar literature, more concerned with content than form. There is no justification of the mode of segmentation into lines, nor of higher level units.

3. I am indebted to Dell Hymes for bringing home to me the hazards of the notion of "loose structure" in the present case.
4. I probed this proposition, making up hypothetical circumstances. For instance, people entering a graveyard invariably pray loudly to the ancestors, so as not to take those powerful spirits by surprise, which could have lethal consequences. I asked if a man entering alone would offer prayers. The only response was that a man would not enter a graveyard alone. In fact, the opportunities for being alone are limited. A desire to go off alone is cause for suspicion of illicit behavior, such as an adulterous liaison. To avoid such suspicion, a child is taken along "for company." Only in hunting are men much alone, and some men are reputed to gain knowledge from jungle spirits. But this communication is specifically not through prayer. Finally, there is an interestingly ambiguous case in the rite of **katé apok** (**katé** means "to throw away," **apok** means "dirt"), in which a newly widowed woman bathes in a secluded spot, and then, so I am told, makes a dirge addressed to her dead husband, asking that no harm befall her or her children. Yet this case can be ruled out on a technicality: Prayer is addressed to spirits, yet the widow is in mourning precisely because her spouse is not yet spirit, but still human, with a soul, **telanak** (Metcalf 1982a:47–48). Such addresses are not made in **píat**.
5. At the rite described in chapter four, shamans sprinkled yellow rice (i.e., rice with saffron) on the crowd. This act was accompanied by prayer rather than constituting prayer. It is comparable to the blood from a sacrificial knife that is dabbed onto the backs of the hands of participants—an act of communion (see chapter two).
6. In none of the societies of central northern Borneo are there unilineal descent groups (Appell 1976). Among the Kayan and Kenyah there are, however, social classes that are ideally endogamous (Rousseau 1978, Whittier 1978). These classes are not found among the Berawan.
7. It should be noted that there are genres among the Berawan that have all the seriousness of Rotinese ritual language, and emphasis on precise recitation. The most obvious of these are the death songs (see introduction), which, if misused, are lethal. Also, there are shamans who do sing special songs. The point here is to pursue the comparison of **píat** per se with Rotinese ritual language.
8. To some readers, the system of numbering synonyms may seem incongruous since we do not associate mathematics with poetry. This system, however, does have several advantages: it is admirably suited to displaying the metrical structures that are my principal concern; it provides a visual representation of what is the most striking feature, namely repetition; and by its strangeness it alerts us to a feature of Berawan prayer that is not found in the same way in our own poetry.

9. This spectrum of borrowing and modification is hinted at in I. N. H. Evans's account of Dusun "sacred language" (1953:495–96), in which he offers a five-part classification of words in the language: 1. "ordinary Dusun words," 2. "special but easily recognizable forms of ordinary words—poetic forms," 3. "words not usually current in the village . . . but found in other villages, near or far away," 4. "loan words from Malay," 5. "words used, as far as known, only in the sacred language, for which derivations are not obtainable." It seems likely that the circumstances that he is discussing are not dissimilar to the Berawan case.

10. It remains possible that **rapule** and **ramule** were not made up at random. Beatrice Clayre points out to me (personal communication) that if the alliterative **ra-** is removed, we can recognize two roots meaning "to return" or "to turn back." This meaning only fits the context with difficulty; it is possible that Tama Aweng meant that the sick child's soul was to return, but the point is that none of my informants recognized his novel words.

11. The notion of rhyming employed here requires some discussion. To achieve a proper rhyme in English, it seems that it is necessary to reiterate all phonemes from the stressed syllable onwards. Berawan however always place stress on the last syllable (with the infrequent exception that the final syllable is comprised of a lone vowel, in which case the preceding syllable is the one stressed). Consequently, it is relatively easy to manufacture rhymes in Berawan.

For present purposes, I consider two Berawan words to rhyme if they share the same final form of V, or VV, or VC, or VVC, as appropriate. Some would argue that a full rhyme also requires replication of the consonant preceding the final vowel, and that the condition specified above is merely a special case of alliteration. I chose to retain the term rhyme because alliteration usually refers to the initial sound group rather than the final one.

There are cases where rhymes occur between lines. For instance, in prayer one, lines 64–67, there are four lines in a row that artfully share final rhymes. Only two are from a dyadic set, the others are unattached. Yet such cases are rare relative to the number of rhyming dyadic sets within lines.

12. For example, the river by which the people of Long Teru live is labeled **Lemiting** on maps, supposedly after the original inhabitants. The Berawan themselves call it **Melîtèng**.

13. Beatrice Clayre has a different hypothesis concerning the origins of **kenumaan:** "I suggest that the root is '**kaan**' meaning 'to eat.' A similar root is found in other languages of Sarawak (Lun Kayeh, Penan, and others); -um- is an infix, usually found in intransitive verbs in north Borneo/Sabah (for example, in Dusun). It is rarely used now in the languages of central

and northern Sarawak, and when it occurs it may also function in transitive
contexts. Hence **k-um-aan** (c.f. Lun Dayeh, Penan, etc.); -en- (or -in-) is a
common infix meaning completed action. Hence **k-en-um-aan.**" Note that
kumaan is the standard Berawan word for "to eat," and that **nakaan** is also
recognizable in everyday speech as the act of making offerings to spirits in
the form of a **pakaan. Kenumaan,** however, was not recognizable to my
informants outside the context of **píat,** but they were younger men. Clayre
contines: "The occurrence of these two infixes raises interesting problems:
(1) I know of no other examples of the co-occurrence of -in- and -um-
south of Sabah. (2) Whereas in Dusun, -in- signals completed action in all
focus clauses, in the languages of Sarawak it is, as far as I know, restricted
on non-actor focus clauses (-um- is an actor-focus infix). I have long
suspected that the languages of central Sarawak once employed more affixes
than they do today. So the question arises—is 'kenumaan' a survival of an
earlier form of the language?" (personal communication) Clayre raises the
possibility that some words that appear to be **píat**-words are actually archaic
forms. If this is so, the prayers may provide interesting data for historical
linguists. No Berawan suggested to me that **píat** contains old or disused
words, although this claim is made concerning the death songs. Moreover,
even if the form **kenumaan** once existed and was then lost, the common
practices for making up **píat**-words could have caused its unwitting
reinvention.

14. There are two exceptions to this, both of them occurring in Sadi Pejong's
    prayer seven. At lines 209 and 211 he really does seem to be asking
    plaintively why it is that his folk are suffering so much. Please refer to the
    conclusion for more details.
15. There a couple of reasons why two-line terraces occurring in midverse are
    not shown with the repeated words underneath each other. First, the
    terrace tends not to be noticeable, and only makes the shape of the verse
    appear irregular. Second, the following line may be so far indented that any
    subsequent parallel structures cannot be indented further without running
    off the page. This presents no problem, however, if the terrace is at the end
    of a verse.

Chapter Two

1. This generalization should be restricted to prayers in the traditional manner
   and not those of the Bungan cult. For example, prayer seven begins instead
   with an announcement of what the prayer is about. Prayer five does not
   begin with the usual phrase, but it does begin with invocation. Prayer three
   has its opening lines missing, but it did begin in the normal way.

2. There are some exceptions to this, but they are explicable in terms of slips. At one point in a list of spirit agencies, Tama Aweng uses **kaam,** the third person plural pronoun, before the formula naming the Creator. But he does so only to reproduce the phraseology of the preceding lines.
3. Hose and McDougall's account does not seem reliable, and one has not been obtained by the techniques of modern fieldwork. It seems unlikely, for instance, that Laki Ju Urip and Laki Jup Urip are really distinct deities. Hose is surely right, however, that there are a number of departmental deities.
4. There were two occasions when I saw prayer sites made with just two **tapo'** sticks. Both were, however, purposely invalidated prayers. One was the act of cursing discussed in the conclusion. The other was for a properly sociable purpose, to secure the welfare of a young man about to depart to the coast for schooling. But he needed to leave right after the prayer, breaching a taboo against leaving the longhouse for twenty-four hours after such a rite. Consequently, his father prepared a nonstandard prayer station, so as not to be caught by the taboo—evidently, it is possible in this way to have your cake and eat it too.
5. I could obtain no gloss for **penusu,** and I can discover no likely cognates in Kenyah tongues.
6. I heard of a couple of cases where chickens had prayers spoken over them in this fashion but were then released alive. In both instances, the prayer was for the continued health of a child. Clearly there was an implication of unfinished business, and also perhaps of the "sacrificial bargain;" if the child stays healthy, the spirits will receive their sacrifice. The semiotic element is also there; when the child is judged safe, that is when the message to that effect will be sent.

Chapter Three: Prayer One

1. This is the standard formula for referring to the collectivity of the ancestral spirits. The formula is discussed in chapter one. The only unusual feature is that Tama Jok reverses the order of the first dyadic set. He does this because he prefers to place the Berawan term first. Others prefer to put the shorter word first, which is still comprehensible because the formula is so familiar.
2. This is a cognate of Malay **pegang** (to hold, grasp, control). Like the Malay word (as used in the watershed of the Baram), it often carries the meaning of rule or political control. For instance, the period of colonial control by Britain is usually referred to in Baram as **pegang Kwin.**
3. This particle, said so rapidly that it is easy to miss, is seldom heard in ordinary speech. Here it signifies that the individual subsequently named is long dead, one of the revered ancestors.

4. In contrast to the name in the next line, this one is constructed in an irregular manner. The personal name (**ngaran usaa**: **ngaran** means "name," **usaa** means "body") of the individual referred to was Ajan. In addition, the teknonym that he used throughout most of his life is added: Tama (father of) Langet. Normally the personal name follows the teknonym, as in Tama Julan Tinggang (Tinggang "father of Julan"). This irregularity is not a slip of the tongue by Tama Jok but reflects the usage at Long Teru. Tama Langet is the only person I came across whose personal name is tagged on to the front of his teknonym, and no one could explain why this is so.

   There is considerable idiosyncratic variation in the use of names and teknonyms. An individual may be eligible during the course of his or her life for many teknonyms. Which ones are actually employed depends partly on the preferences of the owner but also on the vagaries of popular usage. Which teknonyms persist in the collective memory after death, and whether they are usually heard in combination with a personal name, is not systematic. Tama Julan Tinggang is almost always mentioned by both personal name and teknonym, whereas Tama Langet is usually mentioned by the latter only.

   The word **sadì'** here is a different story. It is often used as part of a teknonym; for instance, Sadi Pejong is the grandfather of Pejong. The first letter of Sadi is in capitals to indicate this fact. But in this line of the prayer, Tama Jok is not referring to the man who was the grandfather of Ajan, but to Ajan himself. In this context, **sadì'** is a type of necronym, a term of respect indicating that the person subsequently named is a revered ancestor.

5. Tama Julan Tinggang was another leader at Long Teru in the between-wars period and was a rival of Tama Langet. Tama Jok is tactful to mention them literally in one breath. Each leader had a faction within the longhouse, and those people have descendants who remember the rivalry only too well. While celebrating community solidarity on this occasion, it is necessary to bracket them together so as to offend no one. Tama Langet is a rather colorless figure in Berawan oral history. He was appointed headman on three separate occasions, largely because of the excesses of Tama Julan Tinggang. The latter, however, was a more effective politician in the Berawan mode, and he would scheme and bully until he was once again made headman in place of his weaker but more respectable rival. Tama Julan Tinggang was given to fits of violence in which he would assault people murderously.

6. Consistent with the usage explained in note 4 of this chapter, the man that Tama Jok refers to here is not the grandfather of Lawai but the ancestor Lawai. Throughout his life, Lawai never made much use of a teknonym of the form Tama X or Sadi Y, even though he had both children and grandchildren. This was partly a matter of personal preference, but it was

also a result of the title that was conferred on him at an early age. He was appointed **penghulu** (government-appointed chief) by the last Rajah's representative in the Baram District and held the title until his death in 1955. Consequently, he is most frequently referred to as Penghulu Lawai. He was a wise and popular leader.

On the tape recording of this prayer, it is possible to hear Tama Jok hesitate for a moment after the word **sadì'**. He was perhaps wondering whether to use the title Penghulu before Lawai's name or to use some unfamiliar teknonym. The former might be offensive to some mortal or spirit, because it would give more dignity to Lawai than to Tinggang and Ajan. But the latter would be forced—Tama Jok might not even at this moment have been able to recall the name of Lawai's eldest child, who is the one that should be named in the teknonym. In the event, he used neither title nor teknonym, and the line trails awkwardly.

7. The Lelak moved their longhouse away from the lake and down to the main river, the Tinjar, at the turn of the century, on the instructions of the District Officer. There they intermarried with immigrant Berawan folk and eventually adopted the Berawan language (see note 33 of this chapter). It is for this reason that I describe Long Teru as basically a Berawan community. But the lake is still of great economic and emotional significant to the Long Teru folk. It provides rich supplies of fish, and it is a jealously guarded patrimony.

8. Orang Kaya Luwak was the leader of the Lelak people at the turn of the century, and he brought them successfully through a dangerous period when they were vulnerable to the depredations of more numerous and aggressive upriver folk. Given his prestige, and his remoteness in time, Tama Jok did not hesitate to use an honorific when referring to this leader. Orang Kaya (**orang** means "person," **kaya** means "rich, powerful") is a Malay title acknowledging local preeminence. The Sultans of Brunei, whose hold upon the Baram was always tenuous, frequently conferred this title on leaders of communities that were loyal, or at least not too troublesome. That Luwak possessed this title shows that he was already juggling external forces against his restless neighbors even before the Baram area was ceded to the White Rajahs. He is the only person in this list of leaders who can safely be referred to with his honorific, and indeed he is invariably so named. In addition to this title, his name is also preceded by the particle **ke** (see note 3 of this chapter) and **sadì'** (see note 4 of this chapter). Moreover, he is addressed, uniquely, as a spirit (**bìlì'**). All the ancestors are spirits, by definition. Tama Jok is at pains here to emphasize this fact; Orang Kaya Luwak is a presiding spirit.

I often asked whether the personal name Luwak was derived from the term for the lake (**luvak**) that was so important to the Lelak people, but I was told that the phonetic similarity was a coincidence. I never met anyone called Luwak, but that in itself does not prove much because the Berawan have an apparently endless supply of personal names.

9. This particle, borrowed from Malay, serves to emphasize the word to which it is appended. It is commonly employed in Sarawak Malay. There is a Berawan version of this particle, which is frequently used in the Long Teru and Batu Belah dialect of Berawan. The emphasis particle **ba** is pronounced with stress on the plosive. It is so characteristic that Berawan from other communities tease Long Teru folk by tacking a loud **ba** on to every second word.

10. This is a complex piece of imagery. First, a synecdoche by which the trivet is made to stand for all cooked food and all offerings given to the spirits. **Angaan** and **jakaan** are alternative names in everyday Berawan for the devices—usually a metal ring with three legs—that are used to hold cooking pots above the coals of the fire. We may asky why Tama Jok uses the trivet to stand for food. He is making an analogy between a trivet and the **tapo'** in front of him, which also has legs—the upright sticks that hold the indispensible eggs. The metaphor has several implications: that sacrifice is a kind of cooking (all the comestibles on a **tapo'** are in fact raw); that the **tapo'** is the sort of place that a hearth is; and that the **tapo'** feeds people.

11. Long Teru is so named because it is the place where the Teru river meets the larger watercourse, the Tinjar. **Long** means "river-mouth." This is the standard way of designating places throughout central northern Borneo.

   The term **lía** is elastic: it can mean "family," and it can also mean "nation" or even "race" (with all the ambiguities that these words possess in English). In this prayer it is easy to choose the gloss "community" because these prayers are in the context of a longhouse festival.

12. Both **mída** and **luya** are words in everyday Berawan. The latter means literally "tame." A life that is "tame" and "slow" is one without crises, strife, or disasters.

13. **Ketan** and **kepan** have similar meanings in everyday Berawan. The concept of a "thick" or "deep" life is one of fulfillment and satisfaction.

14. In this list of words—all meaning "luck" or "lucky"—it is hard to be sure which are used in everyday Berawan. In casual conversation, Berawan usually employ some variant of the Malay **nasib** (fortune, destiny). **Lukí** and **melaí** are evidently recognizable outside **píat**, however. **Melubí** and **beluwai** are probably **píat**-words. Rhyming and alliteration occur between lines as well as within them, and this figure recurs frequently in the prayer.

   In the previous figure, all three of the words for money are direct borrowings from Malay, which is appropriate since Malay is preeminently the language of trade. Only **paraí** is a standard Berawan word.

15. In this pair, **nyadu** is evidently concocted so as to provide alliteration.

16. **Pun** is an inseparable particle used in Malay to emphasize the preceding word or phrase.

17. The standard Berawan term for "house" is **lamèng**. Here the cognate form **lamín** is used, borrowed from Kenyah. It properly means the apartment of a coresidential group within the longhouse, but it is used here in a wider sense. **Uma** is borrowed from Kenyah, and does mean "house." **Da** and **lírín** are evidently **píat**-words.

18. The preceding four lines encapsulate an entire theory of blood sacrifice (see chapter two).

19. These four lines are difficult to translate, and their meaning is discussed in detail in chapter two.

20. **Tílong** is a pair word invented to go with **padong**, which is a term in everyday Berawan, although used infrequently. The notion is metaphysical: a **padong** is a place that is "up high," the abode of a god perhaps. It implies security, and that is why I use the gloss "fastness." Apparently, pieces of ritual apparatus may be referred to as **padong**. Many longhouse festivals culminate in the erection of tall posts, for example the status-enhancing ritual of **kaju uran** (**kaju** means "wood," **uran** is untranslatable) that can only be performed by certain noble individuals. These posts evidently can be referred to poetically as **padong**. This usage lends support to the interpretation that such structures provide a point of contact between human and spirit realms.

21. For a discussion of this figure, see chapter two.

22. For the connotations of these words, see the discussion of sacrifice in chapter two.

23. The preceding three lines amplify the imagery in lines 32–43.

24. This particle occurs in several common constructions. It has a range of possible glosses, depending on its syntactical function. I give two examples of ways that it is used: 1. To construct questions: **Co kedíín . . .?** "What sort of?" (**kedíín** means "sort, type, manner"); **Co kuví . . .?** "How long . . .?" or "How long ago . . .?" (**kuví** means "long, long time"). In this construction it can be compared with the use of **apa** in Malay. In some phrases **íno** (what?) can be substituted for **co**: **Ino kedíín . . .?** "What sort of . . .?" 2. In the following phrase **co** appears to function as a kind of preposition: (**ko**) **pulo co luvak** "I'm going to the lake" (**ko** means "I," **pulo** means "go," **luvak** means "lake"). One does not use **co** when the destination has a proper name: **pulo Long Teru** "I'm going to Long Teru." Moreover, in the following phrase there is a readily identifiable preposition present as well: (**ko**) **sakí tuman co luvak nî'é** "I just arrived from the lake" (**sakí** means "arrive," **tuman** means "from," **nî'é** means "before, just now"). **Co** can also appear before abstract nouns: **bíyar, co unyín** means something like "hasten slowly" (**bíyar** means "slow," **unyín** means "desires, emotions, temperament"). In these phrases, **co** resembles a definite article used in front of some nouns only. (See also prayer two, note 9.)

25. **Ubín** means literally a "footprint," or the "spoor of an animal."
26. **Nulong** is cognate with the Malay **tolong** (aid, assistance, help), but it is a widely distributed Austronesian word. **Mejong** also suggests perhaps that the spirits should raise the young men to social prominence.
27. **Usau** is evidently a píat-word designed to rhyme with **urau**, which means literally "to sit down." **Uma** means literally a "house," but the environment requires a verbal form.
28. **Orang puteh** is the standard term in Malay for a European. Occasionally Berawan would translate the phrase into their own tongue (**laké putéé: laké** means "man," **putéé** means "white"), but they often used the familiar Malay. **Bangsa** in the next line is also Malay, and I gloss it as "race" here though it has a similar range of references as Berawan **lía** (see note 11 of this chapter). The image of floating names implies that their owners are widely respected.
29. **Bípì** is a píat-word concocted to go with **mekí**.
30. **Melì** is a Berawan form of the Malay verb **beli** "to buy." The implication is that the sacrifice will purchase the attention of the spirits.
31. See note 10 of this chapter.
32. All four of the words used to describe what the prayer station is full of— **ma, naga, mang, lagang**—drew blank looks from my informants. **Naga** is a term known to the Berawan—it is the mythical dragon used as a motif all over Southeast Asia—but how it fit into this context is a mystery. **Mang** in everyday Berawan means "again." Despite the difficulties of literal translation, it is clear enough what the preceding six lines are driving at: the offerings (blood is emphasized on line 63, but rice wine is mentioned in a similar context on line 71) should be sufficient to make the spirits pay attention to the welfare of the supplicants. At this moment, Tama Jok is pouring rice wine onto the **tapo'** sticks of the prayer site.
33. At this point, Tama Jok is directly associating himself and the entire longhouse with its Lelak heritage. This is entirely appropriate because he has from the outset been addressing his prayer to the spirits of the ancestors, those whose graves lie nearby, in and around the lake. Those ancestors are Lelak, even though the Berawan element is now dominant at Long Teru.

Orang Kaya Luwak (see note 8 of this chapter) led his people to move their longhouse out of the lake area and down to the main river at the request of the Rajah's Resident in Marudi, who needed a village in the otherwise deserted lower Tinjar to provide him with paddlers when he went upriver. Orang Kaya Luwak wished to cooperate with the White Rajah's regime because his community was vulnerable to raids from his more numerous and aggressive neighbors, such as the people gathered under Aban Jau at Long Batan in the upper Tinjar. He calculated, correctly as it proved, that the Lelak could guard their farmlands around the lake as well from the mouth of the Teru stream as from the lake itself. Also their numbers were increased by Berawan immigrants from Batu Belah in the lower Tutoh, another major tributary of the Baram, who intermarried with the Lelak.

He realized that the Lelak community was in a difficult situation demographically. For some reason that is not at all clear, all the small ethnic groups on the lower Baram went through a period of low birth rates in the first decades of this century. Orang Kaya Luwak saw that the best hope for survival was to encourage immigration from closely related downriver peoples, rather than be submerged in a flood of relatively alien upriver folk pushing down toward the coast. Meanwhile, at the Berawan community of Batu Belah there had been serious factionalism following the collapse of a major downriver confederation. Disaffected individuals and families moved to Long Teru, and began a process of amalgamation that was virtually complete by the time of fieldwork between 1972 and 1974. Linguistically, Berawan had won out over Lelak so it was hard to find anyone who remembered much Lelak at all, but the Lelak heritage is still conspicuous in ritual matters.

34. **Ngelaté** looks like a **píat**-word designed to pair with the standard Berawan **tílé**. It adds a syllable, as style demands, using a verbal prefix **ng-**, and reverses the order of consonants in the base. However, Rodney Needham tells me that **ngelaté** is found in Penan, where it has the meaning "to recognize, be acquainted with." Consequently, it may be a loan word from Penan.

35. **La'ít** is evidently a **píat**-word. It rhymes with its pair but does not exhibit an extra syllable. This is not called for here because the word **mulong** is repeated anyway; the effect is pleasing if the syllables are matched.

36. See note 14 of this chapter.

37. These two lines are syntactically and lexically obscure, though the gist is plain enough. The four words stating what the spirits are to give are a mixed bag, etymologically speaking. **Pují** is borrowed from Malay—and ultimately from Sanskrit—and means literally "praise." **Kalawí** (fame) is evidently standard Berawan. **Yan** and **pelukan** are probably **píat**-words, or at least restricted to poetic speech. Both of them, I was told, mean "name" (**ngaran**). The underlying notion is good reputation or respectability.

The repetition of the word **bílì'** four times is puzzling. Tama Jok probably means "you spirits give" praise and so forth, but what he says means literally "you give spirits of" praise, which is the way that I have rendered it.

38. **Tusaa** is standard Berawan (Malay **susah** means "difficult"), and the **píat**-word, meaningless in any other context, is made one syllable long and with the same final vowel.

39. The familiar word for a shield is **utap**. **Agelatang** and **ngelalang** are

unfamiliar and may both be **píat**-words. This is confirmed by their usage in prayer five (see note 3 of chapter five). Evidently, my informants came up with the gloss by considering the context alone.

40. **Mímat** is evidently a pair word constructed to go with **mapat**. Note that the "us" in line 103 is understood in lines 101 and 102.

41. This is a nice example of a prayer responding to events in the immediate vicinity. Just as Tama Jok was saying the previous line, he heard the call of an omen bird (**kutèk** or **sekutèk**, the tailorbird, genus *Orthomus*). The cry did not have any particular significance at the moment, but Tama Jok took this opportunity to include the spirit manifested in the bird's appearance among those to whom he appealed and to whom the blood of the sacrifice is transmitted.

42. **Sío** is a Kenyah word with mystical overtones. Galvin (1967:90) gives these glosses for the term in Lepo Tau Kenyah: "life-elixir, magic, life-giving force." However, Rodney Needham makes this comment regarding the meaning of **sío**: "only in **taban sío** can it be glossed as an elixir (Galvin's "magical" will not do); it connotes "life-giving" in that it characterized the early days of the Kenyah when they were in the ulu Iwan and had no need to farm since spirits did all the work for them; it also characterizes the afterworld, where similarly every kind of foodstuff and good is simply there (for example, in Apo Kesio); in ordinary life, spirits can be induced to descend and 'consecrate' water, which thereby becomes the equivalent of holy water (Kenyah **telang sío**). I have no record of Penan equivalents." (personal communication)

43. This phrase is commonly used, often while waving the chicken that is to be sacrificed above the **tapo'**. **La** is a word borrowed from Kenyah, which means "sacrifice" (Galvin 1967:30). **Líwa** is a cognate form found in some Penan dialects (Needham: personal communication); also **éwa** (Kenyah, Long Nawang).

44. **Mulong** is standard Berawan for "life" or "to live." **Mejong** is a **píat**-word not comprehensible outside this environment.

45. For a description of the **tapo'** or prayer station, see chapter one.

46. **Jat** is familiar everyday Berawan; **nat** is a **píat**-word that is not comprehensible outside this environment.

Chapter Three: Prayer Two

1. Tama Aweng chooses to begin by appealing to the spirits of the omen animals. This is not what one might expect in this social context. It may be that he heard or saw an omen bird just as he was about to begin—as Tama Jok did when he was at the end of his prayer (see chapter three, prayer one, note 41). Another possible motive is that Tama Aweng wanted to emphasize his role as an augur in the community (see chapter seven). It is

not, however, the major omen bird that is addressed here, but only a list of the lesser omen creatures: **lurok** is any of three species of trogons (*Harpactes duvauceli, H. oreskios dulitensis*, and *H. orrhopaeus viduus*) while **penguwèk**—the usual pronunciation is **pengenyok**—refers to two other species of trogons (*H. diardi diardi* and *H. whiteheadi*). **Sírèk** is either of the woodpeckers *Dendrocopus canicapillus aurantiventris* or *Meiglyptes tukki tukki*. I have no record of an omen creature called **lukíng**, despite having talked to several experts. Tama Aweng has hit upon some rare omen creature or an obscure alternative name. **Asé** is either of the kingfishers *Lacedo pulchella melanops* or *Ceyx erithacus rufidorsus*. **Nyawan** is the snake *Maticora intestinalis*. There are about ten important omen birds and about a half a dozen important land creatures. Lists vary from community to community, and interpretation of omens is also somewhat variable. (For full details on Berawan augury see Metcalf 1976b.) Tama Aweng asks that these creatures all appear on the auspicious right-hand side.

2. This string of three paired phrases is a formula that Tama Aweng is fond of; he uses variants of it several times below—for example, see lines 68–71. **Ngajoí, ngeluwok,** and **nyíkí** are words in standard Berawan, but all the other terms are unfamiliar and, we may assume, **píat**-words.

3. See chapter three, prayer one, note 7.

4. The usual word for "unfamiliar" is **tebí**. **Tenebí** looks like a word made up to make a pair with **tebí**, in which case Tama Aweng has forgotten to use the standard Berawan word of which it is a variant. Alternatively, Beatrice Clayre suggests to me that **tenebí** may be an inflected form of **tebí**, now longer used in everyday speech. See chapter one, note 13.

5. **Adèd** is the Berawan form of a word that is found in many languages throughout island Southeast Asia. It is usually written in the Malay, which is **adat**. **Adat** means generally prescriptions for the ways things should be done; it incorporates etiquette, manners, aesthetic principles, law, and rules for the performing of ritual.

6. This is a variant of the familiar **píat** formula for referring to the ancestors as a whole. See chapter three, prayer one, note 1.

7. See chapter three, prayer one, note 24 for a description of this particle.

8. **Ca** is a **píat**-word that pairs with **lía**, the meaning of which is discussed in chapter three, prayer one, note 11.

9. Here **co** is used in another construction, in addition to those described in chapter three, prayer one, note 24. It has here the implication of purpose, so that I render it as "use for" in lines 34–40.

10. A **melígaí** is a small container, hung in the rafters of a longhouse apartment in which are put small food offerings, such as packets of rice, candy, and cigarettes. It is usually made on the instructions of a shaman, who learns during a seance that there is some spirit of a minor or localized

importance that wishes to frequent that apartment, and to receive offerings there. **Melígaí** are often elaborate: little dolls' houses with doors, windows, and model people. What Tama Aweng means by using the term here is generally clear—he refers to the sacrifice of the chicken. But whether he means that the chicken itself is a sort of **melígaí**, or that the **tapo'** is the **melígaí** and the chicken its contents, is unclear. **Melaí** is clearly a **píat**-word made up as a pair, but it also produces an accidental homonym with **melaí** meaning "luck."

11. This passage, delivered at high speed, contains words whose meaning is hard to deduce. **Papì'** is a familiar term for "prayer," but **pamata, boya,** and **palana** are complete mysteries. If I guess that the last is a mangled form of **pelíka** (repair, care for), then the last line may have something to do with restoring health. Tama Aweng is not above using meaningless terms that roll off his tongue in **píat**.

12. See chapter three, prayer one, note 21; and chapter two.

13. See chapter three, prayer one, note 22.

14. **Tulong** (compare Malay: **tolong**) is an everyday word, and **pejong** is its **píat** counterpart.

15. **Paraí** is the standard Berawan term for "unhusked rice," and **uraí** is an invented **píat**-word that would be incomprehensible in any other environment. In the next line, Tama Aweng does not provide a pair word for **wang.**

16. Tama Aweng mentions fishing in his prayer when Tama Jok did not, and he does so appropriately. They are standing near fishing grounds that are very important to the economy of Long Teru. Fish provide an important source of food, and also of cash income. Tama Aweng deftly suggests both utilities in successive lines. People whose farmlands adjoin the shallow waters of the lake set long rectangular nets (**pukat**) between stakes, and catch enough fish for their own needs. The really big catches of fish (sometimes hundreds of pounds in one night, if the water conditions are right) are made in the Bunok river. Large dipping nets (**labau**) are rigged on a balanced frame, which is mounted on a heavy raft. When the frame and net are lowered into the water, the current holds open the bag or seine of the net, and fish swim into it. Then it is raised, and the fish are scooped out. Surplus fish can be dried or salted for future use, or nowadays they can be taken downriver to Marudi and sold in bulk. An ingenious system of huge floating fish cages is used to keep the fish alive until they arrive, and these cages are allowed to drift slowly downriver when the Tinjar and Baram are flowing calmly. Tama Aweng, with the hyperbole typical of **píat**, asks that they catch plenty of fish even if their nets are ridiculously small.

17. See chapter three, prayer one, note 43.

18. The translations of the words **langèt** and **sarèt** are less literal here than in line 42 of the prayer. The former is justified by the notion that shamans are "hot" or "feverish" during a seance, when they are literally "inspired." The formula that appears three lines below is the standard one for referring to the supreme deity.

19. **Nakaan** is a verbal form derived from **pakaan** (see chapter two).

20. This figure is discussed in chapter one.

21. **Nelì** is probably derived from the Malay **beli** "to buy." The implication that the attention of the spirits can be "bought" with offerings may seem odd, but Tama Jok uses the same word in prayer one, line 66. Tama Aweng changes **kappì** (to ask for) into **nappì** so as to make an alliteration. Verbs often begin with **n-** or **ng-**, but **kappì** is already a verb.

22. These are the same words as appeared above as **ngajoí** and **ngaluroí** (see chapter three, prayer two, note 2). The inflection is meaningless.

23. A **belungín** is a mythical creature that often turns up in stories, and as a motif in painting, beadwork, and carving. These representations are also described as **naga**, and the latter is common in myth and art all over Southeast Asia. The Berawan version is a river dragon. His special manifestation is a whirlpool. The most distinguished Berawan families claim descent from a hero born of a river dragon's egg. It is interesting to compare this creature with the Western Penan **berungan**, a malign water spirit (Needham: personal communication).

24. The literal meaning of **dukep** is "grasp," but it is often used with the political implication of rule, or control. Please refer to chapter three, prayer one, note 2 for a comparison to **mígang**.

25. This section, which focuses on the spirit of water dragon, is a little odd. Water dragons are not usually thought of as active in the affairs of men, and are usually mentioned in **píat** only in passing. Tama Aweng pauses before mentioning it or them (line 88), and I guess that he stuck the phrase in out of desperation since he was unable to think of anything else to complete his phrase. After he does that, he justifies himself, as it were, by talking about the control that the **belungín** have in the river. These phrases are reminiscent of those used about the ancestors.

26. **Icung** is a variant of **kícung** "to give."

27. **Turíp** and **takíp** are both **píat**-words. The former is derived from **urip**, which in many Kenyah dialects means "life" (Galvin 1967:104). **Takíp** is a pair for **turíp**.

28. See chapter three, prayer one, note 16.

29. **Tepíon** is the famous rhinoceros hornbill *Bucerus rhinoceros*, with its massive upturned casque. **Temenggang** is any of several smaller species of hornbill found in Borneo, such as the black hornbill *Anthracoceros malayanus*. Oddly enough, the hornbills are not particularly important

birds for the Berawan. They do not figure prominently in myth or in ritual, and they are not used as omen birds. This is in contrast to other Bornean peoples. Berawan do prize the tail feathers of **tepíon** for decorating war cloaks.

30. This phrase **bulu mulong** (**bulu** means "hair," **mulong** means "to live") is used, even in everyday speech, to mean all peoples, humankind in general. It is a metaphor that does not translate well. A common variant is **bulu lamulong.**

31. This is, of course, a reference to the god of Islam. Tama Aweng is going against normal practice in mentioning Allah in **píat**, but it does not make him a convert. When Berawan speak of their Creator Spirit in Malay, they render him as Tuan Allah (**tuan** means "sir, mister"). Tama Aweng often incorporates Malay words and phrases into his **píat**. A like example is the appearance of **tudu** in the preceding line, by which he seems to mean a "revelation." The literal meaning of the word in Malay is "to follow a course unswervingly."

32. **Mutong** is derived from **butong**, which means a statuette that is usually a small carving of a human or an animal. **Butong** are used in a number of ritual contexts, and the word is familiar in everyday speech. The verbal form **mutong** would not, I think, be readily comprehensible outside **píat**. One of the names for the Creator has the same root.

33. This whole section (lines 96–106) is awkward. Basically, Tama Aweng is saying that Berawan sacrifice chickens rather than hornbills because it is the will of the Creator. One is left wondering who ever suggested hornbills as sacrificial animals. Despite lines 96 and 97, hornbills are not at all plentiful, and they are not taken alive when they are hunted. Tama Aweng's flowery language does not disguise the underlying non sequitur. The reference to elbows and upper arms in lines 104 and 105 is ambiguous; I would guess that what he is suggesting is that we are made "entirely" by the Creator—head to toe, as we might say. Lines 99–104 are said very fast, virtually all in one breath.

34. **Sepèk** is a common small bird. I gloss it as "sparrow." **Lusalèk** is evidently a **píat**-word designed to accompany it.

35. **Awang** is the open sky where there are no clouds.

36. All these four terms meaning bad or evil are unfamiliar. **Angat** or **amat** might be derived from **jat**, the standard word for "bad." For a discussion of the word **latang**, see chapter three, prayer one, note 39. **Lebang** is a concocted pair.

37. One of these words for "scatter" is probably standard Berawan, and the other is an invented pair. The notion here is that the community will be split by internal quarrels, and so become dispersed and vulnerable. This poetic passage is more successful than the previous one (see chapter three,

prayer two, note 33). It is a variant on Tama Jok's pro forma statement about the effectiveness of one drop of sacrificial blood (see chapter three, prayer one, note 18). Tama Aweng argues that even if the chicken was a tiny speck, like a bird high in the sky, it would still have vast spiritual power.

38. **Pírèng** is a triangle of wall that extends up into the gables of a roof. In a longhouse, only the two end rooms have them, and they are usually light structures of palm leaves sewn onto a frame so that they can be moved as necessary to keep the rain out or to let a breeze through. **Ngelírèng** is an invented pair-word, given a verbal form.

39. In this passage, Tama Aweng skillfully continues the celestial imagery of the previous one. Even if the chicken is as tiny as a bird in the heavens, its power will still cover the longhouse as if it were a cloud.

40. There are no tigers in Borneo, but interior folk must have heard of the power and speed of the animal from Malays. The tiger is often used as a symbol of vigor and of leadership. **Maccì** is a cat that is found in Borneo jungles, is much respected by hunters, and is the subject of special taboos.

41. See chapter three, prayer one, note 14.

42. The imagery in lines 118 and 119 is again poetic and original. There is a modal personality that is appreciated in young men: quick, energetic, impetuous to the point of rashness. This concept is summarized in the Berawan term **sagem** "vigorous." Surely the young people with this vigor will achieve everything they desire, both wealth and fortune.

43. **Kenajíu** is an elaborated form of the standard **jíu** "to say." **Kelaríu** is a pair word that would be incomprehensible outside this environment.

44. See chapter three, prayer one, note 17.

45. See chapter three, prayer one, note 20.

46. This passage is difficult to follow. Tama Aweng seems to strike a note of humility; human beings are proud but actually insignificant compared to the spirits.

47. Both **sau** and **dacíen** are evidently mythical water creatures. **Sau** was described as a sort of huge fish. Rodney Needham points out to me that **dacíen** may be related to Penan **sian**, meaning a "tortoise" (personal communication), but my informants were vague about the nature of **dacíen**, and I know of no context in which the tortoise is accorded any special religious significance.

48. **Uvì'** is evidently a variant of **vì'** (grandparent).

49. What Tama Aweng is talking about here is the special role or office that is unique to Long Teru. As discussed in note 16 of this prayer, fishing is important to the Long Teru folk for subsistence and as a way of earning cash. Fishing sites along the river are the property of individual families, and unscrupulous individuals can increase their own catches at the expense of others by changing the shape of the riverbed. This is done by setting

stakes into the bottom just upriver from your own raft, so as to make the river more shallow there. The current will run faster so the fish will be more likely to be swept into your net. The job of the man who **dukep** the Bunok river is to watch out for such abuses, to make sure that the banks are maintained, and occasionally to prohibit fishing for reasons of conservation. The man that held this role in 1973 was Gumbang, a leading figure at Long Teru.

Tama Aweng's language is flattering to Gumbang. Gumbang is described as "propping up" (line 154) the whole Bunok—a phrase we last heard used about the awesome spirits of the ancestors (prayer one, line 12). The spirits are asked to make his words "spiritually powerful" (line 163).

50. **Ngelabau** is a verbal form that is used in everyday Berawan. It is derived from **labau,** a "seine net" (see note 16 of this prayer).

51. The preceding five lines are difficult to understand. The gloss of **síngala** is uncertain. **Bísa** might be glossed as "ability" (derived from the Indonesian **bisa** meaning "can"), giving the implication that what Gumbang says ought to be able to influence people. **Muléí** (return) implies perhaps that his words should influence people later, when they are contemplating a wrongdoing.

52. Here again Tama Aweng inappropriately uses spiritual language to refer to Gumbang: in line 42 above, it is the sacrifice that is said to be "feverish" and to "quiver," here it is speech about mundane matters (see note 49 of this prayer). Also note that three lines below Tama Aweng uses the plural pronoun in referring to the Creator, but only to preserve the phrasing used in adjacent lines.

53. As Tama Aweng is saying these words he is burning the hair on the back of the pig's neck, releasing smoke that rises in a thin column to the jungle canopy.

54. Tama Aweng is mixing up cosmologies. For the origin of the names of the deities mentioned, see chapter two.

55. This is the first occasion when Tama Aweng addresses the spirit of the pig directly. For the implications of this, see the section on sacrifice in chapter two.

56. In its most familiar usage, **a an** is simply a more emphatic way of asking "where?" **An** can occur alone, but a more common word for "place" is **atak. A an** sometimes occurs in everyday speech in a context that requires an English gloss of "why." The gloss of the unfamiliar word **puku** is based on the context.

57. This is a frequently heard verb of motion. Berawan habitually orient themselves by reference to the nearest large watercourse. With that as a reference point, motion is either upriver (**kraí**) downriver (**kíng**), or away from the river (**kellajjì'**). If the river is winding, as most are, the direction considered to be upriver will vary according to how far one is from its

banks. Complications also arise when there are several watercourses nearby. Since long distance travel is usually by river, Tama Aweng's instruction to the pig not to "wander away from the river" amounts to a warning not to get lost.

58. This word is perhaps a contraction of **maccì** "to paddle a canoe." This usage emphasizes movement in the correct direction for a long journey (see note 57 of this prayer).

59. This is a further example of the tendency, marked in the case of Tama Aweng, to amalgamate the names of deities borrowed from other traditions (see chapter two).

60. **Udíp** is a modified form of the Kenyah word **urip** "life" (see note 27 of this prayer). **Típ** is probably a **píat**-word, but it may be related to the Penan (Long Buang) word **tipah,** meaning "custom" (Needham: personal communication).

61. This combined name amalgamates different deities in the manner noted in note 59 of this prayer.

62. **Uko** is a word borrowed from Kenyah; a cognate form, **ukun,** is used in the standard formula for the ancestors (Kenyah Lepo Tau: **uko,** Kenyah Long Wat: **ukun,** Kenyah Sebop: **ukun;** Urquhart 1956). The particle **pa** is a suffix that gives emphasis to the following word, and it too is borrowed from Kenyah languages (Galvin 1967:67). These loan words are appropriate because Bungan is a Kenyah deity.

63. Berawan **du'an** "the world" is probably derived from Malay **dunia,** which in turn comes from the Arabic. The phrase **bulu du'an** repeats the form of **bulu mulong** mentioned in note 30 of this prayer.

Chapter Four: Prayer Three

1. See chapter three, prayer two, note 62.

2. See chapter three, prayer two, note 60. **Lakíp** is a **píat**-word designed to make a pair with **uríp**. Tama Aweng uses **típ** instead.

3. **Bulu mulong** means "human beings." See chapter three, prayer two, note 30.

4. The translation here is less than literal. A word-for-word gloss would be "destination seat destination walk."

5. See chapter three, prayer two, note 59.

6. **Tupo'** is a term of address for grandchildren or great grandchildren. Tama Avit is not in fact a grandparent of Ukat, but he is married to the child's grandmother.

7. This line repeats the form of line 8, and in a similar context. A word-for-word gloss would be: "I this come walk come seat." The translation is not literal, but it preserves the redundancy of the original.

8. These names are both constructed with a teknonym and a personal name. See the discussion preceding prayer three.

9. Berawan has an extra series of pronouns not found in English. They are neither singular nor plural. They specify instead that the subject is two persons or two things. **Suvéí** means "we two," including the person addressed; **maséí** means "we two," excluding the person addressed and including some third person; **kaséí** means "you two," including the person addressed and some third person; and **díséí** means "they two," which brackets two people together who can be identified by context. Here, **díséí** clearly refers to Gumbang and Keleing, the parents of Ukat. Married couples are often referred to using this pronoun. For instance, Gumbang and Keleing could be called Gumbang **díséí**, or, just as easily, Keleing **díséí**.

10. See chapter three, prayer two, note 56.

11. "Worry" is the gloss offered by my informant for the word **pava** in the previous line. He may have guessed it by comparison with the next line, where a piece of parallel speech clearly signals a similarity of meaning with **tusaa**. Tama Avit, however, probably borrowed the word from Kenyah. Galvin (1967:67) glosses the Lepo Tau Kenyah word **paba** as "dilemma, uncertainty."

   In Malay as spoken in the Baram river area, **susah** is frequently used, and with a wide range of meaning. In different contexts it can mean: "hard, difficult, uncomfortable, uneasy, anxious, sad." **Kena susah** (**kena** means "knock into, encounter") means to run into difficulties or discomforts, or to suffer misfortune or grief. **Tusaa** in this line is a variant of the familiar Malay word. The best gloss here appears to be "anxiety."

12. **Kumaan selamat** is here rendered as a "celebration."

13. This is yet another alternative name for the supreme deity borrowed from a neighboring group, probably the Sebop. Hose and McDougall (1912, 2:6) note that their Kayan informants said that **Pa Silong** is the equivalent of their **Laki Tenangan** and the Kenyah **Bali Penyalong**. Unfortunately, they attribute the first of these titles only to the "Klemantans," a ragbag category of their invention that includes many disparate groups. **Pesalong** is evidently a corruption of **Pa Silong**, and the suffix points to a Kenyah-related group so I suspect that the name was originally Sebop. At Long Jegan, a Berawan community once closely allied with the Sebop, there is a powerful rice charm called **Aping Pesalong**. **Jalong** may be a pair-word of Berawan invention. It is a sad comment on our knowledge of the traditional religions of interior Borneo that we cannot even attribute confidently names for the supreme deity.

14. For a discussion of **daren** and **bíto' tíloí**, see the section on prayer stations in chapter two.

15. This line, like the next, presents a rapidly recited list of spirits assumed to be associated with certain places, creatures, or things. For **bíli' ca bíli' lía,** see chapter two. A **lasaan** is a simple shelter that consists minimally of a raised bamboo floor and a thatched roof, such as are built on hunting expeditions or at the farms. Here Tama Avit refers to the latter. By mentioning whatever spirits that are present at the farms, Tama Avit neatly balances the prior reference to spirits of the longhouse: town and country, as it were. **Síkíp** are part of the contents of bundles of charms that are attached to the sheaths of war swords (**belílík takèng**). These bundles are supposed to confer valor and immunity from the enemy's weapons. They are brought out whenever major sacrifices are made in the longhouse so that their efficacy can be renewed. Note that in this and in the succeeding line the repeated phrase "spirits of" has been left out to save space in the translation.

16. Another rapid list of spirits: **belungín, sau,** and **dacíen** are all mythical water creatures. **Belungín** is a **naga**-like dragon (see chapter three, prayer two, note 23). **Sau** is a huge fish. Tama Aweng also speaks of **dacíen**; see chapter three, prayer two, note 47.

17. There are many spirits associated with mountains. The Dulit range on the upper Tinjar is associated with the journey to the land of the dead. **Junyang** apparently means a "guide, someone who can show the way through remote areas" (see Metcalf 1982a:213–22).

18. This reference to spirits of the sun and the moon is unusual. I gloss them in the singular, a spirit of each, but there is nothing in the phrase to make that necessary.

19. This is the verbal form of **papì'** (prayer). Since prayer occurs in all rites, the term implies ritual generally.

20. See chapter three, prayer one, note 43.

21. For a discussion of **Penyalong,** see chapter three, prayer two, note 61; for **Jalong,** see note 13 of this chapter. At this time, Tama Avit is glancing around, looking for the sacrificial pig. As line 46 indicates, he cannot see it.

22. **Cì' ya** means literally "go to him." The personal pronoun is a variant used at Long Jegan.

23. The terms that appear after **telang** are mostly familiar from other prayers, but two are not new. None of my informants recognized **dèíng** or **nèíng,** and I did not check back with Tama Avit for clarification. Thus, my glosses are guesswork.

24. For the meaning of this figure, see chapter two.

25. In the preceding ten lines, Tama Avit produces yet another string of assorted spirit agencies. See note 16 of this chapter for **dacíen** and **sau.** For a discussion of "spirits of dreams," see the prayer summary. For **síkíp, ca,**

and **lasaan**, refer to note 15 of this chapter. See chapter two for a description of prayer stations.

26. This is a nice example of the unequal sacrificial bargain of which Valeri speaks (1985:65). The parents solemnly promise a jar of rice wine in exchange for the life of their son.

27. See chapter three, prayer two, note 19.

28. This phrase is syntactically difficult. As described in chapter two, the **kaju unong** (**kaju** means "wood", **unong** means "life") is an element in the structure of a **tapo'**. After he mentioned it, Tama Avit tags adjectives on to the word **unong**, as in the familiar formula: **ulong jìn ulong genín** (see line 52 for instance). **Unong** in this line provides a double service.

29. The four words here following **unong** all refer to social class. **Maren** is the Kenyah term meaning someone of the upper or noble class (Galvin 1967:42). **Tíga** means "good" in Lepo Tau Kenyah, and is found in the phrase **panyín tíga**, "good commoners," the elite of Kenyah freemen (Whittier 1978:110). **Lenga** and **seken** are evidently **píat**-words with similar meanings.

30. This line contains some compact imagery. A **rèng** is a mystical fence erected by a shaman, usually consisting of lengths of thorny creeping plants wrapped around short posts. It resembles nothing more than a barbed wire entanglement, but it is designed to keep out supernatural influences. Tama Avit asks that the body of the child be spiritually fenced in this manner. Both **tubo** and **batu** are borrowed from Malay. The former is clear enough, it means simply "body." The latter, however, is mysterious: I do not know what Tama Avit means by the "stones" of the child. Perhaps he refers to bones in contrast to flesh, or to the major internal organs.

31. This line repeats the puzzling form of line 8, discussed in note 4 of this chapter.

32. Both these words for "travel" are unfamiliar. **Lasat** is evidently usable in everyday Berawan, and **penalat** is a concocted pair word.

33. The closing six lines are delivered at high speed and in one breath as a final flourish.

Chapter Five: Prayer Four

1. See chapter three, prayer one, note 3.

2. See chapter three, prayer one, note 8.

3. **Mé** is a **píat**-word designed to go with **supé**.

4. **Melígat** is a **píat**-word designed to go with **tanyat**. The latter is a variant of **tanyít**, "healthy."

5. In this line, and in lines 7 and 9, Uking mentions the three ethnic groups that strike him as relevant in the present context, namely three of the four

main Berawan communities. That ethnic group name is a Malay version of the true autonym, which is Melawan. The people who now live at Long Jegan, upriver from Long Teru in the Tinjar, offer no other autonym. Since Uking is from Long Jegan, he probably refers to it alone in this line. This reference is ambiguous, however, since almost all those present consider themselves to be Melawan, even if they also have alternative autonyms (see notes 6 and 7 of this chapter).

6. In the lower Tutoh there is a community of Berawan people whose village is usually referred to by non-Berawan as Batu Belah. This is a Malay version of autonym **Bíto' Kala** (**bíto'** means "stone," **kala** means "red"). This name is explained in stories of migration from a location near a source of mineral dyes.

7. The Lelak were the original inhabitants of Long Teru, who later intermarried with Berawan immigrants from Batu Belah (see chapter three, prayer one, note 33). When Uking mentions them, he completes his list of the groups or the communities involved in the present ritual.

8. See chapter three, prayer one, note 5.

9. See chapter three, prayer one, note 6. It is interesting that Uking produces a list of luminaries of the Long Teru community that is similar to the list given by Tama Jok at the beginning of prayer one, despite their different backgrounds.

10. The man referred to here is Tama Avit. Tama Avit's personal name (see chapter three, prayer one, notes 4 and 6) was Bellalang, and Alang is an abbreviation that is only suitably used by someone who enjoyed an affectionate relationship with the man before his death. Notice that the word **tama** here is not capitalized. That is because Uking is talking about Alang himself, not the father of Alang. Alang is Uking's father only in a metaphorical sense, principally as his mentor in ritual matters.

11. See chapter three, prayer one, note 11.

12. We might gloss **tua** as "elder," and **kampong** means "village." Both terms are Malay. The **Tua Kampong** is an officially recognized but unpaid position. The candidate is usually chosen by the community, and then the selection is ratified by the local District Officer. The **tua kampong** is to mediate between government and villagers, speaking on behalf of the community.

13. Kajan was the protegé of Oyang Ajang (see note 35 of this chapter), and duly succeeded him as headman when Oyang Ajang died in 1971. Kajan had received some secondary education, and Oyang Ajang promoted him as a man to deal with modern conditions. But Kajan was much younger than the usual headman, and insecure about his control. Uking is exploiting this circumstance.

14. **Nacau** is a Berawan form of the Malay **kacau**, "disturb."

15. Uking refers to the difficulty that Kajan was having in collecting rents that

Iban settlers on Berawan land had agreed to pay. Uking knew very well that Kajan had been subject to much criticism for not being forceful enough in dealing with these settlers, but the truth is that no one could have done much better. Kajan had few sanctions to apply. His people were already outnumbered and surrounded, and the settlers had never had any intention of honoring their agreements.

16. The "people upriver and down" of Long Teru are Iban. The Iban are numerous and have a long history of expansion and encroachment. In Uking's lifetime, Iban had settled by the upper Teru stream and near the main Tinjar river. These settlers invited ever more to join them. There have been several court cases, but the decisions are not enforced. The final stronghold is the lake, **co luvak**, access to which the Long Teru folk jealously guard. In 1987 the Sarawak state government removed the lake from Berawan ownership and opened it up for development, despite the unwavering resistance to this move by the people of Long Teru.

17. See chapter three, prayer two, note 62.

18. **Bang** is difficult to gloss, and seems to occur always in this construction. Its implication may be flattering: "such a reputation . . . that . . ." Or it may be chiding: "You call yourself a . . . but . . ."

19. Uking is jumping to the conclusion that the names Luwak and **luvak** are the same. However tempting this piece of etymology may be, my informants at Long Teru insisted that it is wrong. Luwak is, they say, a personal name like any other. Orang Kaya is a Malay title that prefixes a personal name (see chapter three, prayer one, note 8). **Luvak** is simply the word for "the lake." Uking makes the curious suggestion that the lake is named after the man. This would suggest that there is another word for "lake" with which to build the phrase "lake Luwak," but there is not. I also do not know of any topographical feature named after a person, as we sometimes name mountains and lakes. It is possible that Uking does not mean his suggestion seriously, and is engaged in some form of verbal play.

20. See chapter three, prayer two, note 56.

21. This loud, deep calling noise is usually made at the beginning of a prayer, but Uking uses it in the middle for a dramatic effect.

22. This word is a variant of **bulu mulong** (see chapter three, prayer two, note 30). The hero Tot Manyem (also called Anak Tau) is the subject of a cycle of myths that explain the origins of various geographical features and ritual usages. However, it is never suggested in the myths that Tot Manyem is the ancestor of all Berawan, let alone all humans. The use of **kaam** before Tot Manyem in line 48 is a grammatical error. **Kaam** is a plural pronoun, but Tot Manyem is singular. The error is repeated in line 58 when he is addressing the spirit of the chicken. It is not, in fact, uncommon in **píat**.

23. The preceding eight lines are difficult to gloss, largely because the syntax is muddled. Uking refers to two different episodes in the myth of Tot

Manyem, and at the same time twists them around so that he can harp on his favorite theme, the Iban settlers. In the myth, the animals (**aman**) that provide omens are the spirit familiars of Tot Manyem. As he paddled down the Bunut Stream, the Sambhur deer (*Cervus unicolor*, in Berawan **payau**) bailed water out of the bilges of his canoe. Where the deer threw water out, left and right, he created tributary streams. This is the episode alluded to in lines 55 and 58. Near the lake, Tot Manyem fought with and destroyed a gang of quasihuman creatures. Uking chooses to identify them with the Iban, regardless of the fact that Iban have arrived in the area of Long Teru only in the last generation or two. His general point seems to be that there are Iban in every tributary of the Teru river nowadays, and that Berawan should oppose them just as Tot Manyem opposed his enemies in the mythic past (see note 16 of this chapter).

24. See chapter three, prayer one, note 24.

25. This passage is remarkable because of the task that it assigns to the spirit of the chicken, which is normally charged only with delivering messages. Usually messages of this type appeal to the Creator and other agencies for aid, but here the chicken itself is told to "cast away bad spirits." The usage is eccentric.

26. The usual formula for the unitary supreme deity is **bilì' puwong bilì' ngaputong** (see chapter two). It is rare to use only the first part of the formula, as Uking does here. Uking uses the full formula in line 48 above, with a vowel substitution characteristic of the Long Jegan accent.

27. **Pekena** means "repair, restore, set to right." **Pelíka** is a **píat** pair word.

28. This line makes the hypocrisy of Uking's prayer blatant. It is always spirits that are invoked and addressed in prayers. Yet here Uking directly appeals to the crowd, like a politician on the campaign trail.

29. Uking, the visitor from Long Jegan, is exhorting the men and women of Long Teru not to distrust their leaders—a remarkable piece of impudence.

30. Again the spirit of the chicken is given unusual responsibilities (see note 25 of this chapter).

31. **Pang buno** are gifts exchanged by two communities to seal a peace treaty. Frequently, a young woman of noble birth was spoken of as **pang buno** if she went in marriage from her own village to a previously hostile one. No one offered a gloss of the words separately, and it is possible that the phrase is borrowed in toto from another ethnic group since Berawan villages did not fight among themselves. In Kenyah, **pang** means a "gathering" (Galvin 1967:70).

32. **Bangsa** is a Malay word meaning "ethnic group, race, family."

33. **Kaman** is heard only before the names of the dead; it is a necronym like that discussed in chapter three, prayer one, note 4. Note that Uking refers to the late Penghulu Lawai, who was an important figure at Long Teru (see chapter three, prayer one, note 6), as an uncle while he dignifies the

recently dead Tama Avit as "father" (**tama**). When Long Teru folk mention Lawai they call him grandfather (**sadï'**). Uking is again less than respectful.

34. For the political implication of **dukep**, see chapter three, prayer two, note 24. **Bïtang** refers to anything long and substantial, such as a tree trunk, and refers here to the longhouse with its great timbers.

35. Oyang Ajang was the previous headman; see note 12 of this chapter.

36. This is a further jab at Kajan; see the prayer summary.

37. The word I gloss here as "morale," **unyïn**, has a wide range of meanings. Generally, it means temperament, but it can also refer to feelings and emotions. In line 107 we hear of **bïlï' unyïn**, which I gloss as the "spirits that rule emotions."

38. In this passage (lines 90–94) the syntax of the first two lines is tangled but the meaning is plain enough.

39. **Pa'a** is evidently borrowed from Penan **pa'an**, "thigh" or "haunch of an animal," but it is from a common Austronesian root (Rodney Needham: personal communication).

40. In the preceding four lines, Uking had launched into a familiar formula concerning the efficacy of sacrifice, but he cuts it short here. In the four lines before that (99–102), he offers an unusual disclaimer.

41. Uking's closing appeal for "bad feelings" to be "cast out" is a final piece of hypocrisy.

Chapter Six: Prayer Five

1. Note that Lian does not begin with the usual calling noise because he does not want to draw the attention of the spirits. He feels that it is better to leave the ancestors undisturbed.

2. See chapter three, prayer two, note 56.

3. See chapter three, prayer one, note 24.

4. Standard Berawan has two words that are commonly used to mean "disturb," **kabé** and **nacau**. **Ngelabang** and **ngekalang** are not familiar, and my informants may well have derived the gloss that they offered strictly from the context. Two similar words in prayer one—found at line 101—are probably of the same nature, exclusive to **pïat** and negotiable in meaning.

   These opening lines are elliptical. Lian Yang fears a demon called **telasak** that tries to invade corpses and to nightmarishly resuscitate them.

5. **Ka** is a particle indicating futurity or intention.

6. **Ukuk** is a room within the longhouse, belonging to a particular family. At the same time **ukuk** is the members of the family, that is, the coresidents of the room.

7. See chapter three, prayer one, note 6.

8. See chapter three, prayer one, note 5.

9. See chapter three, prayer one, note 7.
10. This particle is a suffix that gives emphasis to the following word. It resembles **pa,** which is borrowed from Kenyah languages (see chapter three, prayer two, note 62).
11. See chapter five, notes 5 and 6.
12. **Selakík** is a **píat**-word made up to go with **ukuk.**
13. In the opening lines, Lian's anxiety is that "some other" might have disturbed Tama Suleng. Here he is anxious that Tama Suleng will "disturb" the living. Since Tama Suleng had been dead many months, the dangerous, vindictive phase should be over. Even so, the possibility is almost unmentionable—Lian rushes through line 26. Properly speaking, **lamèng** means only "house;" longhouse is **lamèng kuvít** (**kuvít** means "long").
14. The preceding five lines tactfully remind Tama Suleng of the efforts that the community must make in order to put on the ritual that is just beginning. A whole agricultural cycle may be necessary in order to accumulate stocks of rice to feed the crowds of participants for many days. Other food must also be sought just prior to the event through intensive hunting and gathering. Tama Suleng is asked to promote these activities.
15. Ikiung Pete is a place next to the Bunok stream near the lake (**luvak**) where there is an extensive graveyard containing the tombs of important people.
16. This is another line said with embarrassed rapidity.
17. Lian Yang alludes to the many meetings at Long Teru to discuss whether a **nulang** would be conducted for Tama Suleng, and under what conditions.
18. This line refers to the belief that the recently dead are dangerous and liable to turn viciously on their nearest and dearest. Lian encourages Tama Suleng to feel emotions to them similar to those he showed when alive.
19. See chapter three, prayer one, note 9.
20. **Pínyít** is an euphemism; what Lian means is that the rites are about to begin.
21. The relationships of the individuals listed by Lian to Tama Suleng is explained in the summary of the prayer.
22. My translation "transport" is an amalgamation of **mala,** "get," and **maccì',** "paddle." What they actually did was to load the coffin into a barge made of two canoes lashed together side-by-side. An outboard motor was used to propel the barge back to Long Teru.
23. There are a string of words in the preceding three lines that make reference to the fact that the people Lian is talking about are all long dead, part of the company of revered ancestors. For a discussion of **ke,** see chapter three, prayer one, note 3. **Leta'** is the everyday Berawan word for "dead," but it tends to be avoided in connection with human beings, other than strangers. When discussing the deaths of people to whom those present felt an

emotional attachment, the word is circumlocuted in a manner familiar to Westerners. Lian Yang uses the word in line 59, but then corrects himself in line 60, substituting the more dignified **param,** "the late." Surai (or perhaps it is Sadi Surai, see chapter three, prayer one, note 4) was evidently a distinguished ancestor of Lanau.

24. **Ba** is a particle that is common in everyday speech at Long Teru and at Batu Belah. It serves to emphasize the word or the phrase that precedes it. See chapter three, prayer one, note 9.
25. This is one of Lian Yang's few poetic sallies.
26. **Lamulong** is a variant form of **bulu mulong** (see chapter three, prayer two, note 30).
27. The **gu** are a complex cycle of songs that are performed during the rites of secondary treatment of the dead.
28. The word **uted** is heard infrequently. It is more common to hear about **telanak,** the souls of the recently dead. However, there is a clear understanding of what an **uted** is: it is a soul that makes itself visible to humans, often to remind them of their duties; hence "ghost".
29. The preceding eight lines are talking about the decision some months before to discontinue the singing of the death songs, and its subsequent reversal. See the prayer summary for more details. In the final four lines Lian Yang asks that all of this indecision will not be held against them and cause problems for the living.

Chapter Seven: Prayer Six

1. See chapter two for details of construction of prayer stations and associated ritual apparatus.
2. Tama Aweng is fond of using these four words, meaning "to shout" or "to call out." They occurred several times in his prayer in chapter three. Only **ngajoí** is standard Berawan, the other three are **píat**-words. See chapter three, prayer two, note 2.
3. It is unusual for the word **ca** to appear without its pair **lía** because **ca** is not heard in everyday speech. **Lía,** by contrast, is a familiar term (see chapter three, prayer one, note 11). The two words are heard together in the usual way in line 17 below.
4. See chapter three, prayer one, note 43.
5. Note the shift from a plural second person pronoun in line 8 to a singular one in line 9, a shift that cannot be registered in English, but which in Berawan neatly marks the speaker's shift of interest away from the multiple spirits of the prayer station to the spirit of the eagle.
6. The **aman** are the augural creatures.
7. The term **kèta'u** refers to social rank; it is cognate with Kenyah (Lepo Tau)

deta'u (Whittier 1978:110). **Sekotèk** is any of four local species of the tailorbird *Orthotomus*. Tama Aweng addresses the bird—in flattering language—only because he sees one across the river.

8. See chapter four, note 14, and chapter one.

9. See note 3 of this chapter.

10. Tama Aweng substitutes a Kenyah form of the name for the spirit of the eagle, and he does so repeatedly later, making a kind of chorus out of the phrase. The use of the Kenyah form gives a note of sophistication, and has some phonetic advantages (see the discussion of Tama Aweng's style). The Kenyah term **bali** means a "spirit" or "deity" (Galvin 1967:5), and the principal omen bird is usually written as **flaki** (Hose and McDougall 1912, 2:256).

11. **Pu'ong** is cognate with Malay **bohong**, "to lie, false." But the Berawan term is less bald; I could have rendered it here as "exaggerate." Of the four words glossed here as "call," only one is familiar in everyday Berawan. **Metun** has been taken over by Christian converts to describe the act of calling people to pray. Note that the pair of words glossed as "to call" in line 4 of this prayer are not restricted to the act of calling a spirit, whereas these have that association, especially in "calling" the major omen bird. Nevertheless, they are numbered as part of the same sequence of synonyms, and there are more to come.

12. See chapter three, prayer two, note 30.

13. There appears to be a contradiction here about the child's name. In line 27 Tama Aweng calls his grandchild Ukat, but in line 29 says that the child was given the name Balleng. The latter is correct. Ukat is a generic name, used of male infants who are too young or too frail to bear a proper personal name (see the discussion of naming children in chapter four). Tama Aweng's grandson had been given a personal name, but it was seldom used because the child was frequently sick.

14. This particle serves to emphasize the preceding word, a variant of the Kenyah **pa**. See chapter three, prayer two, note 62 for another example.

15. Tama Aweng draws attention to the fact that he chose his grandson's name while acting in his role as shaman. This practice is one in which Berawan demonstrate a weakly formulated belief in reincarnation. The shaman inquires of his familiars whether the soul that animates the child is new to them or was it previously possessed by an individual remembered by those present.

16. **Buwan** are songs in a Kenyah style, sung with a lead and a chorus and using a number of rhythms. **Tekena'** are legends and myths that take an hour or two to tell. Like **buwan**, they are the metier of particular old people, and they invariably tell of the great deeds of heroes of the past. The spirits of these songs are presumably those of the mythical heroes, one or

more of whom share the name that Tama Aweng picked out for his grandson.

17. This is **píat**-word concocted to make a pair with **ngaran**.
18. Significantly, this word is usually used about a corpse in a state of rigor mortis. It was precisely these deathlike symptoms that so disturbed the child's parents. Death is not supposed to come and go in this fashion, hence Tama Aweng's plaint in lines 24–27.
19. The preceding six lines are Tama Aweng's attempt to characterize the symptoms of his sick grandson. He is probably describing an epileptic fit (see prayer summary).
20. See chapter three, prayer two, note 56.
21. See chapter three, prayer one, note 24.
22. Here are two more words meaning "to call" to add to those discussed in note 11 above. **Míka** is derived from **bíka**, an assembly of the entire community that would gather for instance to hear a piece of litigation. **Mínya** is not standard Berawan and is probably borrowed from Penan **menya'**, "to ask for, beg" (Needham: personal communication).
23. **Metok** is a word used in everyday speech, and its invented pair is **semílok**, which is peculiar to **píat**. Another pair with the same meaning occurs in line 146.
24. The **telejang** are three sticks set in the ground in front of Tama Aweng so as to frame sections of the sky from his viewpoint.
25. Of the three terms here glossed as "disturb," only one is familiar in everyday speech, namely **kabé**. **Kelabé** is a **píat**-word derived from **kabé** by adding the usual epenthetic syllable. Another common term used in standard Berawan to mean "bother" or "disturb" is **nacau**, which is cognate with Malay **kacau**. Tama Aweng's term **kenacau** is a **píat**-word constructed by amalgamating the Malay and Berawan verbs. His objective is probably to have a three syllable word to go with **kelabé**.
26. The term **bulu** does not distinguish between fur or hair or feathers. **Lècu** is a **píat**-word made up to pair with it.
27. An individual becomes **tekena'** if his or her soul is dislodged by some potentially destructive agency. When I asked for an example, the one offered concerned the danger of looking at rainbows. The notion is that they are so visually dramatic, so captivating, that the soul may be attracted away from the body. (This is a nice example of the Berawan fear of mixing colors, see Metcalf 1982a:102, 187–88.) Note that there is no suggestion of an anthropomorphic genius of the rainbow that intentionally entraps the unwary soul. Though supernatural from our point of view, the action of the rainbow is automatic, and it is this feature that puts **tekena'** in the same category with **palé**, which is discussed next. The gloss "bespelled" should not be taken to suggest the presence of a magician or witch. Berawan know

of witches among some of their neighbors but deny their presence among themselves.

28. **Palé** is a state of susceptibility to affliction that an individual enters because of the breach of a taboo. In the Berawan view, these prohibitions are part of the natural order. The results of an infraction are automatic, and there is no hint of a guardian spirit who looks out for breaches of taboo and then metes out punishment. It is this unmediated quality that makes **palé** like **tekena'**.

29. See chapter four, note 9.

30. There are innumerable taboo acts, the commission of which will cause someone (not necessarily the offender) to become **palé** (see note 28 above). Despite the long lists of taboo acts that I collected during fieldwork, I am sure that my inventory is incomplete, especially as some categories allow for the invention of new ones by the extension of a general rule of some kind. Nevertheless, fully half of all those I collected concern pregnancy—things that the expecting mother or father must not do. Significantly, the word for an act that is taboo is the same as the word for "pregnant" (**nyílèng**). Mothers-to-be must avoid seeing rotting or decaying things, lest the fetus appear in similar condition; fathers must not tie things up, or screw in nails or bolts, or hammer nails, or anything similar, lest they block the birth canal; and so on.

    In the preceding four lines Tama Aweng has been instructing the eagle to fly over the middle **telejang** stick if the root cause of his grandson's odd illness is of the **tekena'-palé** type.

31. This and the preceeding line are mumbled and unclear. Nevertheless, the intent is clear. Tama Aweng sets up a third category for etiologies of his grandson's illness, and it is a residual category—whatever is not covered by the first two. The reference to **díséí** (they two) at the end of line 68 is puzzling. Evidently Tama Aweng wants to include other sources of affliction whether they have to do with the parents or not.

32. **Meluwan** is a **píat**-word concocted to go with **seluwan**. In line 47, the latter is paired with **uram**.

33. **Sengílok** is a **píat**-word devised to make a pair with **sengetok,** both adding to the pair discussed in note 23 above. I gloss them as "hide," but the basic notion is of avoidance, of pretending not to be aware of something.

34. This calling noise is different from that produced at the outset of this and most other prayers. The latter is low, as loud as possible, and sustained only briefly. This one is high-pitched, and sustained for as long as possible. It has a warbling quality, which is produced by moving the tongue up and down slightly. This noise is characteristic of calling **plaké** and heard in no other context. It may be made, as here, in the middle of **píat**, where it is run into the following phrase. Or it may be made unaccompanied by **píat,** as the augur sits there hour after hour, waiting for a bird to appear.

35. **Matok** means a short while, a "minute" as in "come here a minute." **Sarok** is a pair word not used in everyday speech.

36. The translation of this line appears to depart from the literal, but in fact corresponds to everyday usage. The phrase **íno kedíín** is commonly used in just such a way.

37. **Usaa** means simply "body," but here it acts as a quantifier, meaning "individual." Where we say "eight people" or "eight souls," Berawan would say **maré usaa**.

38. In this list of three words glossed as "fly left," there is only one that is commonly understood in technical but non-**píat** discussions of the meaning of omens by both augurs and laymen alike. That word is **ngabèng**. The other two terms are **píat**-words that would not be used or understood in other contexts.

39. See chapter three, prayer one, note 16.

40. For the sake of brevity I gloss **líma** as "window." It refers to daylight generally, though not the direct rays of the sun.

41. A **tapaan** is a wide, shallow bowl made of loosely woven rattan. It is used as a sieve to remove stalks and husks from threshed rice. A **sagín** is a block of wood on which meat, fish, or vegetables are chopped up.

42. The everyday word for "sky" is **mílèk**, and it was used only a couple of lines previously. I suspect that my informants simply deduced the meaning of **langít** from its context. Of the four adjectives qualifying **langít**, only one is familiar. **Putéé** means "white," or in this context, "bright." **Buwéé** can be assigned a similar meaning since it is paired with **putéé**. Neither **manèng** nor **marèng** meant anything to my informants, and the meaning assigned in the running translation is a suitable guess.

43. **Ekor** is a familiar word borrowed from Malay. **Dètor** is a **píat**-word invented to make a pair. **Kepík** is a **píat**-word invented to make a pair with **pawèk**, which means "arms" or "wings." Presumably **peca, tíma, tegen,** and **aren** are parts of a bird, but not one of these terms is familiar. Their assigned glosses are suitable guesses.

44. See chapter three, prayer one, note 9.

45. My informants provided this gloss, noting that the word is Kenyah. Galvin (1967:44) says that **mejong** means "to lift, to raise." That word is presumably in the Lepo Tau dialect of Kenyah, though one cannot be sure because Galvin mixes words from various isolects. My informants said this and subsequent words come from the Kenyah of Long Ikang, who have long maintained contact with the Berawan. According to my informants, **iko, tau,** and **saga** have the same provenance. The first two terms appear in Galvin's dictionary with the same glosses that I was given (1967:17, 94). The phrase **mejong saga Kayan** is used in everyday conversation. The style of dancing favored by upriver folk (**ngajat**) involves solo performance, and is often the principal entertainment of a late night party. Both the men's and

women's versions are slow and controlled, but the men's is also extremely athletic. The desired effect is of liquid, effortless motion, and it requires strength and coordination. Throughout the Baram river area, the Kayan are reputed to have the most skilled dancers, so that the phrase "as graceful as a Kayan dancer" has general currency. Tama Aweng means to suggest that the flight of an eagle, turning and swooping, shows the same elegant mastery.

46. Of the eight terms in this parallel structure, only **pela** and **katé** are in everyday Berawan. **Ngabat** may be derived from Penan **nabat**, "to medicate, administer medicine" (Needham: personal communication). **Masat** is a **píat**-word made up to go with **ngabat**. **Ngabo, maso, nga,** and **konga** all drew shrugs from my informants, and their glosses are guesses based on the context.

47. **Lunaa** is a **píat**-word devised to make a pair with **usaa** (body), which is a familiar word in everyday Berawan.

48. Two more unrecognizable **píat**-words in a phrase spoken at high speed. The translation "cure him" is a guess based on the context. For an alternative explanation of these terms, see chapter one, note 10.

49. **Pulé** is a **píat**-word made up to pair with **katé**, which is an everyday word. **Lígat** and **masat** are both **píat**-words that would be unrecognizable outside this context, but a meaning was already assigned to the latter because it appears in line 118 paired with a different term that evidently means "to heal." **Ngíso** has no pair word. **Ngelabé** is a **píat**-word whose meaning is deducible because it was paired with **kabé** in line 129. The implication of the word **manaí**, repeated six times, is that a bird should appear that is proficient, rather than some novice that might make a botch of the assignment. Note the implication that a skilled bird will bring about a cure.

50. Each of the four musical instruments mentioned in this stanza is supposed to produce sweet music, in contrast to the forcefulness of percussion instruments such as gongs and drums. **Keluné** and **pagíng** are associated with courting. The **keluné** is a wind instrument with six or eight pipes coming out of a gourd. By blowing into the gourd and sounding individual pipes, a noise similar to a mouth organ is produced. The **sapé** is a stringed instrument with the neck and soundbox carved from one piece of wood. It makes a sound somewhat like a banjo. A **kurèng** is a mouth harp made of bamboo. A **pagíng** is made from a single node of bamboo of the largest diameter that can be obtained. Strings are fashioned by carefully prying a filament of the fibrous outer layer of the bamboo free from the woody interior. These filaments are held away from the bamboo and also tuned with wooden frets that need constant adjustment. Plucking the strings produces a sound much like a small harp.

51. For details on **da, uma, lamín,** and **lírín,** see chapter three, prayer one,

note 17. For **padong**, see chapter three, prayer one, note 20. **Dong** is a **píat**-word invented to go with **padong**. The formula that asks that Tama Aweng's musical voice arrive at the house of **balí plakí** is an adaptation of the one used in several preceding prayers (see prayer one, lines 34–35). But in those cases it was sacrificial blood that was being transmitted, and only to the ancestors or to the Creator Spirit.

52. According to my informants, **nyíbu** means "taking shortcuts," and hence not doing a conscientious or effective job. **Muju** is evidently a concocted pair word not recognizable in any other context. Similarly, **keléjéo** apparently means "offhand" with a suggestion of unpleasant condescension, and **selurío** is a **píat**-word.

53. Both **laan** and **kelabaan** are unrecognizable, and their translation is a guess.

54. What Tama Aweng means by asking for a bird that has "old wings" is a bird with experience, one that must have given omens many times before. Note that once again a clear distinction is being made between the eagle that will answer Tama Aweng's call and **balí plakí** himself.

55. See chapter three, prayer one, note 1, which discusses these words for "grandparent" or "ancestor." Tama Aweng here adapts another formula often used in connection with sacrifice. In prayers one and two, the spirits are repeatedly reminded that they have received "blood of the chicken, blood of the pig" from the community since "long ago." Tama Aweng's message seems to be that **balí plakí** has also participated in those sacrificial offerings.

56. See chapter three, prayer two, notes 54 and 61. Tama Aweng again emphasizes that he wants an effective emissary sent to him, an eagle familiar with the abodes of the supreme deity.

57. See chapter three, prayer one, note 43.

58. See chapter four, note 2. **Takíp** and **lakíp** are alternative pair terms, and **turíp** is a variant of **uríp**.

59. For more details on **pakaan**, see chapter two. **Supa'** are the small packets in which portions of betel nut are kept ready to offer to guests. **Laam** is a term that my informants did not recognize, and its meaning is a guess.

60. A **sanang** is a medium-sized gong about a foot or so in diameter. **Agung** is evidently a pair word made up to go with **sanang**. The offerings that Tama Aweng describes in the previous line are contained in a gong at his feet.

61. **Síngau** and **sapau** are both unrecognizable. The gloss of the pair is a guess.

62. The first term in this pair is evidently devised to go with **gíto'**, "hundred."

63. Tama Aweng points out that the eagle was invariably summoned prior to warfare.

64. Lines 193 and 195 are hard to make out, and both the transcriptions and the translations are approximate.

Chapter Eight: Prayer Seven

1. For **adèd** see the introduction.
2. See chapter three, prayer one, note 24.
3. See chapter three, prayer two, note 62. **Ma** is a variant of **pa**; it serves to emphasize what follows, namely that there are two religions at Long Jegan.
4. **Sebayang** is derived from Malay **sembahyang**, "to pray." Christianity is **adat sembahyang**, "praying custom."
5. I use the word "Bungan" to cover what Sadi Pejong calls the "religion of the Creator Spirit and grandmother Bungan."
6. **Staat** is the English word, just as it appears to be. It is used in Baram Malay and in Berawan because of the name assigned to a part of an outboard motor; the gear lever at the side of a motor, which sets it in forward, neutral, or reverse, is called **go-staat**. In these riverine societies, everyone is familiar with outboard motors.
7. What Sadi Pejong is referring to here is the initial adoption of the Bungan cult at Long Jegan.
8. **Caang** is the leaves of a common palm tree. Bundles of these leaves are used in various ritual contexts, most notably to wrap the trophies of a headhunt. (see Metcalf 1982a:117). There are no heads at Long Jegan, but Sadi Pejong has made the **caang**, "whip" (a loose bundle of fronds) into an element of his prayer. **Kelupéí** is a delicacy prepared for special occasions, and often included on a tray of offerings (**pakaan**) to a spirit. It consists of little packets of savory rice cooked in a succulent leaf.
9. **Supa'** here refers to a little bundle of chopped up betel, inside a leaf smeared with lime. **Borèk** is an alcoholic drink made by fermenting cooked rice. In this passage, Sadi Pejong addresses the various items on his list with the second person singular pronoun **kau** (cf. Berawan Long Teru **no**). The effect created is quaint, but the intention is clear: he is checking off a list of items that should be on the table in front of him as offerings to the spirits.
10. **Lotí** is Sadi Pejong's rendition of the standard Malay term for "bread," **roti**, derived in turn from a Hindustani root.
11. **Arak** is a liquor made by distilling rice wine. It is usually clear, as opposed to the milky look of **borèk**, and can be very potent. Upriver folk often prepare **arak** themselves, especially before large festivals, using a simple still made out of jars and bamboo. At other times they purchase it from upriver traders.
12. It is a fact of some significance for the study of Berawan politics that there is no word meaning "leader" or "chief" per se. Instead these men are referred to under the rubric **dé lo kíjì'** (Long Teru dialect), which literally

means "they who are big." Just who is included in this category varies with context. If one is looking at a graveyard, it will probably mean the single greatest man of each generation. In a legal proceeding it might mean all the heads of households. Here, Sadi Pejong refers to the half dozen most prominent men in the community. Hence the use of "leaders" in the running translation.

13. The importance of Sadi Ulau is explained in the introduction to this chapter.

14. This use of the pronoun to mean "those people" is common in everyday Berawan.

15. **Dínak** are the unmarried youths.

16. Sadi Ujan was nearly left out, evidently. Sadi Pejong had started off on a different tack, when he noticed another elder sitting behind him. So he sneaks in the elder's name before returning to his topic.

17. In the preceding seven lines, Sadi Pejong is looking around the room, and mentioning people as he sees them. This haphazard presentation, which lacks balanced phrases or meter, is the result. Sadi Pejong's phraseology is again quaint in line 22 when he describes the audience as **ra jat,** "not bad." In line 30, note that the true autonym is Melawan.

18. This is something of an exaggeration. This opening prayer of the Bungan festival was in fact less well attended than later gatherings that involved food and entertainment.

19. Both **ngabenar** and **ngabesar** are **píat-**words evidently manufactured from Malay; **besar** meaning "large," and **benar,** "right, accurate." The prefix **nga** often indicates a verbal form.

20. See chapter three, prayer two, note 56.

21. **Lava** is evidently a pair word designed to accompany **suva.**

22. Sadi Pejong implies that the offerings listed below entitle him to make requests of the Creator and of Bungan.

23. In the preceding line, **ngusaí** is derived from the Malay word **usai,** meaning "to set in order, to arrange," with the addition of a Berawan verbal prefix. **Ngalamaí** is similarly derived from Malay **ramai,** "crowded, well attended, festive." I gloss both as "celebrate." In this line, **makan** is the Malay word for "eat;" the everyday Berawan for which is **kumaan.** **Nguman** is a **píat-**word made up to go with it, and I gloss both as "provision."

24. The usual gloss of **tero** would be "already;" it functions to indicate a past tense.

25. **Ngasan** is probably derived from Malay **asal,** "origin," itself with an Arabic root. Sadi Pejong uses **ngasan** transitively. The ancestors originated the current community by migrating from the hilly interior and setting up villages in one place after another down by the river, hence "settled." Since, in the Berawan view, the clearing of virgin jungle gives rights to

the land in perpetuity, the Long Jegan folk think of themselves as owners of the entire river.

26. **Pang** is not usually paired with **lía** because it implies a less permanent grouping.

27. I could obtain no gloss for **uran**; it may be derived from the Kenyah word **uyan,** which means "to fashion, to make" (Galvin 1967:105). The **kaju uran** is a monument erected by an important man, supposedly as a result of dream inspiration. It consists of a tall, carved post with a wooden representation of a jar on top of it. The erection of a **kaju uran** is the only ritual in Berawan culture that directly focuses on high status. There is one in front of the longhouse at Long Jegan, originally erected by the forebears of Sadi Ulau, and renewed several times since. Significantly, Sadi Ulau is the first person mentioned in Sadi Pejong's list of notables in line 24. During the annual festival of Bungan, prayers and sacrifices are made by Sadi Ulau's family in front of the **kaju uran.**

28. This phrase is syntactically odd, but its meaning is clear.

29. Dreams are taken seriously as omens. Sadi Pejong has a particular reason to mention them since his own prophecy was dream inspired.

30. **Seluyok** is made up to make a pair with **tutok.**

31. Sadi Pejong introduces a metaphor that is repeated frequently, and which expresses a concept of worship. Both words are derived from Malay. **Menamba** is derived from **sembah,** "respectful salutation." The inflected form **menyembah** means "to perform the salutation of homage." **Menabi** is derived from **tabek,** "greeting (from an inferior)." Neither term is used in everyday speech, but a simpler version of the latter, **tabí,** is used throughout the Baram watershed to mean "shake hands."

32. The phrase "spirit(s) of fullness" is eccentric. Sadi Pejong invents it because he is talking about food, and asking for full bellies for the coming year.

33. **Nyululok** is another **píat**-word invented to make a pair with the standard **tutok.**

34. See chapter four, note 9.

35. Note that the preceding verse is spoken almost in a whisper. See the section on style accompanying this prayer.

36. Note the simple parallelism by repetition in the preceding two lines. **Semup** is a **píat**-word, making a pair with **cukup,** a Malay word frequently used in everyday Berawan.

37. **Nacau** in the preceding line is derived from Malay **kacau,** "to disturb." The substitution of **n** for **k** makes it resemble a Berawan verb. **Kenacau** is a further variant or possibly an archaic inflected form (see chapter one, note 13). **Berapa** is a Malay term meaning "how much?" or "how many?" When it is incorporated into Berawan, it takes on the meaning "much," as

in the phrase **ra berapa,** "not much." Dry rice farming is a risky business, as Sadi Pejong's pleas indicate. Too much rain at one season, or too little at another, can easily ruin the crop. As it begins to ripen, there is anxiety about various blights that frequently recur. Wild animals, particularly a troop of monkeys, can devastate a field in one night. The people at Long Jegan repeatedly failed to harvest enough for their annual needs. Berawan are, in general, not particularly effective rice farmers, and have since time immemorial relied on the wild sago palm as an additional subsistence staple. But sago is food of low prestige, and Berawan frequently resort to buying rice from neighboring peoples. In view of the fears of Iban invasion on Berawan land (see chapter five), it is ironic that it is often these selfsame Iban who provide extra rice for the Long Jegan folk—at a price.

38. **Legan** is a concocted pair word for **an.**
39. Two more terms that I gloss as "celebrate" are derived from a Malay root. **Ramai** means "crowded, well attended." In Sarawak Malay, it is frequently used to mean a "party" or "festivity." **Ngalamaí** Berawanizes it in a verbal form, and **ngusaí** provides a pair. I do not think either term would be recognizable in an everyday context.
40. The stones referred to here are evidently supernaturally powerful ones. Sadi Pejong may be thinking of the sacred house stones, **bíto' tíloí,** in the Long Teru isolect (see chapter two). There are also magical stones that are used by shamans, or the stones can be attached to swords to make their owners invulnerable. Sadi Pejong may mean any or all of these.
41. **Peno** is borrowed from the Malay **penoh,** "full." The tailorbird *Orthotomus* is one of the omen creatures (**aman**). It is mentioned here because it is small.
42. See chapter three, prayer two, note 29.
43. See chapter three, prayer one, note 21.
44. Neither **luvat** nor **balat** is familiar, and my informants may have deduced a meaning based on context. The poor chicken will need to be strong to carry all the items listed below.
45. **Usaa** is the everyday word for "body," and **lenaa** is concocted to make a pair.
46. **Lakau** is a common word meaning "to walk," while **cíe** means simply "to go." I gloss them together as "to travel." **Ngusau** is an invented pair for the former.
47. **Dítaí** is everyday Berawan, and **selaí** is concocted to form a pair.
48. **Kíku** is used in everyday speech; **ngapulu** is invented to make a pair.
49. **Pabéí** is familiar in everyday speech, **peréí** is a concocted pair word.
50. **Mucau** is another pair word devised to go with **lakau.** See note 46 of this chapter.

51. **Tíléí** is the standard word for "see." **Ngelatéí** may be a **píat**-word, or possibly it is borrowed from Penan **ngelaté**, "to recognize, be acquainted with." See chapter three, prayer one, note 34.

52. In the preceding three lines, the chicken is instructed to watch out for the paths of the dead, which are "all to the left." The paths of the dead are left-handed in the sense that they are "sinister."

53. **Numau** has the sense of peering, and **metau** means "to make something out at a distance." The two make a nice pair without need of invention.

54. **Temaga** is a Berawan form of the Malay term **tembaga**, meaning "copper, bronze," or "brass." Brass is properly **tembaga kuning** (**kuning** means "yellow"), but Berawan are unfamiliar with copper or bronze. Brassware brought in from the coast by trade was a traditional symbol of high status.

55. The Creator is conceived as living in a house resembling those of humans, with a floor raised six or more feet off the ground. No doubt his house is particularly lofty, with many steps leading up to it. **Mat** is Sadi Pejong's pronunciation of the Malay **mas**, "gold."

56. **Kellèjjé** is the Berawan form of Malay **kerja**, "work," which can be used in several contexts. Here I gloss it as "products," meaning the offerings described earlier.

57. **Melí** is the Berawan form of Malay **beli**, "buying." It seems a bit bald of Sadi Pejong to suggest that humans "buy" favors from the Creator and from Bungan, but the expression occurred earlier. Tama Jok uses it in prayer one, line 64. I gloss it as "seek."

58. The phraseology here briefly follows that found in Tama Jok's and Tama Aweng's prayers (see for instance prayer one, lines 22–28).

59. **Ngabayan** is a Berawan form of the Malay **bayar**, "pay, paying," which utilizes a verbal prefix. Again we have the strange connotation of commercial dealings with the Creator. **Gajjíe** is another borrowing from Malay: **gaji**, "wages." Since Malay is the language of trade in the Baram river area, it is not surprising that Berawan borrow words from Malay to describe commercial dealings. **Budíe** might be glossed as "debt." The implication is a donation that is customary, such as one to help cover the costs of a ritual. The tone of these two lines is distinctly peevish; Sadi Pejong seems to be castigating the Creator for not doing his part when the Berawan are dutifully spending their wages to do theirs.

60. The new year referred to is the Chinese new year (see the introduction to this chapter).

61. Sadi Pejong's phraseology is curious, but his meaning is plain enough. His expression "from their feet to the crowns of their heads" is similar to our "from head to toe." He means simply that their salutations are sincere.

62. "Brave" is a somewhat colorless gloss for **lakín**, which has the specific meaning of possessing many trophies as a result of prowess at headhunting.

63. In the preceding six lines, Sadi Pejong is talking about a frequently remarked correlation between the seasonal appearance of certain common jungle flowers and epidemics of viral diseases. It is not clear why there is an association. It is a rainy time of the year, but then again much of the year is rainy. It is not a season when there is much ritual activity, which can contribute to the spread of disease by bringing people together from different longhouses. The connection that Sadi Pejong makes is through **bílíe busèk**, "the spirit(s) of the flowers." This is not so naive or so animistic as it may at first appear. Sadi Pejong does not imagine that every flower has a spirit, or that the flowers somehow release a spirit like a genie from a lamp. What is deducible for him is that the flowers evidently attract a spirit agency, the precise nature of which he does not know. These epidemics are not trivial. Although healthy adults do not usually suffer more than a few days, children are vulnerable.

64. The word **puwíeng** usually means "to hold" or "to own," as in one name for the Creator. Yet here Sadi Pejong uses it as a pair for **tajun**, "reason." Though unusual, it is comprehensible in a phrase meaning "what is the cause?"

65. See chapter four, note 9.

66. **Nasib**, "luck," is a borrowing from Malay, which in turn had borrowed it from Arabic. **Sa'ín** is borrowed from English, perhaps from Catholic missionaries. That information hardly elucidates the metaphorical usage here: when Berawan say **nyí cukup sa'ín** (**nyí** means "he, she, it;" **cukup** means "enough"), they mean something like the English expression "his time's up," i.e., someone is dead or dying. An informant explained it as a book in which so many pages had to be filled. The individuals referred to here are those who died in the previous year (see line 213 in this prayer).

67. This line sounds sarcastic in translation, but I doubt that is intended. The next line expresses the theme more positively. Note that the preceding passage contains more parallel language that is familiar from prayers one and two (see note 58 of this chapter).

68. The usual word for "if" in Berawan is **mo**. Less frequently, **bí** is heard. Sadi Pejong's word **jau** is used infrequently and is a contraction of the Malay **jikalau** or **kalau** (if). **Ríbelí** is a Berawan form of the Malay word **iblis** (devil), itself borrowed from the Arabic. **Shaítan** may have been derived from the words of Christian missionaries about Satan, or more likely, from the Malay **shaitan**, which was also borrowed from the Arabic. Note that a concept of a unitary devil has no place in preconversion Berawan cosmology, and that Sadi Pejong almost certainly refers to evil spirits of all kinds.

69. Again, Sadi Pejong adapts a Malay word in order to refer to religious concepts. **Ampun** means "pardon, forgiveness, a privilege granted by a ruler."

70. The usual word for "speak" is **pattéí**. In order to make the words in this line alliterate, Sadi Pejong adds a redundant verbal prefix.
71. See note 81 of this chapter.
72. **Ngeluok** is a pair word invented to go with **tunok**.
73. **Sakèk unyín** means literally "sick feeling," but a literal gloss is inappropriate. Even in everyday speech the phrase is common, meaning upset or worried.
74. **Pecaya** is borrowed from the Malay **percaya**, "trusting, believing in," which has a Sanskrit origin. It is significant that there is no Berawan word that means "believe" or "belief."
75. See note 23 of this chapter.
76. Normally, to speak of someone having a "bad soul" implies an antisocial temperament (Metcalf 1982a:52). However that is not what Sadi Pejong means here. He is evidently concerned with souls that are "bad" because they allow their owners to become ill.
77. In Berawan concepts of the causes of illness and misfortune, "soul loss" figures prominently.
78. **Petalau** is presumably an invented pair word for **katau**, although neither term is familiar.
79. In this line, "close to" is a reading of **co** that seems best to convey the meaning. A more literal gloss might be "by."
80. The parallelism between lines 267 and 268 is lost in the translation because **usaa** and its pair **lenaa** are glossed differently. The underlying idea is of counting individuals by bodies.
81. There is a curious implication in the preceding seven lines. For an individual to be healthy, his or her soul should remain in its body, or at least leave only for brief periods. Illness will result from the soul being stolen away by evil forces, and Sadi Pejong asks the Creator and Bungan to rescue such ambushed souls. But a soul that is "close to" the Creator and/or Bungan is still absent from its owner's body. There is no need to resolve this nice theological problem. What is interesting is the parallel with the biblical passages where God or Jesus are described as calling lost souls to Themselves.
82. **Pelíka** is a **píat**-word invented to make a pair with **pekena**.
83. A **tebukau** is a length of line or string with a number of knots in it. In days gone by, it was used to reckon the appointed time for a rendezvous or a major ritual. Each interested party had a line with a similar number of knots, and untied one knot each day. Young Berawan are unfamiliar with the term. Sadi Pejong's image of the Creator's role is as a tally keeper: he has a **tebukau** for each human, and unties a knot everyday until their time is up (see the discussion on **cukup sa'ín** in note 66 above). But having suggested that determinist view, Sadi Pejong charmingly subverts it by suggesting that the Creator can always tie on a few more knots.

84. **Kuréí** is a pair word concocted to go with **mukéí.**
85. **Peneka** is another concocted pair word for **pekena** (see note 82 of this chapter).
86. Neither **míkat** nor **mera** are **píat**-words, but their meanings are apparently similar.
87. **Gítau** (Long Teru **gíto'**) is a standard Berawan word; **tangau** is a **píat**-word invented to make a pair with it.
88. This is one of two occasions in the prayer where Sadi Pejong talks about himself in the third person, here in order to be modest. In fact, he had extensive knowledge of who lived in the community, and how they were related. Any leader of a Berawan community is bound to have such knowledge. He seems to be apologizing for not reciting the names of all the members of the community. What he may be thinking of is the special song that is performed during the rites of secondary treatment that does exactly that, recalling each soul individually to its owner (Metcalf 1982a:214, 227–28). Since Sadi Pejong abolished the rites, he also threw out the songs, and this may be a backhanded acknowledgement of their loss.
89. **Sebutok** in line 293 is another concocted pair word for the familiar **tutok.** What is brought together is the "signs" of each life, in another bookkeeping image. The Creator is now seen with a book of names (**ngaran**) to look over. But he also has to keep track of their **sa'ín** (see note 66 of this chapter) to make sure that their time is not up.
90. **Lakanak** refers to the descendants of some ancestor. **Ukuk** is a family apartment within the longhouse. Berawan language lacks the numerical coefficients characteristic of Malay, but Sadi Pejong seems to be using one here with **lukíng.** The word "hole" is used as a classifier for longhouse apartments in many of the languages of central northern Borneo.
91. People from Long Jegan travel both up- and downriver seeking modern medical attention. If an outboard motor is available, it takes about three hours to go by canoe up to the Roman Catholic mission station at Long Loyang, where simple medical aid is available. More serious matters necessitate the more arduous trip (six to eight hours) down to the hospital in the small township of Marudi on the main Baram river. Such trips are expensive because of the high cost of gasoline.
92. Sadi Pejong speaks from the heart here. He is part of the generation that is made anxious by the absence of children for long periods. He was worried about who would do the hard work on the family rice farm when he was no longer able to do it, and who would then feed him and his wife.
93. Translated literally, Sadi Pejong says that he "calls the speech" of those who are absent. The word he uses for calling was last seen in prayer six, when Tama Aweng was calling the omen bird.
94. At any given time, a good part of the population of Long Jegan is away

from the longhouse. Young people may be away at the residential secondary school at Marudi if they did well in the local elementary school. Young men often seek work in lumber camps in order to earn a sum of money, and they may be located anywhere in the Baram river watershed. Older men go downriver to sell carving or jungle produce. There is no doubt that the increasing tendency of people to stay away from the longhouse for extended periods undermines the cohesiveness of the community. Sadi Pejong is painfully aware of this, and he urges the Creator to look after absent members also. He explains that their nonparticipation in the festival does not indicate a lack of faith. In fact it is very hard for a Berawan away from home to meaningfully continue being an adherent of the old faith or the Bungan cult.

95. Again it is the Malay term **percaya** that must be used to express belief or trust.

96. Note the order of events here: the Creator and Bungan are asked to represent human beings to the "spirits of the land." The latter are not assumed to be evil or necessarily harmful. They are not the "devils" that Sadi Pejong talks about earlier, and they are greeted in the same terms as the Creator and Bungan. In fact, place spirits are at least in part ancestral spirits. But Sadi Pejong does not appeal to them directly, as would be the case at Long Teru.

97. Although not evil, it is still the negative aspects of the place spirits—their quirkiness—that is foremost in Sadi Pejong's mind. Note that the particle **ka** here indicates intentionality.

98. Long Jegan is located in the middle Tinjar, just on the edge of the mountainous interior. Big mountains are clearly in view, but the land around the longhouse is mostly flat, even swampy, as it is at Long Teru. However, there is one striking conical mountain just across and downriver from the village. On it is the principal graveyard of the community. The school is built on a flat area below the longhouse, and is consequently close to this mountain. There is a large cleared area in front of the school where the children can play soccer. It is usually in the morning and the evening that the playing field is most used, rather than in the heat of the day.

99. The spirits whose possible anger worries Sadi Pejong are those of the hill across the river from the school where the graveyard is located. Once again, he deals with the ancestral spirits only through the Creator and Bungan, and there is no mention of the positive benefits to be gained from them.

100. Ba'ín is a **píat**-word invented to go with the familiar **unyín** (feelings).

101. The prefix **dí-** used before **arap** is borrowed from Malay in order to produce a passive voice. It is not used in Berawan, and constitutes a speechy affectation. **Melaín** is a **píat**-word designed to go with **mulíín**.

102. **Ngadèng** is a **píat**-word designed to go with **merèng**. For details of the mystical meaning of "fence," see note 103 below.

103. **Kampong** is a borrowing from Malay. It is a familiar word because every community has a government appointed official called a **tua kampong**, or headman (**tua** or **ketau** means "old, senior, elder"). Sadi Pejong's reference to "fencing" the community has more significance than meets the eye. In several ritual contexts a mystical barrier (**rèng**) is set up to prevent malign spiritual influences from entering the protected space. I have seen shamans construct a low wall of woven thorny creepers, like barbed wire, all around a patient. In former times, when cholera epidemics were a great scourge, whole longhouses were fenced in in this fashion, and no one was allowed to cross in either direction.

104. **Musíng** is a word familiar in everyday speech. Nevertheless, it is derived from Malay **pusing**, which has the primary meaning "to revolve," and derivatively "to cheat." Note that the particle **ka** again indicates intentionality.

105. Sadi Pejong seems here to be talking about spirits that are "devious" and want "to create bad feelings." In this line he makes the subject ambiguous; no doubt he is thinking of human beings who do these things, in particular the same Uking whose prayer at Long Teru is recorded in chapter five, and who constantly stirred up trouble at Long Jegan.

106. **Selalu** is borrowed from Malay. It has already been noted that Berawan take dreams seriously as portents of the future.

107. As in note 105, Sadi Pejong is more likely to be thinking of human enemies of the community that are "devious" and "slander, attack" the community, rather than spirits that are. In addition to internal disruption by people like Uking, the community has external enemies, particularly the Iban and Kayan who are trying to move on to their land.

108. It is not clear why Sadi Pejong wants to say that Berawan land is bad. Though inevitably there are places in any farm that are difficult to work because of a steep incline, or lack top soil, or rapid growth of weeds, these problems are universal in Borneo. In fact, the Berawan of Long Jegan possess some very good farm land.

109. Again **melí**, "to buy," is rendered as "seek."

110. **Sío** is a word loaned from Kenyah isolects. See chapter three, prayer one, note 42. **Sa'an** means "to carry on the shoulder." In these two lines Sadi Pejong again borrows language from traditional prayer. These phrases are repeatedly used in prayers one and two (for instance in prayer one, lines 40–47), but with a much more mystical impact. Here it is only rice that is referred to, but in the other prayers it is the sacrament of the blood of the pig or chicken.

111. Neither **petatau** nor **pelalau** are familiar, but the context makes it easy to

assign a meaning to them. For details of the anxieties over loss of land to interlopers, see chapter five.

112. Sadi Pejong does not mean to imply that he owns the entire veranda of the longhouse. He means only that the food offerings to the Creator and to Bungan are set up on the veranda outside his **ukuk** or family apartment.

Conclusion

1. There are exceptions to this. I have seen a shaman sell a verbal charm to a customer with every show of secrecy. I have also seen small, crudely carved statues (**butong**) supposedly used in magic. The Berawan say that these things are not indigenous, but imported from coastal peoples, mainly Moslems. The striking feature overall is how little concern there normally is with such things.

Appendix: First Lines of Verses by Theme

This listing is a supplement to the account of the identification of verses offered in chapter one. It shows first lines or constructions of each verse in the corpus, theme by theme. The theme of divination is excluded because it is found in only one prayer. Unclassified verses are excluded. Prayer seven is also excluded because it is in the new Bungan style. The lines are identified by prayer and then verse (prayer, verse).

	Invocation		1,28	You spirits
			2,1	Where are you
1,1	Where are you		2,2	We are calling
1,2	Grandfather X		2,4	Thus I call
1,3	Spirit of grandfather X		2,11	This is what I call

2,15	That's what I call	4,16	It's for you to make
2,16	That's what I say	4,17	Have pity
2,23	This is what I say	4,18	. . . set things right
2,25	You spirits	4,20	Try to restore
2,26	Where are the spirits	4,22	Pity and care for
2,29	You spirits	4,23	Try to look out for
2,32	I'm not calling carelessly	4,26	. . . throw away bad
3,8	Because made so by	5,7	Lest you disturb
3,11	To you	5,8	Let them have
3,12	You spirits	5,11	Give them
4,3	That's what I say to	5,12	. . . let your feelings
4,9	Grandfather X	5,16	Don't disturb
4,11	All you spirits	5,18	Pity the people
5,1	Where are you X	5,20	Be skillful in explaining
6,1	Where are you spirits	6,22	In order to expel
6,3	All you spirits	6,23	It's for you to cure

Supplication

1,5	Give us
1,6	Let us have
1,11	. . . lift them up
1,12	. . . let their names float
1,17	Let us all be secure
1,18	Let us have
1,19	You give
1,20	You spirits shield us
2,7	Take care of
2,8	. . . let them have rice
2,9	Even if . . . push fish
2,13	Give us
2,14	. . . we ask for
2,22	. . . let young people be
3,3	To ask for
3,18	May X live
4,1	Have pity
4,2	Don't fail to make
4,7	It's for you to make
4,8	Don't let X
4,13	. . . cast away bad spirits
4,14	. . . set things right

Offering

1,4	Come all of you eat
1,14	This is the food
1,15	Let this rice wine enter
2,17	See the eggs we give
3,14	These are the eggs
3,15	This is the offering
3,16	This is the rice wine
3,17	This is the tree of life
4,17	This is the rice wine
6,21	This is the tobacco

Sacrifice

1,7	Even if only a drop
1,8	Charge with power
1,9	Let the blood enter
1,13	This blood
1,22	This blood
1,23	Charge it with power
1,24	Take it to be charm
1,26	This is the chicken

1,25   Make it powerful
1,27   This is the blood
1,28   Charge it with power
1,29   Make it powerful
2,5   This chicken
2,6   Take it to be charm
2,10   This is the chicken
2,18   This is the chicken
2,19   Many are the hornbills
2,20   However small our chicken
2,21   Huge let its power be
2,30   This order of singed pig
2,32   . . . spirit of pig
3,1   Go to
3,2   Your destination
4,24   Not because we want to eat
4,25   . . . let the blood enter
5,6   This is the chicken
6,2   This is the chicken
6,20   This is the chicken

Identity

1,10   Look at your grandchildren
1,16   We the Lelak
2,3   We are your children

2,12   It's not me alone that calls
4,5   These are your grandchildren
4,6   This is X

Explanation

3,5   I am coming because
3,6   That's the reason
3,7   They celebrate because
3,13   Because we said
4,4   Our father is dead now
4,19   Father is dead now
5,2   It is I here to tell you
5,3   This is why
5,4   It's true that
5,5   Just because
5,9   . . . that's why
5,10   Not that . . . but
5,13   That's why
5,14   This is the first day of
5,15   The whole longhouse of
5,19   Although we said . . . yet
6,5   Because we humans
6,6   Because my grandson
6,7   Because he that is sick
6,8   That's why

Bibliography

Alter, Robert. 1985. *The Art of Biblical Poetry*. New York: Basic Books.

Appell, George. 1976. *The Societies of Borneo: Explorations in the Theory of Cognatic Social Structure*. Washington, D. C.: American Anthropological Association.

Austerlitz, Robert. 1958. *Ob-Ugric Metrics*. Folklore Fellows Communications no. 174. Helsinki.

Bachofen, J. J. [1859] 1967. *Myth, Religion, and Mother Right*. Princeton: Princeton University Press.

Banks, E. 1935. Some Kalimantan Vocabularies. *Sarawak Museum Journal*. 4:247–59.

Beidelman, Thomas. 1974. *W. Robertson Smith and the Sociological Study of Religion*. Chicago: University of Chicago Press.

Berlin, Adele. 1985. *The Dynamics of Biblical Parallelism*. Bloomington: Indiana University Press.

322

Best, Elsdon. [1924] 1976. *Maori Religion and Mythology*. Wellington: A. R. Shearer.

Boas, Franz, and George W. Stocking. 1974. *The Shaping of American Anthropology, 1883-1911: A Franz Boas Reader*. New York: Basic Books.

Bolinger, Dwight, ed. 1972. *Intonation*. Middlesex: Penguin.

Brandstetter, R. 1928. "Die Hymnen Dayakischen 'Tiwah'-Feier." *In Festschrift fur P. W. Schmidt*, 189–92. Berlin: Kotta.

Cruttenden, Alan. 1986. *Intonation*. Cambridge: Cambridge University Press.

Dunselman, D. 1954. "Kana Sera of Zang der Zwangerschap." *Bijdragen tot de Taal-, Land-en Volkenkunde* 110:52–63.

———. 1959a. "Gesangen behorend tot het huwelijks ceremonieel der Mualang-Dajaks." *Anthropos* 54:460–74.

———. 1959b. *Uit de Literatuur der Mualang-Dajaks*. The Hague: Martinus Nijhoff.

Ellis, William. 1839. *Polynesian Researches*. London: H. G. Bohn.

Elshout, J. M. 1926. *De Kenja-Dajaks uit het Apo-Kajanebied*. The Hague: Martinus Nijhoff.

Evans, I. N. H. 1953. *Religion of the Tempasuk Dusuns of North Borneo*. Cambridge: Cambridge University Press.

Fallaize, E. N. 1919. "Prayer (Introductory and Primitive)." *Encyclopaedia of Religion and Ethics* 10:154–58.

Fortes, Meyer. 1987. "Prayer." *In Religion, Morality and the Person: Essays on Tallensi Religion*. Cambridge: Cambridge University Press.

Fortune, Reo. 1935. *Manus Religion: An Ethnological Study of the Manus Natives of the Admiralty Islands*. vol. 3. Philadelphia: Memoirs of the American Philosophical Society.

Fox, James J. 1971. "Semantic Parallelism in Rotinese Ritual Language." *Bijdragen tot de Taal-, Land-en Volkenkunde* 127:215–55.

———. 1974. "Our Ancestors Spoke in Pairs: Rotinese views of Language, Dialect and Code." *In Explorations in the Ethnography of Speaking*. Edited by R. Bauman and J. Sherzer, 65–86. Cambridge: Cambridge University Press.

———. 1975. "On Binary Categories and Primary Symbols." *In The Interpretation of Symbolism*. Edited by Roy Willis, 99–132. London: Malaby Press.

———. 1977. "Roman Jakobson and the Comparative Study of Parallelism." *In Roman Jacobson: Echoes of His Scholarship*. Lisse: de Ridder.

———. 1982. "The Rotinese Chotbah as a Linguistic Performance." *In Papers from the Third International Conference on Austronesian Linguistics*. Edited by Amran Harris, Lois Carrington, and S. A. Wurm. 3:311–18.

Fox, James J., ed. 1988. *To Speak in Pairs: Essays on the Ritual Languages of Eastern Indonesia*. Cambridge: Cambridge University Press.

Frazer, James. [1890] 1963. *The Golden Bough*. New York: Macmillan.

Freeman, J. Derek. 1960. "Iban Augury." In *The Birds of Borneo*. Edited by B. E. Smythies, 73–98. Edinburgh: Oliver and Boyd.

Furness, William. 1899. *Folklore in Borneo: A Sketch*. Pennsylvania: privately published.

———. 1902. *The Home-Life of Borneo Head-Hunters*. Philadelphia: Lippincott.

Galvin, A. D. 1967. *A Dictionary of Kenyah (Leppo Tau)*. Miri: RC Mission.

———. 1968. "Mamat Chants and Ceremonies, Long Moh (Upper Baram). *Sarawak Museum Journal* 16:235–48.

———. 1974. "Prayers for the Erection of a New House." *Sarawak Museum Journal* 22:353–69.

Geertz, Clifford. 1960. *The Religion of Java*. Chicago: University of Chicago Press.

Haddon, Alfred Cort. 1901. *Headhunters Black, White and Brown*. London: Methuen.

Hardeland, A. 1858. *Versuch einer Grammatick der Dajakschen Sprache*. Amsterdam: Martinus Nijhoff.

de Heusch, Luc. [1972] 1982. *The Drunken King: Or the Origins of the State*. Later edition translated by Roy Willis from the French. Bloomington: Indiana University Press.

Hocart, Arthur Maurice. [1936] 1970. *Kings and Councillors: An Essay in the Comparative Anatomy of Human Society*. Reprint. Edited and introduced by Rodney Needham. Chicago: University of Chicago Press.

———. 1952. *Life Giving Myth*. New York: Grove Press.

Hose, Charles, and William McDougall. 1912. *The Pagan Tribes of Borneo*. 2 vols. London: Macmillan.

Hubert, Henri, and Marcel Mauss. [1899] 1964. *Sacrifice: Its Nature and Function*. Later edition translated by W. D. Halls from the French. Chicago: University of Chicago Press.

Hudson, Alfred. 1978. "Linguistic Relations Among Bornean Peoples with Special Reference to Sarawak." *Studies in Third World Societies* 3:1–44.

Hymes, Dell. 1960. "Ob-Ugric Metrics." Review article concerning Austerlitz 1958. *Anthropos* 55:574–76.

———. 1981. *"In Vain I Tried to Tell You": Essays in Native American Ethnopoetics*. Philadelphia: University of Pennsylvania Press.

Jakobson, Roman. 1960. "Closing Statement: Linguistics and Poetics." *In Style in Language*. Edited by Thomas Sebeok, 350–77. New York: Wiley.

———. 1966. "Grammatical Parallelism and Its Russian Facet." *Language* 42: 398–429.

———. 1973. *Questions de Poetique*. Paris: Editions de Seuil.

Jensen, Erik. 1974. *The Iban and Their Religion*. Oxford: University of Oxford Press.

Kauffman, Donald T., ed. 1957. *The Dictionary of Religious Terms*. London: Marshall, Morgan and Scott.

Kern, W. 1956. *Commentaar op de Salasilah van Koestai*. The Hague: Martinus Nijhoff.

Kuipers, Joel. 1980. "The Division of Labor in Language and Society: How Speech 'Works' for Men and Women in Weyewa, Eastern Indonesia." Paper given at the annual meeting of the American Anthropological Association, Washington, D.C.

Kugel, James L. 1981. *The Idea of Biblical Poetry: Parallelism and Its History*. New Haven: Yale University Press.

Leach, Edmund R. 1950. *Social Science Research in Sarawak*. Colonial Research Studies no. 1. London: Colonial Office.

Levi-Strauss, Claude. 1966. *The Savage Mind*. Chicago: University of Chicago Press.

Lewis, E. D. 1987. "A Quest for the Source: The Ontogenesis of a Creation Myth of the Ata Tana Ai." In *To Speak in Pairs: Essays on the Ritual Languages of Eastern Indonesia*. Edited by James J. Fox, 246–80. Cambridge: Cambridge University Press.

Lewis, Gilbert. 1980. *Day of the Shining Red: An Essay on Understanding Ritual*. Cambridge: Cambridge University Press.

Lyons, John. 1981. *Language, Meaning and Context*. Suffolk: Fontana.

Malinowski, Bronislaw. 1935. *Coral Gardens and Their Magic*. New York: American Books.

Mallinckrodt, J., and L. Mallinckrodt-Djata. 1928. "Het 'Magah-liau' een Dajaksche preisterzang." *Tijdschrift voor Indische Tall-, Land-en Volkenkunde* 68:292–346.

Mauss, Marcel. 1968. "La Priere et les rites oraux." In *Oeuvres*. vol. 1, *Les fonctions sociales du sacre*. Paris: Editions de Minuit.

Metcalf, Peter. 1974. "Berawan Adoption Practices." *Sarawak Museum Journal*. 22:275–86.

———. 1976a. "Who are the Berawan? Ethnic Classification and Distribution of Secondary Treatment of the Dead in Central Northern Borneo." *Oceania* 47:85–105.

———. 1976b. "Birds and Deities in Borneo." *Bijdragen tot de Taal-, Land-en Volkenkunde* 132:96–123.

———. 1982a. *A Borneo Journey into Death: Berawan Eschatology from Its Rituals*. Philadelphia: University of Pennsylvania Press.

———. 1982b. "Supernatural Etiologies of Illness in Central Northern Borneo." *Journal of the Malaysian Branch of the Royal Asiatic Society* 15:115–25.

Moerenhout, J. A. 1837. *Voyages aux iles du Grand Ocean*. Paris: Bertrand.

Nadel, S. F. 1957. "Malinowski on Magic and Religion." In *Man and Culture*. Edited by Raymond Firth, 189–208. London: Routledge.

Needham, Rodney. 1960. "A Structural Analysis of Aimol Society." *Bijdragen tot de Taal-, Land-en Volkenkunde* 116:81–108.

———. 1972. *Belief, Language, and Experience.* Chicago: University of Chicago Press.

Pawley, Andrew. 1974. "Austronesian Languages." In *Encyclopedia Britannica.* 15th edition. *Macropaedia* 2:484–94.

Pei, Mario. 1966. *Glossary of Linguistic Terminology.* New York: Anchor Books.

Perry, W. J. 1923. *The Children of the Sun.* London: Methuen.

Phillips, D. Z. 1966. *The Concept of Prayer.* New York: Schocken.

Pollard, R. H., and F. E. Banks. 1937. "Teknonymy and Other Customs Among the Kayans, Kenyahs, Kelamantans, and Others." *Sarawak Museum Journal* 4:395–409.

Reichard, Gladys A. 1934. *Prayer: The Compulsive Word.* Monograph of the American Ethnological Association no. 8. Seattle: University of Washington Press.

Rivers, W. H. R. 1906. *The Todas.* London: Macmillan.

Rousseau, Jerome. 1978. "The Kayan." In *Essays in Borneo Societies.* Edited by Victor King, 78–90. Oxford: Oxford University Press.

Rubenstein, Carol. 1973. *Poems of the Indigenous Peoples of Sarawak: Some of the Songs and Chants.* 2 vols. Special monograph no. 2. *Sarawak Museum Journal.* Kuching: Sarawak Museum.

Sandin, Benedict. 1966a. *Tusan Pendiau.* Kuching: Borneo Literature Bureau.

———. 1966b. "A Saribas Iban Death Dirge (Sabak)." *Sarawak Museum Journal* 14:15–80.

———. 1968. *Leka Sabak.* Kuching: Borneo Literature Bureau.

———. 1972. *Gawai Antu.* Kuching: Borneo Literature Bureau.

Sapir, David. 1985. "The Politics of Translation." Paper given at the annual meeting of the American Anthropological Association. Washington, D.C.

Sapir, Edward. 1921. *Language, An Introduction to the Study of Speech.* New York: Harcourt, Brace, & Company.

Schärer, Hans. [1946] 1963. *Ngaju Religion: The Concept of God Among a South Borneo People.* Later edition translated by Rodney Needham from the German. The Hague: Martinus Nijhoff.

———. 1966. *Der Totenkult Der Ngadju Dajak In Sud-Burneo: Mythen zum Totenkult Und Kie Texte zum Tantolak Matei.* The Hague: Martinus Nijhoff.

Sebeok, Thomas A., ed. 1971. *Current Trends in Linguistics.* vol. 8, *Linguistics in Oceania.* The Hague: Mouton.

Seitel, Peter. 1980. *See So That We May See: Performance and Interpretations of Traditional Tales from Tanzania.* Bloomington: Indiana University Press.

Smythies, B. E. 1960. *The Birds of Borneo.* Edinburgh: Oliver and Boyd.

Staal, J. 1927. "A Heathen Dunsun Prayer." *Anthropos* 22:127–201.

Stokhof, W. A. L., ed. 1982. *Holle Lists: Vocabularies in Languages of Indonesia*. vol. 8, *Kalimantan (Borneo)*. Canberra: Australian National University Press.

Stort, P. van Genderen. 1912. "Nederlandsch-Kenja Dajaksche Woordenlijst." *Verhandelingen van het Bataviaasch Genootschap van Kunsten en Wetenschappen* 59:1–33.

Tambiah, S. J. 1968. "The Magical Power of Words." *Man* 3:175–208.

Tedlock, Dennis. 1972. *Finding the Center*. New York: Dial Press.

Turner, Victor. 1967. *The Forest of Symbols: Aspects of Ndembu Ritual*. Ithaca: Cornell University Press.

Urquhart, I. A. N. 1955. "Some Interior Dialects." *Sarawak Museum Journal* 5:193–204.

———. 1956. "Some Baram Kinship Terms." *Sarawak Museum Journal* 6:33–46.

Valeri, Valerio. 1985. *Kingship and Sacrifice: Ritual and Society in Ancient Hawaii*. Translated by Paula Wissing from the French. Chicago: University of Chicago Press.

Watson, Wilfred. 1984. *Classical Hebrew Poetry: A Guide to Its Techniques*. Journal for the Study of the Old Testament Supplement Series no. 26. Sheffield, England: JSOT Press.

Waugh, Linda R., and C. H. van Schooneveld, eds. 1980. *The Melody of Language: Intonation and Prosody*. Baltimore: University Park Press.

Weber, Max. 1968. *On Charisma and Institution Building*. Edited by S. N. Eisenstadt. Chicago: University of Chicago Press.

Weiner, Annette B. 1983. "From Words to Objects to Magic: Hard Words and the Boundaries of Social Action." *Man* 18:690–709.

Whittier, Herbert L. 1973. Social Organization and Symbols of Social Differentiation: An Ethnographic Study of the Kenyah Dayak of East Kalimantan (Borneo). Ph.D. dissertation, Michigan State University.

———. 1978. "The Kenyah." In *Essays on Borneo Societies*. Edited by Victor King. Oxford: Oxford University Press.

Williamson, Robert W. 1937. *Religion and Social Organisation in Central Polynesia*. Cambridge: Cambridge University Press.

Wilson, Monica. 1957. *Rituals of Kinship Among the Nyakyusa*. London: Oxford University Press.

Index

328

Glossary

This glossary is designed to facilitate further study of the prayers. It is not a complete dictionary. For brevity's sake, most Berawan words are provided with only one English gloss. There may well be others that are equally appropriate, or even more appropriate for the word in general usage, but is the use of the words in the texts that governs the glosses selected. The glossary does not provide etymologies. However, since borrowing is characteristic of **píat,** the probable origins of loan words is indicated. In some cases, the language from which **píat** borrows a word may in turn have borrowed it; this applies, for instance, to Malay words borrowed from Arabic or Sanskrit, but only Malay is shown as the source of the word. In other cases, a word is adapted from some root that is widely distributed in the languages of central northern Borneo. Many sources are possible, but only the most likely is given. Loan words are written as they are pronounced in Berawan.

Since the information in the glossary is presented in a compact form, a few examples are useful in explaining its conventions. Berawan words are shown in the Long Teru isolect. If a Long Jegan variant occurs in the texts, it is shown enclosed in parentheses directly after the Long Teru term. For example: **acì'** (**acíe**) one. If the word is a **píat**-word as defined in chapter one, the word it is paired with is shown enclosed in parentheses immediately following the English gloss and preceded by an asterisk. For example: **da** house (*uma). If the Berawan word is a variant of some other word, that word is given in parentheses after the English gloss. For example: **ato'** here (variant **lato'**). If the gloss of a Berawan word is uncertain, it is followed by a question mark in parentheses. For example: **palana** to care for (?). Berawan words that cannot be translated have their function indicated within the parentheses. For example: **ka** (particle indicating futurity). Finally, the likely origin of a loan word is indicated in parentheses after a gloss. For example: **kampong** village (Malay).

A

a	where
abang	open, clear
abun	cloud
accì	outside
acì' (**acíe**)	one
acín	steps
adang	actually
adèd	custom, law, ritual, religion, festival
agang	brave
agung	gong (*sanang)
akí	because
alé	harm
aman	omen, omen creature
amat	bad (* jat)
an	place
anak	child
andang	origin
ané	there
angaan	trivet
angat	bad (*amat)
ano' (**anau**)	to make (variant **mano'**)
anyam	grandchild
anyí	to receive
apabíla	whenever (Malay)
apan	to take
apíu	above
apo	plateau, watershed (Kenyah)
apun	forgiveness (Malay)
arak	distilled liquor
arap	to hope, trust in
aren	pinions (*tegen)
aroo	many
asé	kingfisher
atak	place
atan	for
atau	or (Malay)
attéé (**atteí**)	to say, speech
ato'	here (variant **lato'**)

atong	throughout, along, around
awa	veranda
awang	aerial space, sky

B

ba	(intensifier particle)
baco' (bacau)	variety
ba'ín	feelings (*unyín)
balat	strength (*luvat)
balí	spirit (Kenyah)
bang	reputation
bangsa	race, nation (Malay)
banyak	much, many (Malay)
barang	thing
batu	stone (Malay)
bawa	to fight, war
bawaa	sweet
belungín	river dragon
belurí	to get
beluwaí	luck, lucky (*melaí)
benau	scream
berapa	much, how much? (Malay)
bí	if
bí'é	lest
bíjì'	crocodile
bíkín	to make
bíkuí	pig
bílì' (bílíe)	spirit
bílo'	widow
bí'o	smell
bípì	sacrifice (*mekì)
bíra	to ask, ask for
bísa'	to be able to
bítang	trunk of a tree, log
bíto' (bítau)	stone
bíto' tíloí	house stones
bíyaí	don't want

borèk	rice wine
boya	offering (?) (*pamata)
budí' (budíe)	gift
bukan	not (Malay)
bukeng	crown of the head
bulíín	moon, month
bulu	hair, feathers
bun	first
buno	see pang buno
busèk	flowers on a tree
butí	scrap, grain
buwan	narrative song
buwau	to migrate
buwéé	white (*putéé)

C

ca	community (*lía)
caang	leaves of a certain palm
cen	animal
cí' (cíe)	to go
cín	money
co	(indicative particle)
cukup	enough (Malay)

D

da	house (*uma)
dacíen	mythical water creature
daíyung	shaman
dapat	fathom (i.e., six feet)
daré (daréí)	is not, are not
daren	red-leafed shrub *Dracoena*
dé (déí)	they
dèíng	to grow, augment (*nèíng)

dekat	near (Malay)
dètor	tail (*èkor)
díccem	night
díccì	before (past tense)
díccu	woman
díek	chicken
díken	father-in-law
díku	tune
dínak	bachelor, unmarried young person
dínu	cooked food
dísa	soil, earth
díséí	those two (pronoun)
díta' (dítaí)	plain
dítíu	aforementioned
dong	fastness (*padong)
du'an	world
duít	cash (Malay)
dukep	grasp, hold, rule
dupun	grandparent (Kenyah)
duvé (duvéí)	two

E

èkor	tail

F

flakí	eagle (Kenyah)

G

gajjì' (gajjíe)	wages (Malay)
gaté	to replace
gau	thunder
gaya	appearance (Malay)
gejen	shivering
genín	cool

gímad	foot
gíku	hundred (*gito')
gíto' (*gítau)	hundred

I

íccem	night (variant díccem)
ícío	day
ícung	to give (variant kícung)
íjìn	permission
íko	you (singular) (Kenyah)
ílaan	to bring (variant kílaan)
íno	what, whatever

J

jaga	guard, watch (Malay)
jajjì'	to promise
jaka	period, season
jakaan	trivet
jalan	path
jat	bad
jau	if
jìn (jíen)	good
jíu	to say
jíwé	face
jo	guts, stomach
jumé (juméí)	in front of
junyang	to guide

K

ka	(particle indicating futurity)

kaa	don't
kaam	you (plural)
kabé	to disturb
kabí	to carry
ka'é	who?
kaju	wood
kakíng	left
kala	red
kalawí	fame
kaman	uncle (deceased)
kamé (kaméí)	we (exclusive)
kampong	village (Malay)
kan	right
kanaan	food
kanaí	to know
kapan	thick
kappì (kappíe)	to ask for
kara' (kara)	all, each
karoo	many (variant **aroo**)
kaséí	you two (pronoun)
katé	to throw away
katta	to say
katau	to call (*petalau)
kau	you (singular)
ke	(particle indicating individual named is dead)
keda	below
kedíín	sort, type
kedung	just, only
kelabé	to disturb (*kabé)
kelaríu	to talk (*jíu)
kelaroí	to shout (*kernajoí)
keléjéo	offhand, careless
kellajjí'	to go inland
kellèjjé (kellèjjéí)	to work, work
kelo'	you (plural) (variant **tekelo'**)
keluné	mouth organ
kelupa	underneath
kelupé (kelupéí)	savory rice

kena	to come into contact with, encounter
kenacau	to disturb (*nacau)
kenajíu	to talk (*jíu)
kenajoí	to shout (*ngajoí)
kenumaan	to feed (*nakaan)
kepík	wing (*pawèk)
ketan	deep
kèta'u	noble
keta'un	mass, volume
ketí	charm, amulet
ketu'o	right side
kícung	to give
kíjì' (kíjíe)	big
kíku	to follow
kílaan	to bring
kílong	to bail
kín	at
kína	to keep
kíng	downriver
kísau	to run (?)
kíta	we (inclusive)
kíta'	to look
konga	to eject (*nga)
kraí	upriver
ko	I
kulong	to stare
kulèk	skin, bark
kumaan	to eat
kura	how many?
kuréé (kuréí)	open (*pukéé)
kurèng	mouth harp
kutèk	tailorbird
kuva	to try
kuvít	long

L

la	sacrifice (Kenyah)
la'a	left, remaining
laam	tobacco (?)

labau	seine, net	líwa	sacrifice (Penan)
lacík	scared	lo	that, who, which
lagang	again (*mang)	lotí	bread (Malay)
la'ít	healthy (*tanyít)	lunaa	body (*usaa)
lakanak	family	luppéé	dream
lakau	to walk	(luppéí)	
laké (lakéí)	man	lupo' (lupau)	to appear
lakíp	life (*uríp)	lukí	lucky
lakín	brave	lukíng	hole
lamèng	house	lum	in
lamín	room (Kenyah)	luro'	to leap
lamulong	people	lurok	species of trogon
langèt	feverish, hot	lutok	to float
langít	sky	luvak	lake
lapíu	above (variant apíu)	luvat	strength (*balat)
lasaan	farm house	luya	tame, calm
lasat	to travel		
lasoo	weak		
lasulèk	small bird (*sepèk)		
latang	evil	**M**	
lato'	here		
lava	pride (*suva)	ma	(intensifier particle)
lebang	evil (*latang)	maccam	sour
lécu	feathers (*bulu)	maccì'	to paddle
legen	place (*an)	maccì	lynx
lenaa	body (*usaa)	mada	to show
léng	taste	makan	to eat (Malay)
lenga	good (*tíga)	makíng	to prevent, guard
lèngaí	stick figure	makípík	to lift up
leta' (leta)	dead	mala	to get, to take
leto'	to ring	malaí	to be accustomed to
lía	community, group, nation	malaí	spirit house (*melígaí)
lìèk	upper arm	malam	night, last night (Malay)
lígat	to heal (*masat)		
lígìt	dollar (Malay)	manai	skillful, adept
líkang	business	mané	thus
líko' (líkau)	river	manèng	blue (*marèng)
líma	daylight	mang	again
lìrèk	farm	mano'	to make, do
lírín	house (*lamín)	mapan	to startle
lít	length	mapat	to throw down
lívaí	to come (variant vaí)	mapau	to answer

mara	angry (Malay)	metun	to call
maren	noble, upper class (Kenyah)	mída	slow
		mígang	to hold, control
marèng	blue (*manèng)	mígín	to call (*melín)
masak	to enter	míka	to call
masat	to heal, medicate (*ngabat)	míkat	to tie
		mílèk	sky
maséé	to pity	mímat	to throw down (*mapat)
maso	to expel (*ngabo)		
matang	powerful	mínya	to call (Penan)
matelo'	us, we (exclusive)	miran	plenty (*kapan)
matok	a moment	místí	must
matta	eye	mo	if
mattacèk	to roll up the eyes	mucau	to walk (*lakau)
mattacío	sun	muju	lax (*nyíbu)
mawa	anyway	mugun	to call (*metun)
mawang	open (*abang)	muké (mukéí)	to open, open
mé	to fail (*supé)	mukong	old
mejong	to lift up (Kenyah)	muléí	to return
mejong	to live (*mulong)	mulíín	wall
meka	angry (*mara)	mulong	to live, life
mekì	sacrifice	mupé	to fail (*supé)
melaí	luck	mupok	to cast out
melaí	spirit house (*melígaí)	musíng	twisting, devious
		mutong	to shape
melaín	wall (*mulíín)	muvíu	to mistrust
meluwan	to dawdle (*seluwan)		
melí	to buy (variant nelí)		
melígat	active (*tanyat)		
melín	to call (*mígín)		**N**
melínan	to trouble (?) (*nelían)		
melubí	luck (*luckí)	na	difficulty (*tusaa)
meluwaí	luck (*melaí)	naa	body (*usaa)
memang	of course (Malay)	na'a	afterwards
menabí	to greet	nacau	to disturb
menamba	to salute	naga	mythical dragon (Malay)
mengada	bright, to be bright		
mengkalí	perhaps	nak	even, up to
mera	to knot	nakaan	to feed
merèng	to fence	naku	to serve
metau	to espy	nalinga	to listen
metok	to hide	nangan	to care for
		nanong	name (*ngaran)

napì'	to pray	ngekalang	to disturb
nappì	to ask for		(*ngelabang)
napíu	rude	ngelabang	to disturb
nasíb	luck, fortune		(*ngekalang)
	(Malay)	ngelagí	to awaken (*nyíkí)
nat	bad (*jat)	ngelalang	to shield
naté	to throw out		(*ngelatang)
nèíng	to grow, augment	ngelatang	to shield
	(*dèìng)	ngelaté	to see (Penan)
neku	sudden	ngelínga	to hear, listen
nelí	to buy	ngelíok	to shout (*ngeluwok)
nelían	to trouble (?)	ngelírèng	gable end (*pírèng)
	(*melínan)	ngeluok	patience (*tunok)
nelíka	to remedy (*pekena)	ngeluwok	to shout
nga	to eject (*konga)	ngenung	to stay
ngabat	to cure, medicate	ngetu	to listen
	(Penan)	ngímaí	to spread, scatter (?)
ngabayan	to pay	ngíso	to move, remove
ngabenar	to celebrate	nguman	to eat (*makan)
ngabèng	to fly left	ngusaí	to celebrate
ngabesar	to celebrate		(*ngalamaí)
ngabo	to expel (*maso)	ngusa	to walk (*lakau)
ngabong	to fly left (*ngabèng)	ní	that, those
ngadèng	to fence (*merèng)	níat	purpose
ngajoí	to call	ní'è	before, just now
ngalacau	to disturb (*nacau)		(recent past)
ngalaí	scatter (*ngímaí)	nulong	to help
ngalamaí	to gather people, to	numau	to peer
	celebrate	nun	path
ngalarak	to oppose	nusíng	to cheat
ngalawèk	curly	nutok	to assemble
ngalíngo	to abandon	nuvang	to meet
ngaluroí	to call (*ngajoí)	nyadu	to push
ngan	with	nyasío	to look after
ngapulu	to follow (*kíku)	nyawan	species of snake
ngaputo	titles	nyí	he, she, it
ngaputong	to create, fashion	nyíbu	lax
(ngaputíeng)		nyíkí	to awaken
ngaran	name	nyíkinaan	food
ngasan	origin	nyílèng	pregnant, taboo
ngattéí	to speak (*pattéí)	nyípang	to gather
ngayan	destination	nyírèng	to fly left (*ngabèng)
ngelabau	to fish with a seine	nyululok	to assemble (*nutok)

O

orang	person (Malay)

P

pa	(intensifier particle) (Kenyah)
pa'a	thigh
pabé (pabéí)	to err, get lost
padong	fastness, retreat
pagíng	bamboo harp
pakaan	a tray of offerings
palana	care for (?)
palé	tabooed
pamata	offering (?) (*boya)
pang	gathering
pang buno	gifts exchanged at a peacemaking
papì'	prayer
paraí	rice (unhusked)
param	deceased, late
pat	four
pattéé (pattéí)	to speak, talk
patut	fair, proper (Malay)
pava	to worry
pawèk	arm (*líek)
payau	Sambhur deer
peca	wing feathers (*tíma)
pecaya	to believe (Malay)
pecco	full, fullness
pegéé (pegéí)	too much
pejong	to help (* tulong)
pekena	to remedy, restore, set to rights
pela	to sweep
pelalau	to take away (*petatau)
pelaya	to set right (*pekena)
pelaya	entirely
peleta' (peleta)	to kill
pelíka	to remedy (*pekena)
pelíta	government
pelukan	name (*ngaran)
penalat	to travel (*lasat)
peneka	to set right (*pekena)
penga	finished, completed
penguwèk	species of trogon
peno	full (Malay)
penusaa	trouble, difficulty
pepat	broken, hilly
peréí	to err, get lost (*pabéí)
pesana	slander (Malay)
petalau	to call (*katau)
petatau	to take away (*pelalau)
pí	water, drink
pì'(píe)	all, entirely
píléo	to transform
pínyít	to attend to
píon	to challenge, defend
pírèng	gable end of a house
plaké	Malaysian black eagle
plakí	black eagle (Kenyah)
pubèd	to heal, medicate
pujì	praise, fame (Malay)
pukat	drift net
puku	reason
pulé	to throw away (*katé)
puléí	to turn back
puloo	to go
pun	(intensifier particle) (Malay)
pungané	later on
pu'ong	to lie
pupang	gathered together
pupok	to strike
purok	rotten

putéé	white	sebarang	carelessly
puwong	to hold, own	sebarèng	part
		sebayang	pray (Malay)
		sebutok	together (*tutok)
		sedang	destination
R		sedía	ready (Malay)
		seken	noble (*maren)
ra	not	sekolaa	school (Malay)
raan	appearance	sekotèk	tailorbird
ramulé	to cure (?) (*rapulé)	selaí	plain (*dítaí)
rapulé	to cure (?) (*ramulé)	selakík	family room (*ukuk)
rè	it	selalu	always (Malay)
rèng	fence, mystical	selamat	safe (Malay)
	barrier	selawan	to dawdle (*uram)
ríbelí	devil (Malay)	selí	variety of grass
		selu	to serve (*naku)
		seluréo	offhand (*kelejéo)
S		seluyok	together (*tutok)
		sema	blood
sa'an	to carry on the	semèk	wet, flooded
	shoulder	semílok	to hide (*metok)
sabèb	reason	semín	hungry
sadeng	although	semup	enough (*cukup)
sadì' (sadíe)	grandparent,	senadu	to push (*sínyu)
	ancestor	senga	influenza
saga	type of dance	sengetok	to hide (*sengílok)
sagem	rapid, vigorous	segílok	to hide (*sengetok)
sagín	cutting board	sepadan	farming areas, land
sa'ín	sign (English)		claimed by right
sakèk	sick, sickness		of usage
sakí	to arrive	sepèk	small bird
sanang	medium-sized gong	shaítan	satan (Malay)
sangakam	breach birth	síju	fish
sapat	overgrown	sígup	tobacco
sapé	stringed instrument	síka	stop
sara	near	síkíp	war charms
sarèt	vibration, shaking	síko'	elbow
sarok	a moment (*matok)	sílo'	fingernails
sarong	among	síndírí	self (Malay)
sau	mythical water	síngala	special (?)
	creature	sínyu	to push
sebang	life (?)	sío	life promoting

sírèk	woodpecker	teleman	suddenly
sítong	type of large jar	telíèk	to receive
spak	branch, tributary	telo'	us, we (variant
staat	start (English)		matelo')
sukau	as long as	temaga	brass
suken	to prop up	temau	tally line (*tebukau)
supa'(supa)	betel	temenggang	black hornbill
supé	to fail	tenebí	unfamiliar
suro	odor	tenítèng	to arrange
susaa	difficult, difficulty,	tepíon	rhinoceros hornbill
	hardship	tepo'	soft
suva	pride	tero	already (past tense)
		tetap	but (Malay)
		tíga	good (Kenyah)
T		tíku	egg
		tílé (tíléí)	to see
tabat	medicine (Penan)	tílo	to tell
tabí	to greet, shake hands	tílo' (tílau)	they
tajun	reason	tíloí	see (?) bíto' tíloí
takíp	life (*uríp)	tílong	fastness (*padong)
tam	each	tíma	wing feathers (*peca)
tapaan	winnowing tray	tína	mother
tapí	but	tína'	happy
tapo'	prayer station	típ	life (*udip)
tanaa	land, soil	to	still, continuing
tangau	hundred (*gitau)	tolong	help (Malay)
tau	year (Malay)	tu	this
tau	day (Kenyah)	tua	luck
tava' (tava)	to laugh	tua kampong	headman (Malay)
tawa	to call, invite	tubo	body (Malay)
tanyat	active	tubor	to take care of
tanyít	healthy	tudu	will, decision
tebukau	tally line, knot		(Malay)
tegen	pinions (*aren)	tugéé (tugéí)	to play
tekelo'	you (plural)	tukung	mountain
tekena	bespelled	tulong	help (variant tolong)
tekena'	legend, myth	tuman	from
tekun	from	tunéí	near
telanak	soul	tunok	patience
telang	power, efficacy	tu'o	true
telejang	stick used in bird	tupaan	all
	augury	tupo'	grandchild

turíp	life (Kenyah)	uraí	rice (*paraí)
turau	to sit	uram	to spend time, dawdle
tusaa	difficulty, hardship		
tusong	to occupy, inhabit	urau	seat
tutok	together	uríp	life (variant turíp)
		uro'	grass
		urok	because
U		usaa	body
		usau	seat (*urau)
ubèd	medicine	utan	to provide
ubín	trace, footprint, spoor, descendent	uted	ghost
		uvì'	uncle, aunt, grandparent (variant vì')
uccíu	fair, just		
udíp	life (*uríp)		
ugeng	stiff, rigor mortis		
uko	grandmother (Kenyah)		
		V	
ukuk	family apartment, coresidents of apartment	vaí	to come, arrive
		vì'	uncle, aunt, grandparent (Kenyah)
ukun	grandparent (Kenyah)		
ulan	worms		
ulo' (ulau)	head		
ulong	to live, life (variant mulong)	**W**	
uma	house (Kenyah or Kayan)	wakíl	deputy (Malay)
		wang	money (Malay)
umí	small	wat	guts, intestines
umok	to want to, desire	wong (wíong)	to be
uní	long ago		
unong	to live, life (variant mulong)		
unyín	temperament, feelings, emotions	**Y**	
upo'	tiger	ya	him, her
urak	a measure of a hand's width	yan	name (*ngaran)
		yo	because

Conventions of Notation

See the section entitled "orthography" at the beginning of the book for a complete discussion of the diacritics used in the Berawan script.

Lines of Berawan text are tone groups. Changes in loudness and speed occur between lines, and are shown by a graphic device:

- ■ indicates that the line was spoken very loud or was shouted;
- ▪ indicates that the line was clearly audible;
- ‧ indicates that the line was mumbled and barely comprehensible;
- ◆ indicates that the line was spoken rapidly.

For complete details, see page 51.
Lines are numbered every tenth line.

344

In the running translation, synonyms are labeled with a subscript number:

spirits of grandparents$_1$ spirits of grandparents$_2$

These subscripts indicate that there are two different words used in the Berawan that have the same gloss. Since the true connotations of these words cannot be accurately matched, numbers are preferred. The numbers also serve to highlight the parellel language of the original.

Superscript numbers are used in both the Berawan text and the English translation to indicate endnotes.

Punctuation is interpretive and is therefore left out of the Berawan text, which is intended strictly as a phonological transcription. In the translation, no punctuation is used after subscript numbers—even if followed by a superscript number—because commas and periods can be confusing when used with them. Also, no commas occur at the ends of lines that run on: Most lines of prayer are short, but some speakers extend them until they run out of breath. Such lines are shown with a series of periods at the end of them (. . .) in the Berawan text. With those exceptions, lines within verses end with a comma or a colon, and verses with a period.

Verses (see pages 53–57) are separated by one line. These blanks of necessity also appear in the Berawan so that the lines of text and translation remain synchronized.

Indentation is mechanical in the Berawan text, used only to indicate repetition of words in adjacent lines (these repeated words are aligned), and anacrustic lines (see pages 91–93). In the English translation, indentation is used interpretively to reveal internal structure. Generally, two or more lines that participate in a parallel structure are indented a uniform distance from the preceding line. Repetition may be treated as in the Berawan, or by indenting lines uniformly, according to location in the verse. Structured verses usually move away from the left-hand margin in a series of steps, but occasional long lines necessitate a move back to the left. See pages 54–56. Anacrustic lines are deeply indented when they occur within verses. When these lines occur between verses, they stand alone on the left-hand margin, and are not counted in the tally of verses. Generally, the first line of a verse stands against the left-hand margin unless that verse has the same theme as the one preceding it, in which case it is indented one step. A move back to the margin indicates a new theme.